U.S. ARMY AIRCRAFT

SINCE 1947

U.S. ARMY AIRCRAFT

SINCE 1947

An Illustrated Directory

by

STEPHEN HARDING

specialtypress

This book is dedicated to
Mary, Sarah and Ian

Printed in England by Livesey Ltd.
90 91 92 93 94 5 4 3 2 1

ISBN 0-933424-53-1

First published in the United Kingdom in 1990 by
Airlife Publishing Ltd.

Published in the United States in 1990 by
Specialty Press, Inc.
P.O. Box 338
123 North Second Street
Stillwater, MN 55082 U.S.A.
In Minn 612-430-2210
Toll-free 800-888-9653

Book trade distribution by Voyageur Press, Inc.

Specialty Press books are also available at discounts for quantities for
educational, fundraising, premium, or sales-promotion use. For details
contact the marketing manager. Please write or call for our free catalog of
publications.

Contents

APPENDIX: ARMY AIRCRAFT DESIGNATION

ACKNOWLEDGEMENTS

The author wishes to thank all the people and organizations listed below for supplying the information, photos, and other data without which this book would have been far less complete:

Peter M. Bowers; Jim Sullivan; Duane Kasulka; William T. Larkins; Bob Pickett; Peter Russell-Smith; Roger Besecker; Gordon S. Williams; Georg Fischbach; Peter Mancus; Sharon Shaw of De Havilland Canada; British Aerospace; Jennifer Norton of Fairchild Industries; Florence Piazza of Piasecki Aircraft; Lynn Coakly of *Army Aviation* magazine; H. Dean Humphrey of Cessna Aircraft; Marilyn Phipps of Boeing; C. E. Ruckdaschel of Rockwell International; Holly Moore of the American Helicopter Society; Messrs W. Odermatt and U. Wenger of Pilatus Aircraft; Bruce Goulding of Kaman Aerospace; Ira Chart and E. C. Riley of Northrop Corporation; Lois Lovisolo of Grumman Corporation; Jack Isabel and Z. Joe Thornton of General Dynamics; John Gedraitis of Beechcraft; Don Hanson and Harry Gann of Douglas Aircraft; Bell Helicopter-Textron; Boeing-Vertol; Hynes Helicopters; Eric Schulzinger of Lockheed-California; Joseph E. Dabney of Lockheed-Georgia; Dana Mullady of Sikorsky Aircraft; Fokker Aircraft BV; C. Samuel Campagna of Short Brothers; McDonnell-Douglas Helicopter Company; Mississippi State University; Princeton University; George Welsh of the San Diego Aerospace Museum; Cesare Falessi of Aeritalia; Frank Colucci of *Defence Helicopter World* magazine; Ruth Shephard and Ralph Pritchard of the Army Transportation Corps Museum; Thomas J. Sabiston of the Army Aviation Museum; Major Austin R. Omlie of the Army Aviation Engineering Flight Activity; Joseph Avesian of the Army Tank-Automotive Command; Jack Calve, W. Howard DeMere, LTC Thomas Fichter, and LTC Don R. Watson of the Army Aviation Systems Command; Betty Goodson of the Army Aviation Center; and Wayne Dzwonchyk and Dr Robert Wright of the U.S. Army Center of Military History.

INTRODUCTION

In the just over forty years since its creation the air arm of the modern United States Army has grown from a relatively small and ill-equipped liaison and battlefield observation force into a vast, complex and capable organization employing more than 10,000 fixed- and rotary-wing attack, reconnaissance, transport and general utility aircraft. In the course of this transformation Army aviation has been called upon to perform a wide range of tasks both at home and around the world, and has participated in two major armed conflicts and a host of what are popularly known as 'international crises'. These factors, coupled with long-standing governmental restraints placed on the size, complexity and capabilities of its aircraft, have made the Army both innovative and inventive in its approach to military aviation. As a result, over the past four decades the United States Army has acquired and employed a greater variety of aircraft types — experimental and operational, mass-purchase and 'one-of-a-kind', fixed-wing, rotary-wing and, in a few cases, no-winged — than could be found in many larger air forces.

This book is not intended to be a comprehensive history of post-World War II Army aviation activities; that fascinating and complex story is deserving of a far more detailed study than could be presented in these pages and has, in fact, been well told elsewhere*. Still, any directory of the manned aircraft used by the modern United States Army must include at least a brief summary of the events and trends that shaped Army aviation, for the type and number of machines operated by the Army from 1947 onward — their development, use and eventual supplantation by other, more advanced types — was and is determined by those events and trends.

Though United States Army aviation can trace its lineage back to the Federal balloon companies of the American Civil War, and though many of its traditions and not a few of its current tactics were originally developed by organic aviation units flying small 'grasshopper' aircraft in support of Army operations immediately prior to and during World War II, the air arm of the modern United States Army can more accurately be said to have originated with the U.S. Congress' 1947 passage of the National Security Act. Among its other sweeping reforms of the American military establishment, this legislation transformed the World War II-era Army Air Forces into the United States Air Force, a separate military service effectively responsible for the operation of all non-naval U.S. combat aircraft. Under the terms of the Act, the Air Force was made responsible for, among other things, fulfilling all of the Army's close combat, logistical air support, aerial photography and tactical reconnaissance requirements. The Army, for its part, was allowed to maintain a small force of aircraft for liaison and battlefield transportation purposes, though a joint 1949 Army-USAF agreement specified that the Army's fixed-wing machines could not exceed 2500 pounds in weight, nor its helicopters 4000 pounds.

Within a few years of its creation the Air Force became deeply involved in the development of the strategic bombers, ballistic missiles and supersonic fighters needed to meet the growing threat presented by the increasingly aggressive forces of the Soviet Union and her allies. Though obviously necessary, this concentration on 'high-tech' aircraft and aviation programmes nonetheless ensured that the Army co-operation mission did not receive the level of priority the Army felt it deserved. Indeed, the Air Force's perceived inability to adequately fulfill the Army's aviation needs, coupled with the USAF's continuing resistance to the Army's creation of an air arm that would in any way impinge on what the Air Force considered to be its own domain, forced the Army to begin a careful and often circumspect expansion of its own aviation resources and capabilities within and, in some cases, beyond the limits set by the applicable interservice agreements. This expansion, which included such things as a push for the development of an organic tactical cargo transport capability and the formulation of new and innovative doctrine for the combat use of helicopters, was just beginning to flourish when the Korean War broke out.

At the time hostilities commenced in Korea in June of 1950, the Army had some 660 fixed-wing and fifty-seven rotary-wing aircraft in its inventory, though many of the former were either obsolete types dating to World War II or essentially stock commercial designs unsuited for combat use, and most of the latter were small training machines. Moreover, an acute shortage of pilots and ground crews further complicated initial attempts to field the operational aircraft so desperately needed during the early days of the war. Army aviation answered the challenge despite these difficulties, however, and in the first months of the conflict pilots and ground crew hastily recalled from civilian life kept the vintage L-4s and L-5s in the air and working in support of the United Nations forces.

As the months passed the initial period of make-do improvisation gave way to an increasingly rapid expansion of the Army's aviation arm as more funds became available for aircraft acquisition. As an example, in the fiscal years (FY) 1949 and 1950 the Army had procured only 481 aircraft; in FY 1952 the number of machines ordered jumped to more than 3600, with a further 700 machines ordered in FY 1953. Among the first new types procured was the immensely capable Cessna L-19 *Bird Dog*, which began replacing the older observation and liaison machines in combat units in the spring of 1951. The Air Force's October 1951 lifting of the Army aircraft weight restrictions further enhanced the Army's aviation capabilities by allowing the procurement of larger and more capable fixed-wing machines such as the de Havilland of Canada L-20 *Beaver*, as well as clearing the way for the establishment of the Army's first five helicopter transportation companies.

The war in Korea was a proving ground for the Army's embryonic air arm. Throughout the course of the conflict Army fixed-wing aircraft did yeoman service in the traditional liaison, observation and VIP transport roles, and performed equally as well at such new tasks as forward air control of attack aircraft, electronic warfare and, on more than one occasion, improvised tactical air support. The Army's belief in the military value of helicopters was quickly vindicated in Korea, for combat operations with the Bell H-13, Sikorsky H-19 and Hiller H-23 soon proved that rotary-wing aircraft were ideally suited for battlefield surveillance, casualty evacuation and the rapid point-to-point movement of men, equipment and supplies upon which victory in modern warfare increasingly depended.

During the latter stages of the Korean War, and in the years immediately following the end of that conflict, the Army began to put into practice many of the valuable lessons it had learned about the organization and use of organic aviation assets. These years saw the organization and activation of the first independent aviation units, the Army's first operational evaluation of such fixed-wing jet aircraft as the Cessna T-37 and Fiat G-91, and the formulation of a new tactical doctrine that for the first time promised to make full use of the immense potential value of the military helicopter. In addition, the decade following the Korean War witnessed increasing official interest in the development and deployment of new aircraft types intended specifically to meet the Army's particular aviation needs. Indeed, by 1960 the Army inventory included some 5,000 aircraft of fifteen major types. Though many of these new designs were one of a kind flight test support aircraft, surface-effect machines, compound rotorcraft, individual lift devices and other exotic (not to say eccentric) experimental vehicles meant to explore emerging new technologies, during the late 1950s and early 1960s the Army was also developing and introducing other, more immediately useful types. The Vertol CH-21 *Shawnee*, de Havilland of Canada U-6 *Beaver* and U-1 *Otter*, Sikorsky CH-34 *Choctaw*, Bell UH-1 *Iroquois*, Grumman OV-1 *Mohawk* and Boeing-Vertol CH-47 *Chinook* all entered the Army inventory between 1954 and 1962. It was these aircraft, and the tactics developed around them, which were to form the basis of the Army's initial operations in the Vietnam War.

If Korea was a proving ground for the infant Army air arm, Vietnam was a fiery crucible in which the force was tempered and from which it ultimately emerged far stronger and vastly more capable. The first Army aircraft deployed to Vietnam in appreciable numbers — four transportation companies equipped with Vertol CH-21 *Shawnee* helicopters — arrived in South Vietnam in late 1961 and early 1962. Though initially tasked solely with supporting South Vietnamese forces, Army aircraft and aviators soon broadened the range of their activities to match the United States' growing involvement in all aspects of the conflict. And as the level of American participation steadily increased so did the number and type of Army aircraft deployed in the combat areas. In January 1963 there were 222 Army aircraft in-country, 149 of which were helicopters; by the beginning of October 1964 the Army had 406 aircraft in South Vietnam, including 259 helicopters.

This early period of American involvement in Vietnam also saw the first operational application of a new and innovative aviation doctrine known as 'airmobility', a concept that would ultimately change both the fundamental nature of Army aviation and the way in which the Army developed, acquired and deployed its aircraft. The airmobility concept had been under development since the late 1950s, and in 1963 the 11th Air Assault Division was established specifically to test the doctrine and tactics codified the previous year by the Army Tactical Mobility Requirements Board. Based on the use of large numbers of lightly armed transport helicopters to quickly transport troops and supplies into and out of the combat area, airmobility drew its inspiration and many of its tactics from successful French military experiences with helicopters in Indo-China and Algeria. Simply put, airmobility envisaged the use of aircraft organic to Army units to eliminate the traditional reliance on slow and vulnerable ground transport and at the same time provide ground commanders a theretofore undreamed of ability to rapidly find, fix, engage and, if necessary, disengage from the enemy. The use of high-performance attack helicopters to escort the lightly-armed transport aircraft was an integral part of the airmobility concept, and the Army's adoption of the doctrine thus ultimately led directly to the development of the first purpose-built helicopter gunship, the Bell AH-1 *Cobra*.

As first practised in Vietnam, airmobility relied primarily on the CH-21, though by 1964 the ageing and overburdened *Shawnee* had been almost entirely replaced by the newer and vastly more capable Bell UH-1 *Iroquois*. The Huey, as the latter craft was almost universally known, quickly became the dominant Army helicopter type in Vietnam and did yeoman duty as troop and VIP transport, armed escort, medical evacuation aircraft, electronic warfare and special operations support platform, and command and control machine. Other new types which followed the UH-1 into service in Vietnam included the Hughes OH-6 *Cayuse* light observation helicopter in 1965, the first examples of the above-mentioned AH-1 *Cobra* gunship in 1967, and the Bell OH-58 *Kiowa* in 1969. Though Vietnam was primarily a helicopter war for the Army, several fixed-wing types carried out important tasks as well, especially in the tactical transport and electronic warfare roles. Though continued Air Force resistance to Army ownership of de Havilland *Caribou* twin-engined medium transports ultimately led to the transfer of those craft to the USAF, the Army continued to operate such other important fixed-wing machines as the venerable O-1 (L-19) *Bird Dog*, Beech U-21 *Ute*, Grumman OV-1 *Mohawk*, and even electronic warfare variants of the Lockheed P-2 *Neptune* naval patrol bomber.

Vietnam was indeed a testing ground for Army aviation, and combat experience there led directly to the development and implementation of a wide range of systems that have since become standard for military rotary- and fixed-wing aircraft. These include advanced aircraft protection devices such as radar warning receivers, electronic countermeasures equipment, and chaff and flare dispensers, a variety of target acquisition and designation systems, advanced airborne reconnaissance gear, and a dizzying array of extremely effective weapons. And tactics developed and perfected in Vietnam have also been passed into the post-Vietnam age: nap-of-the-earth flight to defeat enemy detection and anti-aircraft systems, the destruction of enemy armoured vehicles by hunter-killer teams made up of an observation machine equipped with a laser target designator and a missile-armed attack helicopter, the use of specially-equipped fixed- and rotary-wing aircraft to support special operations forces, and the use of highly sophisticated manned and unmanned aircraft for intelligence collection over the modern battlefield. And all of these various developments in both aircraft hardware and aviation tactics have been validated in action, whether during routine peacetime operations in Europe or Asia, during the deployment of Army aircraft and aviators to such areas of tension as Central America, or in actual combat in Grenada and, more recently, the Persian Gulf and Panama.

In the years since the end of the Vietnam War the United States Army has continued to be a leader in the development of advanced purpose-built aircraft. These include types currently in service, such as the Sikorsky UH-60 *Blackhawk* family of utility transport and special operations support aircraft, the McDonnell-Douglas AH-64 *Apache* attack helicopter, high-technology test-beds such as the Sikorsky Rotor Systems Research Aircraft, and such still-evolving machines as the Bell-Boeing V-22 *Osprey* tilt-rotor. The Army also continues to adapt selected civil aircraft such as the Fokker F.27 and Shorts SD3-30 for military use, while at the same time continuing the upgrading and modernization of such existing types as the CH-47 *Chinook*, AH-1 *Cobra* and OH-58 *Kiowa*.

The transformation of United States Army aviation from a small and ill-equipped post-World War II liaison force into a credible independent air arm capable of supporting Army operations worldwide was not easily accomplished, nor have its gains been easily maintained. Early U.S. Air Force envy of the Army's leadership in the development of military vertical flight and opposition to the Army's attempts to develop its own tactical aviation assets, though muted with time, have not entirely disappeared and interservice rivalry continues to cause unnecessary friction. Recurring budgetary restrictions, the increasingly fantastic sums of money needed to acquire, field and maintain modern combat aircraft, the ebb and flow of changing national priorities and, above all, the absolute necessity to remain constantly prepared for action anywhere in an ever more unsettled world, have all played a part in making Army aviation the force it is today. Yet, fortunately, it is a force which, despite the limitations placed upon it, continues to be the most capable of its kind in the free world.

---

* See bibliography for a list of several good general histories.

AUTHOR'S NOTE

In order to provide the most complete coverage possible of the topic, I have included in this volume all manned aircraft types known to have been used operationally by, or evaluated but not ultimately adopted for use by, the Regular Army, the Army Reserve and the Army National Guard. I have also included several air cushion vehicles and ground effect machines which, at first glance, might not seem to qualify as true aircraft. However, these vehicles were considered aircraft by the Army and were, with only a few exceptions, assigned aircraft designations and serial numbers.

In the interests of clarity I have listed the aircraft in both alphabetical and chronological order. This is, the aircraft are listed alphabetically by manufacturer's name and, when several aircraft from the same manufacturer are included, they are listed within the manufacturer's grouping in the chronological order in which they were first obtained by the Army. The reader will note that although in some cases this method of listing will cause several aircraft from the same manufacturer to be seemingly out of order — for example, the Sikorsky H-39, which the Army first acquired in 1954, is listed before the Sikorsky H-34 and H-37, which were acquired in, respectively, 1955 and 1956 — it allows a more accurate indication of when each aircraft type was actually acquired. In compiling the alphabetical listing I have chosen to use the manufacturer's name that was in use during the majority of the time each aircraft was in the Army's inventory, rather than using either the original or the most recent version of a given manufacturer's corporate identity. I have thus, for example, listed several aircraft designed and originally built by Piasecki Aircraft under the Vertol Aircraft heading, for the aircraft in question were acquired and used by the Army after Vertol bought out the original Piasecki concern. I have likewise listed the AH-64 *Apache* attack helicopter under McDonnell-Douglas Helicopter Company, the firm that is currently producing the aircraft for the Army, rather than under Hughes Helicopters, the firm that originally developed the machine.

In still another attempt to impose greater clarity on an often confusing topic, I have listed each aircraft under the most recent basic type designation it held or, in the case of current machines, holds at the time this volume is going to press. This is a necessity because many of the aircraft used by the Army since 1947 have carried a variety of designations, depending on the period in which they were introduced, the use to which a particular variant of the basic machine was being put, and so on. Thus, for example, the de Havilland of Canada *Caribou* is listed under the C-7 designation assigned to the type in January 1967, and which the few examples still in Army service in 1990 still carry, rather than the CV-2 designation the *Caribou* carried for the initial part of its Army service. Similarly, helicopters are designated by the basic prefix H in the top line of each entry, rather than as 'CH' for cargo helicopter, 'TH' for training machine, and so on. Then in the body of the text for each machine I have covered the designations assigned to the variants of each individual type. In the same vein, in the top line of each entry I have listed only those aircraft nicknames that were officially recognized by the Army. The Bell UH-1 is therefore referred to in the heading line by the official nickname *'Iroquois'*, rather than by the admittedly more widely used *'Huey'*.

In the technical data section for each of the various aircraft I have used those dimension figures supplied by the aircraft manufacturer, but have relied on performance figures determined by the Army itself. This was a conscious decision on my part, for though an aircraft's measurements are more accurately determined by the firm that built the craft, the same machine's top speed, service ceiling, or load-carrying capacity in actual operational service is often vastly different to that calculated by a sales-minded manufacturer. Having said this, however, I must remind the reader that specific performance figures cited for any particular aircraft represent the optimum performance of which that machine was capable under the best possible conditions. Speed, service ceiling, range, fuel consumption, and maximum payload figures are never absolute, for they are dependent upon such factors as the fuel load and number of crewmen carried by the aircraft, the geographic area in which the machine is operating, the number and type of weapons carried, whether or not the aircraft is flying in formation, and so on. Two otherwise identical aircraft will often have differing performance capabilities under exactly the same circumstances. The figures cited in this volume are therefore based upon the United States Army's determination of each aircraft's optimum performance under ideal conditions.

All information contained in this book was obtained from non-classified open sources. This applies especially to the designations, capabilities, and numbers of those Army aircraft formerly or currently used for classified intelligence-related activities and special operations, and to the designations and capabilities of intelligence-gathering, navigation, avionics, and other systems fitted to such aircraft.

Finally, I must admit that, despite my attempts to include all relevant information about every applicable airplane, this book is almost certainly incomplete. As the reader will surmise after even a brief review of the contents of this book, the United States Army has used a dizzying array of aircraft types and subtypes. In many cases a single example of a particular airplane was borrowed from another military service, used extensively in Army markings, and returned to its original owners, all without ever having been officially transferred to the Army. As any aircraft buff can attest, trying to track down accurate information on such borrowed airplanes can be extremely difficult, and trying to locate suitable photographs of said airplanes in Army markings can be virtually impossible. The same sort of problem is encountered when one seeks information regarding the approximately twenty-seven aircraft the Army has acquired through the U.S. Government's Confiscated/Excess Aircraft Programme (C/EAP). These machines (which are known to include at least one Gates Learjet, a Short 330, a Brittan-Norman Islander, and a variety of light piston models) were transferred to the Army after being seized by the Federal Government from drug smugglers and other law breakers and are apparently used by the Army to support on-going U.S. anti-drug operations. The Army has steadfastly declined to offer specific information about the aircraft for fear of compromising the confidentiality of the C/EAP and American anti-smuggling operations and methods, and I have therefore chosen not to include them in this volume.

I would welcome any information on, or photos of, additional Army aircraft types, as well as any corrections to the information contained in this volume. Readers may contact me via the publisher, and may rest assured that I am always happy to be corrected.

Stephen Harding
Springfield, Virginia.
December 1989

AERO DESIGN AND ENGINEERING U-9 AERO COMMANDER

Type: Twin-engined utility transport

Manufacturer: Aero Design and Engineering Corporation, Bethany, Oklahoma.

HISTORY

One of the more advanced light twin-engined commercial aircraft to appear in the years immediately following the end of the Second World War, the Aero Design and Engineering Model 3805 first flew in 1948. Modifications made to the original design were incorporated into the more advanced commercial Model 520 Aero Commander introduced in early 1951. In October 1952 the Army acquired three examples of this attractive and capable all-metal light transport for evaluation in the general utility role. Designated YL-26, the aircraft (serials 52-6217, -6218 and -6219) were powered by twin 260 hp Lycoming engines, and were capable of carrying five passengers or up to 1700 pounds of cargo.

This immaculate U-9C staff transport, pictured at Fort Bragg, North Carolina, in the summer of 1963, shows the U-9's general layout to good advantage. This particular machine was later used as an APS-85 SLAR testbed. *(U.S. Army Transportation Corps Museum)*

1

Despite the YL-26's creditable showing during its evaluation the Army chose not to procure the type in quantity at that time. Indeed, it was not until 1956 that the Aero Commander entered regular Army service, when four commercial Model 680 aircraft were acquired. Designated L-26C, these four machines (serials 56-4023 to -4026) differed from the earlier YL-26s primarily in having more powerful 320 hp engines, a better performance, higher all-up weights, and redesigned tail units with swept surfaces. Used as staff transports, the -C model machines were redesignated U-9C under the 1962 Tri-Service designation system.

The Army acquired its final four new-build Aero Commanders in early 1957. The first of these was a single 'militarized' commercial Model 560A (57-1791) which, owing to the type's 1955 purchase by the Air Force, was designated L-26B despite having entered the Army inventory after the later model L-26Cs. The L-27B (redesignated U-9B in 1962) was essentially similar to the L-26C, though it was powered by twin 270 hp engines. The Army also purchased three additional Model 680 aircraft; two of these (serials 57-6183 and -6184) were used as testbeds for the Motorola APS-85 Side Looking Airborne Radar (SLAR) then under development for use with the new 0V-1 Mohawk (q.v.) and were operated with the designation RL-26D. Army records indicate that three of the four original L-26Cs were at least temporarily modified to RL-26D standard; in 1962 all aircraft carrying that designation were redesignated RU-9D. The third new-build Aero Commander acquired in 1957 (serial 57-6531) was designated NL-26D (NU-9D after 1962) and served as an electronic systems development platform. The Army paid for two additional new-build RL-26Ds (serials 58-5512 and -5513) in the fiscal year 1958, but both of these aircraft were destroyed in pre-delivery accidents and never officially entered the inventory.

TECHNICAL DATA *(All versions, except where noted)*

Engines:
Two 260 hp Lycoming G0-435-C2B1 (YL-26)
Two 270 hp Lycoming GSO-480-1 (L-26B)
Two 320 hp Lycoming GSO-480-B1A6 (L-26C, RL/NL-26D)

Dimensions:
Wingspan: 44 ft (YL-26, L-26B)
49 ft 6 in (L-26C, RL/NL-26D)

Wing Area: 242.5 sq ft (YL-26, L-26B)
268.5 sq ft (L-26C, RL/NL-26D)

Fuselage length: 34 ft 4.5 in (YL-26, L-26B)
35 ft 2 in (L-26C, RL/NL-26D)

Weight (empty/gross, in lbs):
3800/5500 (YL-26)
3900/6000 (L-26B)
4475/7500 (L-26C, RL/NL-26D)

Performance:
Speed (cruising/maximum, in mph):
197/211 (YL-26)
200/209 (L-26B)
198/255 (L-26C, RL/NL-26D)

Service Ceiling: 24,000 ft (YL-26)
22,000 ft (L-26B)
22,900 ft (L-26C, RL/NL-26D)

Range: 1150 miles (YL-26)
1100 miles (L-26B)
1500 miles (L-26C, RL/NL-26D)

Armament: None

Accommodation:
Pilot and co-pilot, plus up to five passengers

AERONCA L-16

Type: Single-engined light observation and liaison aircraft

Manufacturer: Aeronca Aircraft Corporation, Middletown, Ohio.

HISTORY

The Aeronca L-16A, a militarized version of the firm's Model 7BC Champion light sports airplane, first entered Army service in 1947. The machine incorporated many features that had first appeared on the company's hugely successful L-3 series of light observation and liaison aircraft, a type that had seen extensive Army service in World War II, and shared the L-3's simplicity of design. The L-16A had a metal-tube fuselage framework covered by fabric, a high strut-braced wing, tandem seats for pilot and observer, and was powered by a single 85 hp Continental piston engine. The Army acquired a total of 509 L-16As and one hundred somewhat heavier L-16Bs, the latter a military variant of the commercial model 7EC that had a slightly larger wing, more powerful 90 hp engine, and a small dorsal spine for added directional stability.

An L-16B trainer (serial 48-450) awaits its next student on a Texas field, circa 1951. The -B model differed from the earlier L-16A in having a more powerful engine, a slightly larger wing, and a small dorsal spine for added stability. (U.S. Army Transportation Corps Museum)

The Army had procured the L-16 primarily for use by the National Guard and had never really intended that the craft serve as a frontline observation and liaison machine. But the outbreak of the Korean War created an immediate and urgent need for large numbers of fixed-wing aircraft and many L-16As were therefore drafted into combat service. The L-16Bs were used mainly as stopgap crew trainers in the United States, though several also saw service in the Far East. The L-16 did not prove a great success as a crew trainer or combat aircraft, however, and both versions were withdrawn from service as quickly as they could be replaced by more capable machines. Most L-16s were turned over to the Civil Air Patrol between 1952 and 1954, and the type had virtually disappeared from the active Army inventory by 1956.

TECHNICAL DATA *(All versions, except where noted)*

Engines:
One 85 hp Continental O-190-1 piston (L-16A)
One 80 hp Continental O-205-1 piston (L-16B)

Dimensions:

Wingspan:	35 ft
Wing Area:	158 sq ft (L-16A)
	170 sq ft (L-16B)
Fuselage length:	21 ft (L-16A)
	21 ft 6 in (L-16B)
Height:	7 ft 8in (L-16A)
	7 ft (L-16B)

Weight (empty/gross, in lbs):
860/1300 (L-16A)
890/1450 (L-16B)

Performance:
Speed (cruising/maximum, in mph):
60/87 (L-16A)
87/110 (L-16B)

Service Ceiling:	12,500 ft (L-16A)
	14,500 ft (L-16B)
Range:	180 miles (L-16A)
	350 miles (L-16B)
Armament:	None

Accommodation:
Pilot and observer

4

AMERICAN HELICOPTER H-26

Type: Twin-engined light observation and rescue helicopter

Manufacturer: American Helicopter Division of Fairchild Corporation, Manhattan Beach, California.

HISTORY

The design of the Model XA-8 single-seat lightweight helicopter was undertaken in 1951 with the sponsorship of both the Army Transportation Corps and the USAF. The Army specification to which American Helicopter had responded in 1950 had called for a light, collapsible machine which could be used as both a light observation craft and as an air-droppable rescue vehicle for downed aircrew. American Helicopter was awarded a development contract in June 1951, and the first of an eventual five XH-26s flew for the first time almost exactly one year later.

The XH-26's compactness is well illustrated in this shot of the first machine, 50-1840, preparing to lift off on a factory test flight prior to delivery to the Army. The craft's blade-tip pulse-jet engines are partially visible, though the rapidly revolving tail rotor is virtually indistinguishable.
(U.S. Army Transportation Corps Museum)

The XH-26 was designed from the beginning to be both collapsible and air-droppable and its construction and diminutive size reflected both requirements. Only twelve feet long and just six feet tall, the helicopter could be transported in a five foot by five foot by fourteen foot container and could be unpacked and assembled by two men in less than thirty minutes. The machine's fuselage was built primarily of aluminum and fiberglas and featured an extensively glazed, pyramid-shaped cockpit. The XH-26 was powered by two 36 lb st pulse-jet engines, one fixed to the tip of each main rotor blade, and could burn virtually any type of fuel.

The Army and Air Force jointly evaluated the five XH-26 prototypes (serials 50-1840, -1841, and 52-7476 through 7478) from 1952 to 1954. The machines were found to be robust in construction and relatively simple to operate, but neither service procured the type in quantity.

TECHNICAL DATA *(All versions, except where noted)*

Engines:
Two 35 lb st American Helicopter XPJ49-AH-3 pulse jets

Dimensions:
Main rotor diameter: 27 ft

Tail rotor diameter: 2 ft 2 in

Fuselage length: 12 ft 3 in

Height (to top of main rotor hub): 6 ft 2 in

Weight (empty/gross, in lbs):
300/710

Performance:
Speed (cruising/maximum, in mph): 70/80

Service Ceiling: 7,500 ft

Range: 100 miles

Armament: None

Accommodation:
Pilot only

AVRO CANADA VZ-9

Type: Twin-engined VTOL
research vehicle

Manufacturer: Avro Aircraft
of Canada Ltd, Malton,
Ontario, Canada.

HISTORY

During the late 1950s both the Army and the Air Force began taking an increasingly active interest in the military applications of jet-powered vertical takeoff and landing (VTOL) aircraft, and the Avro Canada Avrocar is one of the more exotic examples of the experimental platforms subsequently developed with the sponsorship of both services.

Design of the flying saucer-shaped Avrocar began in 1955 with Army and USAF funding, and in 1958 Avro Canada was awarded a joint-services contract for the production of a single flying prototype. This sole VZ-9 (serial 58-7055) was powered by three J69 turbojets ducted to drive a single central lift fan, and had accommodation for two crew members seated in separate enclosed cockpits located on either side of the fan duct. The craft began tethered flight trials in December 1959, and made its first non-tethered flight ascent in May 1961. Avro Canada had

The VZ-9 hovers just above the ground during a June 1961 test flight. Note the three sets of dual-wheeled landing gear.
(U.S. Army Transportation Corps Museum)

intended the VZ-9 to be a true flying saucer capable of high altitude flight at speeds in excess of 300 mph, but the machine was plagued by mechanical difficulties and never succeeded in operating out of ground effect. In 1963 both the Army and Air Force withdrew from the VZ-9 development programme and the sole example was subsequently withdrawn from service and transferred to the Army Transportation Corps Museum at Fort Eustis, Virginia.

TECHNICAL DATA

Engines:
Three 920 lb st Continental YJ69-T-9 turbojets

Dimensions:
Diameter: 26 ft 10 in

Height (from bottom of saucer to top lip of duct):
5.5 ft

Weights and performance figures
unknown

Armament: None

Accommodation: Two crew

The VZ-9 on display at Fort Eustis following the cessation of flight testing. The aircraft's 'front' is to the right; one of the faired-over cockpits can be seen just below the large central fan.
(U.S. Army Transportation Corps Museum)

BEECH C-45 EXPEDITER

Type: Twin-engined utility transport

Manufacturer: Beech Aircraft Corporation, Wichita, Kansas.

HISTORY

During the course of the Second World War both the Army Air Forces and the U.S. Navy acquired considerable numbers of twin-engined Beech C-45s for use in the light utility transport and crew trainer roles. The C-45, a military version of the successful commercial Model 18, was a low-wing cabin mono-plane characterized by twin endplate tail fins and large circular engine nacelles projecting from the wing leading edges on either side of the cockpit. Many C-45 variants remained in U.S. military service well past the end of World War II, and in the decade following the end of the Korean conflict more than a dozen Expediters ended up in the Army's inventory even though there was no official procurement of the type.

The C-45s operated by the Army are known to have included examples of the following variants:

C-45H:
Designation applied to early model USAAF/USAF crew trainers converted for use as general utility and liaison machines, one example of which (52-10748) was acquired by the Army in 1953.

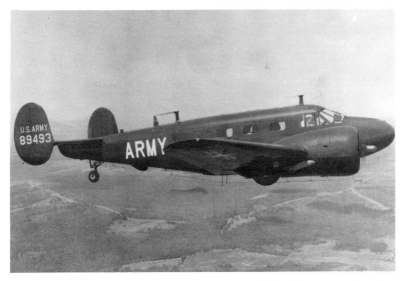

C-45J 89493 in flight. This machine had quite a varied military career, having been built in 1944 as a C-45F transport for the USAAF, transferred to the Navy as a JRB-4, modified by the USN to SNB-5 crew trainer configuration, and then acquired by the Army and reconverted for use as a utility transport. (U.S. Army)

9

One of perhaps three UC-45J (ex-TC-45J) Expediters equipped with tricycle landing gear. This particular aircraft was given a new serial number, redesignated NC-45J (as was a second, non-tricycle machine) and assigned to permanent testing duties. Note the lengthened nose, slightly smaller endplate fins, and more streamlined cockpit windscreen.
(Peter M. Bowers Collection)

C-45J:
Three ex-USN SNB-5s modified for use as utility transports. Two of these machines (BuNos 23822 and 51312) had been built as SNB-5 crew trainers, while the third aircraft (89493) originated as a USAAF C-45F transport, was acquired by the Navy as a JRB-4, and ultimately modified to SNB-5 standard. All three machines were powered by two Pratt & Whitney R-985-B5 radial engines and had accommodation for two crew members and six passengers.

RC-45J:
A single ex-USN SNB-5P photoreconnaissance trainer (BuNo 12375) used by the Army to develop airborne intelligence-gathering systems and techniques. During the course of its Army career this aircraft was fitted with a variety of cameras and ELINT sensors, the latter of which almost certainly included the prototypes of the LEFT JAB and LEFT FOOT systems.

TC-45J:
Six ex-USN SNB-5 aircraft (BuNos 12385, 23829, 39767, 39829, 39935 and 51288) used for general utility and liaison duties beginning in 1958. At least one of these machines (39767) was later fitted with tricycle landing gear, reserialed, and given the unofficial but widely used designation C-45T. All six TC-45Js were redesignated UC-45J in 1962.

NC-45J:
Two of the UC-45Js mentioned above (BuNos 23829 and 39829) were given this designation in the mid-1960s after being modified for use as flying testbeds.

VC-45J:
Designation applied to a single ex-USN SNB-5/UC-45J Expediter (BuNo 23783) used by the Army as a VIP/staff transport.

The C-45s used by the Army were acquired as stop-gap utility transports and were gradually withdrawn from service as more modern helicopters and fixed-wing aircraft became available. The last Army Expediter was retired from service in the late 1960s.

TECHNICAL DATA *(All versions, except where noted)*

Engines:
Two 450 hp Pratt & Whitney R-985-AN-3 radials
Two 450 hp Pratt & Whitney R-985-B5 radials (C-45H/J)

Dimensions:
Wingspan:	47 ft 8 in
Wing Area:	349 sq ft
Fuselage length:	34 ft 3 in
Height:	9ft 8in

Weight (empty/gross, in lbs):
5900/7800
5770/8750 (C-45H)

Performance:
Speed (cruising/maximum, in mph):
211/230

Service Ceiling: 20,500 ft

Range: 750 miles

Armament: None

Accommodation:
Two crew plus up to six passengers

BEECH U-8 SEMINOLE

Type: Twin-engined utility transport   Manufacturer: Beech Aircraft Corporation, Wichita, Kansas.

HISTORY

In January 1952 the Army began the operational testing of the first of four Beech commercial Model D50B Twin Bonanzas acquired 'off-the-shelf' for evaluation in the liaison and utility transport roles. The aircraft, which were designated YL-23 and allocated the serial numbers 52-1800 to -1803, were low-wing cabin monoplanes powered by twin 260hp Lycoming piston engines. The YL-23 proved well suited to its intended roles, and was adopted for operational use in the variants listed below.

L-23A:
First production model, fifty-five of which entered service beginning in mid-1952. These machines had accommodation for up to six passengers, and several examples served as VIP transports in the Far East during the closing stages of the Korean War.

One of four Model D50B Twin Bonanzas evaluated by the Army with the designation YL-23, 52-1801 was later brought up to L-23A standard. At the time of its acquisition the L-23 was the largest fixed-wing aircraft in Army service. *(Beech)*

This machine, 57-6073, was built as an L-23A but was modified to L-23D standard in 1957 (note the additional cabin window). In 1962 all surviving L-23Ds were redesignated U-8D. *(Beech)*

L-23B:
Essentially similar to the -A model, but had two-bladed propellers of metal rather than wood. The Army acquired 40 examples of this model beginning in 1954.

L23D:
Military version of the commercial Model E50 Twin Bonanza, which differed from the L-23B primarily in having 340hp Lycoming engines. Beech began delivery of eighty-five new-construction aircraft in 1956, and upgraded a further ninety-three older -A and -B model Seminoles to -D standard as well. Those L-23Ds remaining in the Army inventory in 1962 were redesignated U-8D.

L-23E:
Designation applied to six commercial Model D50A Twin Bonanzas acquired in 1956. Each was powered by two 295 hp Lycoming engines, and all six aircraft were redesignated U-8E in 1962.

RL-23D:
Twenty L-23D aircraft were allocated this designation in 1959 and 1960 following their modification for use as electronic

intelligence (ELINT) platforms. Two of the machines were experimentally fitted with the AN/APS-85 Side-looking Airborne Radar (SLAR) system, while at least sixteen of the other aircraft received the more advanced AN/APQ-86 SLAR. Both systems used long, rectangular antennae housed in faired ventral pods. In addition, at least one RL-23D was fitted with a ventral blister housing an AN/UPD-1 ground surveillance radar, while yet another of the aircraft was equipped with a nose-mounted AN/AVQ-50 weather-avoidance radar. All RL-23Ds remaining in the inventory in 1962 were redesignaed RU-8D.

L-23F:
Designation applied to three commercial Model 65 Queen Airs acquired for evaluation in 1959, and to the seventy-six production machines procured thereafter. These aircraft were powered by twin 340 hp Lycoming engines, and could each carry up to seven passengers in addition to the two crew members. All surviving L-23Fs were redesignated U-8F in 1962, a designation also applied to a single slightly-modified Queen Air 65 transferred to the Army from the Federal Aviation Administration in 1964. In 1984 Excalibur Aviation Company of San Antonio, Texas, was awarded an Army contract on behalf of the National Guard Bureau for the modification of all surviving National Guard U-8F aircraft to commercial Model Queen Air

The Army's single NU-8E, shown here at the Naval Air Test Facility at Lakehurst, New Jersey, in September 1971, was a commercial Model J50 Twin Bonanza acquired in 1966 for use as an electronics testbed. The extended nose was used to house various special instrumentation packages. *(Roger Besecker via Jim Sullivan)*

800 standard. This included the installation of uprated Lycoming IO-720-A1B engines, new engine mounts, three-bladed Hartzell propellers, and other detail changes. A total of fifty-one machines had been so modified by early 1986.

U-8G:
Designation given to upgraded, re-engined U-8D, RU-8D, and U-8F aircraft (the latter then being further modified as outlined above). The rebuild included installation of twin 340 hp Lycoming engines, addition of advanced avionics, and refinement of the passenger accommodations to seat six.

NU-8E:
A single commercial Model J50 Twin Bonanza acquired for 'special electronics testing', often a euphemism for electronic warfare research activities, in 1966. This machine carried the serial 66-15360, though this was a 'bogus' number probably applied for security reasons.

NU-8F:
Designation applied to a single modified commercial Queen Air delivered to the Army in 1964. This machine was the prototype

Based on the commercial Queen Air 65, the U-8F bears only a passing resemblance to the earlier members of the L-23/U-8 family. The -F model Seminole featured a redesigned fuselage, uprated engines, wings of greater span, and various detail changes. This particular machine, 62-3873, was photographed at Northolt, England, in April 1973. The aircraft was assigned to the 207th Aviation Company based at Heidelberg Army Air Field in West Germany, and the emblem on the port engine nacelle is that of United States Army, Europe. *(Peter Russell-Smith via Jim Sullivan)*

for the turbine-powered commercial King Air 65-90, which was itself the basis for the later U-21 Ute (q.v.). The aircraft had the fuselage of a Queen Air 80 and the wings of a Twin Bonanza, and was powered by two 525 shp Pratt & Whitney PT6A-6 turboprops. The NU-8F designation was also briefly applied to a single commercial King Air 90 used for electronic testing in 1965 (and which bore the 'bogus' serial 66-15361).

The U-8 family of utility aircraft has provided yeoman service to the Army for more than three decades, and nearly 70 examples of different variants remained in service with the active Army, Army Reserve and National Guard as of late 1986.

TECHNICAL DATA (All versions, except where noted)

Engines:
Two 260 hp Lycoming O-435-17 pistons (YL-23, L-23A/B)
Two 340 hp Lycoming O-480-1 pistons (U/RU-8D)
Two 295 hp Lycoming O-480-G2D6 pistons (U/NU-8E)
Two 340 hp Lycoming O-480-A1A6 pistons (U-8F)
Two 340 hp Lycoming O-480-CSC6 pistons (U-8G)
Two 525 shp Pratt & Whitney of Canada PT6A-6 turboprops (NU-8F prototype for King Air 65-90)

Dimensions:

Wingspan:	45 ft 3 in
	45 ft 10 in (U-8F)
	45 ft 10.5 in (NU-8F)
Wing Area:	277 sq ft
Fuselage length:	31 ft 6 in
	33 ft 4 in (U-8F)
	35 ft 4 in (NU-8F)
Height:	11 ft 6 in
	14 ft 2 in (U-8F)
	14 ft 8 in (NU-8F)

Weight (empty/gross, in lbs):
4970/7000
4970/7300 (U-8D/E, RU-8D)
4980/7700 (U-8F)
5081/9300 (NU-8F)

Performance:
Speed (cruising/maximum, in mph):
155/180 (YL-23, L-23A/B)
180/233 (U-8D/F/G)
165/210 (U-8E)
239/290 (NU-8F)

Service Ceiling:	24,300 ft
	27,000 ft (U-8D/F/G)
	29,000 ft (U-8E)
	32,000 ft (NU-8F)
Range:	1350-1470 miles
Armament:	None

Accommodation:
Two crew, up to six passengers
Two crew, up to nine passengers (NU-8F)

BEECH T-42 COCHISE

Type: Twin-engined instrument and transition trainer

Manufacturer: Beech Aircraft Corporation, Wichita, Kansas.

HISTORY

In February 1965 Beech's Model B55 Baron was selected as the Army's new twin-engined instrument and multi-engined transition trainer, and shortly thereafter the Army placed an initial order for fifty-five T-42A Cochise production aircraft. This was later increased to sixty-five machines, and in 1971 the Army procured a further five examples for delivery to Turkey under the Military Assistance Programme (MAP).

The T-42A is a low-winged, twin-engined cabin monoplane developed from Beech's earlier Model D95A Travel Air. The Cochise is of all-metal construction and has fully retractable

The first Cochise acquired by the Army, 65-12679, is seen here running up its engines just prior to its Army acceptance flight. The Army purchased a total of sixty-five T-42As for its own use, plus an additional five aircraft for Turkey. *(Beech)*

tricycle landing gear. Accommodation for up to four persons in addition to the pilot is standard, though T-42s used as instrument trainers normally only carry two students in addition to the instructor pilot. The aircraft is powered by two 260 hp Continental piston engines, and is fitted with dual controls and extensive instrumentation.

Though initially procured for use primarily as a trainer the T-42A has seen widespread service as a general light utility transport. Indeed, the majority of the approximately thirty Cochises which remained in the Army inventory as of late 1986 were used almost exclusively as light transports by the Army Reserve and Army National Guard.

TECHNICAL DATA

Engines:
Two 260 hp Continental IO-470-L pistons

Dimensions:

Wingspan:	37 ft 10 in
Wing area:	275 sq ft
Fuselage length:	27 ft
Height:	9 ft 6 in

Weight (empty/gross, in lbs):
3197/5100

Performance:
Speed (cruising/maximum, in mph): 200/235

Service Ceiling:	19,700 ft
Range:	1065 miles
Armament:	None
Accommodation:	See text

BEECH U-21 UTE

Type: Twin-engined utility transport and EW aircraft

Manufacturer: Beech Aircraft Corporation, Wichita, Kansas.

HISTORY

The lineage of the versatile U-21 family of aircraft can be traced directly to the single NU-8F Seminole acquired by the Army early in 1964. As mentioned in the U-8 section of this volume (q.v.), the NU-8F was a hybrid aircraft which incorporated the fuselage of a Beech Model 80 Queen Air and the wings of a Beech Twin Bonanza. The NU-8F was, in fact, the prototype for the Model 65-90 King Air and was the first turbine-powered aircraft in regular U.S. Army service. The Army was quite pleased with the NU-8F (later designated YU-21), and in October 1966 adopted the unpressurized version of Beech's production model as the U-21 Ute. This was the beginning of a long and varied Army career for the type, the several variants of which are listed below:

U-21A:
Initial production version, powered by two 550 shp PT6A-20 turboprops. The first of an eventual 141 -A model aircraft was delivered in May 1967. The U-21A was intended to directly support tactical units and could accommodate up to twelve fully-equipped combat troops, 3000 pounds of cargo, or three stretchers and three ambulatory casualties. All U-21As were built with large cargo doors adjoining the port-side entry door, a feature which greatly facilitated the loading and unloading of cargo and troops. The first Utes began reaching Army units in Vietnam in late 1967.

The first U-21A (66-18000) takes troops aboard during an early field exercise. This particular aircraft has led an eventful career, for it was one of four -A model variants converted to EU-21A electronic warfare configuration and evaluated in Vietnam beginning in early 1968. The machine was eventually returned to U-21A status, and continued to serve as a staff transport (based in Mannheim, Germany) until finally withdrawn from service in early 1987. The aircraft is slated for preservation at the Army Aviation Museum. *(Beech)*

The sixteen RU-21E Utes acquired by the Army in 1970 and 1971 were production RU-21Ds retrofitted with more powerful engines and upgraded EW equipment. This aircraft, 70-15880, was the sixth example accepted by the Army and is shown here displaying the antenna array normally associated with the GUARDRAIL signals intelligence system. *(Beech)*

EU-21A:
The Army's increasing involvement in airborne electronic warfare (EW) activities in Vietnam had by early 1967 created the need for a signals intelligence (SIGINT) and EW aircraft faster and more capable than those then in use. The Army experimentally equipped four U-21As (serials 66-18000, -18013, -18027, and 67-18058) with dedicated EW and SIGINT equipment and designated the craft EU-21As. All were apparently standard -A model machines except for the addition of mission-related electronics.

JU-21A:
A single U-21A (66-18008) modified for use as an aerial testbed for the AN/ARQ-38 LEFT JAB direction finding (DF) SIGINT system.

RU-21A:
Designation allocated to four standard -A model Utes (67-18112 to -18115) used for the operational evaluation of the LEFT JAB system in Vietnam. Two of these aircraft are believed to have remained in the Army inventory as late as 1984.

RU-21B:
Three commercial Model 65-A90-2 King Air machines acquired by the Army for use in Vietnam as part of the Cefirm Leader EW programme. These aircraft (67-18077, -18087, and -18093) were essentially standard -A model Utes fitted with uprated 620 shp PT6A-29 engines and equipped with the AN/ULQ-11 DF and communications-jamming system.

20

RU-21C:
Two commercial Model 65-A90-3 King Airs procured for use in the Cefirm Leader EW programme and operated in Vietnam in conjunction with the three RU-21Bs. The two RU-21Cs (67-18015 and 18089) differed from the RU-21Bs only in electronics carried and antenna configuration. It is believed that one of these machines remained active in the reserve components through mid-1985.

RU-21D:
The development of the RU-21D was a direct result of both the operational success enjoyed in Vietnam by the RU-21A, -B, and -C aircraft and of the ever-increasing need for more sophisticated EW platforms for use in that conflict. The RU-21D was basically an RU-21A with a revised cockpit layout, upgraded avionics, and modified sensor fit. A total of thirty-four examples entered service beginning in the early 1970s; eighteen of these were rebuilt U-21As (67-18104 to -18111 and 67-18119 to -18128), while the remaining sixteen (70-15875 to -15890) were new-construction articles. At least fifteen RU-21Ds remained in Army service through mid-1985.

RU-21E:
Designation given to the sixteen new-construction RU-21D aircraft following their upgrade to commercial Model 65-A90-4 standard through the installation of 620 shp PT6A-29 engines

The Army's five U-21F Utes, purchased 'off-the-shelf' in 1970 for use as general utility transports, retained their civilian interiors and were the service's first pressurized aircraft. The machine shown here is 70-15909, the second example acquired. Note the round cabin windows, a feature which easily differentiates the -F model from earlier Ute variants. (U.S. Army)

The RU-21H is thought to have been the primary platform for the GUARDRAIL SIGINT system prior to the takeover of that task by the RC-12 Huron. Two of the most obvious external differences between the RU-21H and the earlier model Utes upon which it was based, the deletion of the passenger-cabin windows and rearrangement of the antenna array, are clearly visible in this shot of 70-15898. *(U.S. Army)*

and other detail changes. These aircraft are thought to have fielded the LEFT FOOT SIGINT system in Vietnam; current status of the variant is unclear.

U-21F:
Five commercial Model A100 King Airs (70-15908 to -15912) ordered 'off-the-shelf' in 1970 for general utility transport work. The U-21F was the Army's first pressurized aircraft, and is equipped with twin 680 shp PT6A-28 engines, four-bladed propellers, and civilian interior.

U-21G:
Designation given to the last seventeen production U-21A aircraft (70-15891 to -15907) after they had been fitted with upgraded electronics and other detail changes. At least eight of these machines remained in Army service as of mid-1985.

RU-21H:
Approximately twenty-one RU-21D, RU-21E, and U-21G aircraft were allocated this designation after being updated and fitted with 550 shp PT6A-20 engines. The RU-21H is thought to have been the primary platform for the GUARDRAIL SIGINT/DF system prior to the assumption of that task by the RC-12 Huron (q.v.).

RU-21J:
In 1974 the Army acquired three commercial Model A200 Super King Airs (72-21058 to -21060), designated them RU-21H, and used them in the operational evaluation of the Cefly Lancer airborne SIGINT system. Following the abandonment of that system in the late 1970s all three aircraft were modified for use

as VIP transports and redesignated C-12L Hurons (q.v.). These three machines differ significantly from other U-21 variants, having 850 shp PT6A-41 engines, longer fuselages mounting the Super King Air's distinctive 'T' tail, and various detail improvements.

TECHNICAL DATA (All versions, except where noted)

Engines:
Two 550 shp Pratt & Whitney of Canada (PWC)
PT6A-20 turboprops (U/EU/RU-21A/D/G/H)
Two 620 shp PWC PT6A-29 turboprops (RU-21B/C/E)
Two 680 shp PWC PT6A-28 turboprops (U-21F)
Two 850 shp PWC PT6A-41 turboprops (RU-21J)

Dimensions:

Wingspan:	45 ft 10.5 in	
	54 ft 6 in (RU-21J)	
Wing Area:	280 sq ft	
	303 sq ft (RU-21J)	
Fuselage length:	35 ft 6 in	
	35 ft 11 in (U-21F)	
	43 ft 9 in (RU-21J)	
Height:	14 ft 2 in	
	15 ft 4 in (U-21F)	
	15 ft (RU-21J)	

Weight (empty/gross, in lbs):
5300/9650
5300/11,500 (U-21F)
7530/12,950 (RU-21J)

Performance:
Speed (cruising/maximum, in mph):
248/260
285/310 (U-21F)
325/339 (RU-21J)

Service Ceiling: 26,100 ft
35,000 ft (RU-21J)

Range: 960 miles
1390 miles (U-21F)
2271 miles (RU-21J)

Armament: None normally fitted.
RU-21 aircraft are equipped to carry and dispense defensive pyrotechnics

Accommodation:
Two crew plus up to twelve passengers (U-21A)
Two crew plus up to six systems operators (EU/JU/RU-21A/D/E/G/H)
Two crew plus up to eight systems operators (RU-21B/C)
Two crew plus up to eight passengers (U-21F)
Two crew plus up to ten systems operators (RU-21J)

The RU-21J was developed from the commercial Model A200 King Air and, as this shot of 72-21059 well illustrates, much more closely resembles the C-12 Huron than any of the U-21 Ute variants. All three RU-21Js were initially fitted with the Cefly Lancer SIGINT system, though following the Army's abandonment of that programme in the late 1970s the three machines were converted for use as VIP transports and redesignated C-12L. (U.S. Army)

BEECH C-12 HURON

Type: Twin-engined utility
transport and EW
aircraft

Manufacturer: Beech Aircraft
Corporation, Wichita, Kansas.

HISTORY

As mentioned in the U-21 Ute section of this volume (q.v.), the
Army had been quite pleased with the Beech commercial Model
A90 and A100 King Air aircraft it had acquired in 1967 and 1971,
respectively. That satisfaction undoubtedly influenced the 1974
selection of the Beech civil Model A200 Super King Air as the
winner of the joint Army and USAF 'UC/CX-X' competition for a
new 'off-the-shelf' staff and utility transport aircraft. The A200
was larger, faster, and more capable than the U-21 series
machines from which it had been developed, and was also seen
(by the Army) as having great potential value as an advanced
electronic warfare (EW) platform. Several variants of the C-12,
as the A200 was designated, have since been adopted for Army
service:

RU-21J:
As mentioned in the U-21 section of this book, the Army
acquired the first three production A200s in 1974 and used
them, with the designation RU-21J, in the operational evaluation
of the Cefly Lancer airborne signals intelligence (SIGINT)
system. These three machines differed from subsequent
production C-12A models in having more powerful 850 shp
PT6A-41 engines, no provision for auxiliary fuel tanks, and
slightly different factory-installed avionics. After the successful
conclusion of the Cefly Lancer tests all three aircraft were
modified for use as VIP transports and redesignated C-12L.

The first production C-12D, 78-23140, seen during a pre-delivery factory
check flight. The -D model Huron differs from the C-12A and C-12C primarily
in having a large port-side cargo door, high-flotation landing gear, and
provision for wingtip auxiliary fuel tanks. *(Beech)*

C-12A:
The Army took delivery of the first of an eventual sixty -A model production aircraft in July 1975. These machines were intended for the staff and utility transport roles and were fitted with complete state-of-the-art commercial avionics suites in addition to the normal military communications and navigation systems. The C-12As differed from the commercial A200, and from the RU-21J, in having cockpits configured to military standards and, initially, in having less powerful 750 shp PT6A-38 engines.

C-12C:
Designation allocated to -A model aircraft re-engined with the 850 shp PT6A-41 turboprop. An initial fourteen examples were so modified, though the majority of surviving C-12As are to be eventually upgraded to this standard.

C-12D:
Essentially a -C model Huron equipped with a new port-side cargo door, provision for a fifty-two U.S. gallon auxiliary fuel tank on each wingtip, and high-flotation landing gear. The Army's initial order was for thirty-three aircraft, all of which were delivered by early 1983. Most of these machines remain in service as of mid-1987, as do an additional six examples ordered in 1984 and delivered in 1986.

UC-12D:
In 1983 the Army ordered six examples of this variant for use by the Army National Guard, and all six were in service by mid-1984. The UC-12D is almost identical to the standard -D model Huron, but its interior is optimized for the utility transport role. Additional orders are expected as the Army continues to upgrade the aviation capabilities of the National Guard.

RC-12D:
Designation given to Special Electronic Missions Aircraft (SEMA) version of the basic C-12D. At least thirteen of the thirty-three C-12D machines initially ordered by the Army were actually delivered in the RC-12D configuration. A further six examples ordered in 1984 were built to commercial Model B200 standard, which included the substitution of the 850 shp PT6A-42 engines for the PT6A-41 powerplants of the earlier machines. The RC-12D is a standard C-12D Huron fitted with wingtip-mounted sensor pods and the extensive antenna arrays characteristic of the AN/USD-9(V)2 Improved GUARDRAIL V airborne SIGINT/Direction Finding (DF) system. The RC-12D is believed to be the primary platform for this particular EW system, and the aircraft is operationally deployed almost exclusively in West Germany and South Korea.

RC-12G:
Standard RC-12D fitted with upgraded avionics and improved EW systems. Three such conversions are thought to have been completed by the end of 1985.

RC-12K:

Designation applied to nine new-construction ELINT aircraft ordered by the Army in October 1985. Intended for use with the Improved GUARDRAIL V system, these aircraft have a large cargo door and oversized landing gear as standard. Deliveries began in the spring of 1988.

TECHNICAL DATA *(All versions, except where noted)*

Engines:
Two 750 shp Pratt & Whitney of Canada PT6A-38 turbo-props (C-12A)
Two 850 shp Pratt & Whitney of Canada PT6A-41 turboprops
Two 850 shp Pratt & Whitney of Canada PT6A-42 turboprops (later RC-12D)

Dimensions:

Wingspan:	54 ft 10 in
	55 ft 6 in (C/UC/RC-12D, with tiptanks)
	57ft 10in (RC-12D/G/K, with wingtip sensor pods)
Wing Area:	303 sq ft
Fuselage length:	43 ft 9 in (without antennae)
Height:	15 ft

Weight (empty/gross, in lbs):
7865/12,500 (C-12A/C/L, C/UC-12D)
9865/15,500 (RC-12D/G/K)

Performance:
Speed (cruising/maximum, in mph):
310/325 (C-12A)
333/370)

Service Ceiling: 31,000 ft (C-12A)
35,000 ft

Range: 1040 miles (C-12A/C/L)
2000 miles (C/UC-12D)
1750 miles (RC-12D/G/K)

Armament: None
RC-12D/G/K equipped to carry and dispense defensive pyrotechnics.

Accommodation:
Two crew, plus up to ten passengers (C-12A/C/L, C/UC-12D)
Two crew plus four to six systems operators (RC-12D/G/K)

RC-12D 78-23142 in flight. This aircraft was the third production C-12D and, like all such machines converted to RC-12D standard, it carries the antenna array characteristic of the Improved GUARDRAIL V SIGINT system, wingtip sensor pods, and has had its cabin windows faired over. *(U.S. Army)*

BEECH T-34 MENTOR

Type: Single-engined flight test aircraft

Manufacturer: Beech Aircraft Corporation, Wichita, Kansas.

HISTORY

In early 1987 the Army took delivery of the first of six Beech T-34C Mentor trainers acquired from U.S. Navy stocks as replacements for a similar number of T-28 Trojans (q.v.) used as flight test observation and support aircraft at the Army Aviation Engineering Flight Activity (AAEFA) at Edwards Air Force Base, California, and the Army Airborne Special Operations Test Board (AASOTB) at Fort Bragg, North Carolina. The T-28s had originally been acquired in the years between 1966 and 1976, and the Army's decision to acquire the T-34C as a Trojan replacement was based on the Mentor's proven durability, rugged construction, excellent low-speed flight characteristics, manoeuvrability, and relatively modest maintenance requirements.

The low-wing, tandem-seat T-34 Mentor originated as the Beech Model 45, a private venture trainer design which first flew in December of 1948. In 1953 the U.S. Air Force selected the Model 45 as its first post-war primary trainer, and the USAF ultimately acquired some 450 examples of the piston-powered T-34A production version. In June 1954 the U.S. Navy followed the Air Force's lead, awarding contracts for the first of an

The Army's first T-34C (USN BuNo 160959) in close formation with the service's last T-28 in March 1987. The Mentor still wears its gloss red and white Navy trainer colour scheme in this shot, though all three T-34s assigned to AAEFA have since been given the same high gloss green and white markings as those seen on the T-28. The three Mentors operated by AASOTB retain the Navy colour scheme. *(U.S. Army)*

eventual 423 similar T-34B aircraft. In March 1973 the Navy awarded Beech a contract for the development of a turbine-powered version of the Mentor and the first of two YT-34C prototypes made its maiden flight the following September powered by a 715 shp Pratt & Whitney of Canada PT6A-25 turboprop. The Navy purchased a total of 334 T-34C production aircraft between November 1977 and April 1984, all but a handful of which were assigned to various Naval Air Training Command (NATC) squadrons.

The Army's T-34Cs were drawn from NATC stocks, all six having formerly been assigned to Training Air Wing 5 based at Naval Air Station Whiting Field, Florida. Three of the Mentors are assigned to AAEFA for use primarily in air speed calibration testing and as chase planes during the flight testing of new Army aircraft, while the three aircraft assigned to AASOTB are used as camera platforms during the flight testing of new parachute systems and techniques.

TECHNICAL DATA

Engines:
One 715 shp Pratt & Whitney of Canada PT6A-25 turboprop

Dimensions:

Wingspan:	33 ft 4 in
Wing Area:	180 sq ft
Fuselage length:	28 ft 8.5 in
Height:	9ft 7in

Weight (empty/gross, in lbs):
2960/4325

Performance:
Speed (cruising/maximum, in mph): 246/320

Service Ceiling: 30,000 ft

Range: 814 miles

Armament: None

Accommodation:
Pilot and observer

BELL H-13 SIOUX

Type: Single-engined light utility, liaison, observation and training helicopter

Manufacturer: Bell Helicopter Company, Fort Worth, Texas.

HISTORY

The Army's enduring relationship with the Bell Model 47 light helicopter began in December 1946, when the USAAF procured a single example for operational evaluation by the Army ground forces. This essentially standard commercial Model 47A was designated YR-13, and was soon followed into service by seventeen identical aircraft. The YR-13 was powered by a single 175 hp Franklin 0-335-1 piston engine, offered accommodation for a pilot and one passenger, and featured wheeled landing gear and a fabric-covered tailboom. The R-13's performance was judged to be exceptional, and the type subsequently became the first helicopter produced on a large-scale to enter Army service following the 1947 Army-USAF split. Between 1946 and 1970 the Army procured a total of 2197 Sioux of the following variants:

YR-13A:
Three standard YR-13 machines (serials 46-228 to -230) of the first evaluation batch modified for cold weather trials in Alaska

One of the Army's two H-13K research machines hovers above its Fort Rucker pad in late 1961. Though modified for high altitude flight these aircraft retained the pod and open lattice boom layout, bubble canopy, streamlined fuel tanks, and simple skid landing gear that characterized the entire H-13 series. Both H-13Ks were redesignated OH-13K in 1962. *(Bell Helicopter)*

in early 1947. The 'winterizing' process included the installation of improved cabin heaters, cabin insulation, some additional instrumentation, and minor modifications to the engine, transmission, and dynamic components. In 1948 all three aircraft were redesignated YH-13A in accordance with the services' joint adoption of the H-for-helicopter designation prefix.

H-13B:
Designation allocated to the sixty-five production aircraft (48-796 to -860) procured by the Army in 1948. This version was derived from the commercial Model 47D and was powered by a 200 hp Franklin 0-335-3 engine, had the now-distinctive plastic 'bubble' canopy, and incorporated minor detail changes. All but two of these aircraft were delivered prior to the outbreak of the Korean War, and many examples of this and other variants ultimately participated in that conflict.

YH-13C:
Designation given to a single H-13B withdrawn from normal service in 1950 for use as an engineering testbed. The machine was fitted with the now-familiar metal skid-type landing gear in place of the then-usual wheeled undercarriage, its rear fuselage covering was removed, and it was experimentally fitted with various types of external stretcher-carrying devices for evaluation in the casualty evacuation role.

H-13C:
A total of sixteen H-13B aircraft modified in 1952 for service as air ambulances. These helicopters incorporated the skid landing gear and open-lattice tailboom of the YH-13C, and were capable of carrying two stretchers on external racks fitted to the tops of the skids.

H-13D:
This variant was based on the commercial Model 47D-1, and was powered by the 220 hp Franklin 0-335-5 engine. The aircraft was outwardly similar to the H-13C, with the open-lattice tailboom, skid landing gear, and external stretcher attachment points, though not all of the eighty-seven examples procured (51-2446 through -2531, and 51-16642) were used in the air ambulance role. Those examples remaining in the Army inventory in 1962 were redesignated OH-13D.

H-13E:
Designation given to 490 production aircraft (51-13742 to -14231) essentially identical to the H-13D but with dual flight controls and a third seat. Redesignated OH-13E in 1962.

XH-13F:
In 1955 a single H-13D was experimentally fitted with a 240 shp Continental (Turbomeca) XT51-T-3 shaft turbine engine. This modification was not adopted for operational use and the aircraft was eventually returned to H-13D standard.

H-13G:

In 1953 Bell introduced the improved commercial Model 47G, which featured a small tailboom-mounted elevator for improved stability, greater internal fuel tankage, dual flight controls, and accommodation for a third person. The Army took delivery of the first of 265 examples in 1954. Those remaining in service in 1962 were redesignated OH-13G.

H-13H:

This variant was based on the commercial Model 47G-2 and had an uprated 250 hp Lycoming VO-435 piston engine, all-metal rotor blades, dual flight controls, and external stretcher attachment points. The Army acquired at least 453 examples of this variant beginning in 1956. Redesignated OH-13H in 1962.

H-13K:

Designation given to two production H-13H machines modifed to commercial Model 47G-3 standard through the installation of 225 hp Franklin 6VS-0-335 engines, longer rotor blades, and other detail changes. These helicopters were optimized for high-altitude operation and were evaluated at Fort Rucker, Alabama, in 1960 and 1961. Both were redesignated OH-13K in 1962.

A close-up view of the first of 265 OH-13S examples accepted by the Army, serial 63-9072, sitting on Bell's Fort Worth ramp just prior to delivery. These machines were slightly longer than the standard H-13H model, and were powered by turbosupercharged 260 hp engines. Note that this variant also dispensed with the skid-top stretcher supports common to earlier models. *(Bell Helicopter)*

OH-13S:

In 1963 the Army accepted the first of an eventual 265 examples of this variant, which was derived from the commercial Model 47G-3B. The OH-13S was some sixteen inches longer than the standard -H model Sioux and was powered by a turbosuper-charged 260 hp TVO-435-25 piston engine. The OH-13S could accommodate two persons in addition to the pilot, and had a gross weight of 2855 pounds.

TH-13T:

Designation allocated to the last H-13 variant acquired by the Army, a dual-control instrument flight trainer. A total of 411 examples was delivered beginning in 1963. Generally similar to the commercial Model 47G-3B-2, the TH-13T was powered by a 270 hp Lycoming TVO-435-D1B engine and accommodated one student in addition to the instructor pilot.

TECHNICAL DATA *(All versions, except where noted)*

Engines:
One 175 hp Franklin O-335-1 piston (YR-13/13A)
One 200 hp Franklin O-335-3 piston (H-13B, YH/H-13C)
One 220 hp Franklin O-335-5 piston (H-13D/E/G)
One 240 shp Continental XT51-T-3 shaft turbine (XH-13F)
One 250 hp Lycoming VO-435 piston (H-13H)
One 225 hp Franklin 6VS-O-335 piston (H-13K)
One 260 hp Lycoming TVO-435-25 piston (OH-13S)
One 270 hp Lycoming TVO-435-D1B piston (TH-13T)

Dimensions:
Main rotor diameter: 35 ft 1 in
38 ft 4 in (H-13K)
36 ft (OH-13S, TH-13T)
Tail rotor diameter: 4 ft 3 in
Fuselage length: 27 ft 4 in
28 ft 6 in (OH-13S, TH-13T)
Height (to top of main rotor hub): 9 ft 6 in
9 ft 8 in (YR-13/13A, H-13B)

Weight (empty/gross, in lbs):
1560/2100 (YR-13/13A)
1620/2230 (H-13B, YH/H-13C)
1730/2400 (H-13D)
1730/2500 (H-13E)
1730/2600 (H-13G)
1800/2655 (XH-13F)
1830/2700 (H-13H)
1815/2550 (H-13K)
1936/2855 (OH-13S)
1950/2920 (TH-13T)

Performance:
Speed (cruising/maximum, in mph):
62/78 (YR-13/13A)
66/82 (H-13B, YH/H-13C)
70/85 (H-13D/E/G)
88/95 (XH-13F)
85/100 (H-13H)
80/95 (H-13K)
93/105 (OH-13S)
97/110 (TH-13T)

Service Ceiling: 13,000 ft
17,500 ft (XH-13F)
14,500 ft (H-13H)
21,250 ft (H-13K)
18,000 ft (OH-13S/TH-13T)

Range: 150 miles (YR-13/13A)
175 miles (H-13B, YH/H-13C)
200 miles (H-13D/E)
238 miles (H-13G/H)
235 miles (H-13K)
324 miles (OH-13S, TH-13T)

Armament:
None normally fitted, though several H-13s were experimentally equipped with various weapons in the course of operational evaluations of helicopter armament systems. In addition, many H-13s serving in combat areas were fitted with non-standard defensive armament; such weapon fits often consisted of a single .30 or .50 calibre machine gun fixed to the skid tops and rigged to fire directly forward, or a single light machine gun or automatic rifle on a flexible mount in the passenger door.

Accommodation:
Pilot and one passenger (YR-13/13A)
Pilot and two passengers (H-13B/G/H/K, XH-13F)
Pilot and two passengers or two stretchers (YH/H-13C, H-13D)
Pilot, co-pilot, and one passenger (H-13E)
Pilot and up to three passengers (OH-13S)
Pilot and one student (TH-13T)

BELL V-3

Type: Single-engined VTOL
research aircraft

Manufacturer: Bell Helicopter
Company, Fort Worth, Texas.

HISTORY

In mid-1951 the Army and Air Force jointly began funding the development of Bell Helicopter's Model 200 tilt-rotor vertical takeoff and landing (VTOL) research aircraft in the hope that the machine's innovative propulsion system would revolutionize military VTOL flight. It was hoped that the Bell machine's two wingtip-mounted tilting rotors would give the craft both the VTOL capability of a helicopter and the higher speed and increased manoeuvrability of a fixed-wing airplane.

The first prototype (serial 54-147) was initially designated XH-33 in the helicopter category, though this was changed to XV-3 prior to the machine's maiden flight in August 1955. The craft had the fuselage and tail unit of a conventional airplane, with the pilot's position and four passenger seats in the forward section. The single 450 hp radial engine was mounted almost exactly amidships and drove the two fully-articulated, three-bladed wingtip rotors through a series of gear shafts. Both rotors were set in the vertical position for takeoff and landing, and were tilted fully forward by small nacelle-mounted auxiliary motors to produce horizontal flight.

The second XV-3 prototype (54-148) completes the transition to forward flight over the California desert. The rotor masts, seen here rotated almost fully forward, were encased in non-moving streamlined pods. *(Bell Helicopter)*.

The first XV-3 prototype was damaged beyond economical repair in 1956 and its place in the evaluation programme was taken by a second, somewhat modified machine. This aircraft (serial 54-148) differed from the first example in having two-bladed rotors, a small ventral fin, and other detail changes. The second XV-3 was the first aircraft in history to fully tilt its rotors from the vertical to the horizontal while in flight, and the information obtained during its evaluation was of immense value during Bell's development of the later XV-15 (q.v.). The second XV-3 was jointly tested by the Army and USAF (in Army markings) until 1962, at which time it was turned over to NASA for further VTOL research.

TECHNICAL DATA *(Both prototypes, except where noted)*

Engine:
One 450 hp Pratt & Whitney R-985 radial piston

Dimensions:
Wingspan (over
  rotor nacelles):   26 ft

Rotor diameter (each): 33 ft (first prototype)
                       23 ft (second prototype)

Fuselage length: 30 ft 4 in

Height (to top of tail): 13 ft 7 in

Weight (empty/gross, in lbs):
  3600/4850 (first prototype)
  3525/4900 (second prototype)

Performance:
  Speed (cruising/maximum, in mph):
    130/181 (first prototype)
    125/175/(second prototype)

Service Ceiling: 15,000 ft
Range: 140 miles
Armament: None
Accommodation:
  Pilot and up to four passengers

BELL H-15

Type: Single-engined liaison
and observation
helicopter

Manufacturer: Bell Helicopter
Company, Fort Worth, Texas.

HISTORY

Late in 1946 the Army Air Forces ordered three Bell Model 54 light helicopters for evaluation in the observation, liaison, and light utility roles. The aircraft were initially designated XR-15, but this had been changed to XH-15 by the time the first example made its maiden flight in March 1948.

The XH-15 was of conventional pod-and-boom layout, and its metal tube framework was covered with aluminium skin. The craft was characterized by a wheeled tricycle landing gear and an early version of the rounded plexiglass 'bubble' cockpit enclosure that eventually became de rigueur for seemingly all light civil and military helicopters. The XH-15 was powered by a turbosupercharged 285 hp engine, and used the stabilizer bar-equipped two-bladed rotor developed by Bell for the earlier Model 30 helicopter of 1943.

The first XH-15 (46-530) during an early test flight. *(American Helicopter Society)*

Though funded by the Army Ground Forces (AGF) the XH-15 was evaluated almost exclusively by the Air Force, the latter service having taken control of several AGF aviation projects following the 1947 creation of the USAF. Though an essentially capable machine the XH-15 was not adopted for service use, and all three examples acquired were used by the Army as high altitude research vehicles until stricken from the inventory in the early 1950s.

TECHNICAL DATA

Engine:
One 285 hp Continental XO-470-5 piston

Dimensions:
Main rotor diameter: 37 ft 5 in
Tail rotor diameter: 4 ft 3 in
Fuselage length: 25 ft 7 in
Height (to top of
  main rotor hub): 9ft 2in

Weight (empty/gross, in lbs):
2000/2780

Performance:
Speed (cruising/maximum, in mph): 80/95

Service Ceiling: 27,000 ft

Range: 205 miles

Armament: None

Accommodation:
Pilot and up to three passengers

BELL H-4

Type: Single-engined light observation helicopter

Manufacturer: Bell Helicopter Company, Fort Worth, Texas.

HISTORY

In 1960 the Army launched a design competition for a new Light Observation Helicopter (LOH). The specifications called for an aircraft with a 110 mph minimum cruising speed, 400-pound payload and accommodation for up to three passengers in addition to the pilot. Twelve firms submitted design proposals, and in May 1961 Bell, Hiller and, somewhat belatedly, Hughes, were named as finalists in the LOH competition. Each of the three companies was subsequently awarded a contract for the production of five prototype examples of its proposed aircraft; these prototypes were initially designated the YHO-4A (Bell), YHO-5A (Hiller), and YHO-6A (Hughes), though in 1962 they became YOH-4A, YOH-5A, and YOH-6A, respectively.

YOH-4A 62-4203 in the hover during the weapons suitability phase of the LOH competition. Note the extended 'bubble' nose and the dummy machine gun pod fixed outboard of the portside door. *(U.S. Army)*

The YOH-4A, which bore the company model number 206, made its first flight in December 1962. The aircraft was powered by a 250 shp T63-A-5 engine and featured two-bladed main and tail rotors, skid landing gear, and a conventional pod-and-boom layout with a protruding 'bubble' nose. The five Bell prototypes (serials 62-4202 to -4206) were evaluated by the Army in competition with the Hiller and Hughes designs and, after the Hughes YOH-6A was declared the winner of the LOH contest in 1963, all five of the Bell machines were returned to the manufacturer. The loss of the LOH competition did not spell the end of the Model 206's Army service, however, for a much-modified derivative, the Model 206A, was selected as the 'Lot 2' LOH winner in 1968 and subsequently entered the Army inventory as the OH-58 Kiowa (q.v.).

TECHNICAL DATA

Engine:
One 250 shp Allison T63-A-5 turboshaft

Dimensions:
Main rotor diameter: 33 ft 3 in
Fuselage length: 38 ft 8 in
Height (to top of main
  rotor hub): 8 ft 10 in

Weight (empty/gross, in lbs):
1536/2537

Performance:
Speed (cruising/maximum, in mph):
  111/135

Service Ceiling: 20,000 ft

Range: 283 miles

Armament:
The YOH-4A was fitted with several types of weapon systems as part of the LOH competition, including machine gun and rocket pods, door-mounted flexible machine guns, and podded grenade launchers. However, none of the weapons were actually fired in flight.

Accommodation:
Pilot and up to three passengers, or pilot and two stretchers in the medevac role.

BELL H-1 IROQUOIS

Type: Single-engined utility transport helicopter

Manufacturer: Bell Helicopter Textron, Fort Worth, Texas.

HISTORY

It is almost certain that no other single aircraft type is as closely associated by the general public with modern U.S. Army aviation than the ubiquitous UH-1 'Huey'. This is hardly surprising, given the fact that the Army has procured more than 9440 Iroquois of different variants since 1958. Furthermore, the linkage in the public mind of the UH-1 and the Army was firmly established during the course of the Vietnam War, for the Huey was truly the workhorse of that highly visible conflict and was a monotonously familiar sight, via television, for literally millions of people around the globe. Indeed, the image of heavily-laden American troops leaping from a hovering UH-1 into some long since forgotten battle is perhaps one of the most universally recognized representations of that most painful, confused, and frustrating chapter in American history.

The beginning of the Army's continuing relationship with the UH-1 was almost prosaically routine given the level of recognition eventually achieved by the type. In June 1955 Bell's Model 204 was named the winner of the Army's utility helicopter competition and the company was awarded a contract for the production of three prototypes. These aircraft, which were designated XH-40, were each powered by a single 825 shp XT53 turboshaft engine. In accordance with the Army's original specification the XH-40 could be configured for the aeromedical evacuation, general utility, and instrument trainer roles. The three XH-40s were followed into service by six YH-40 service test aircraft beginning

One of three XH-40s evaluated by the Army in 1957, 55-4461 is seen here during a pre-delivery factory test flight. The Huey's well-known profile is already much in evidence. Note the 'humped' rotor mast fairing, a feature not passed on to later variants. *(Bell Helicopter)*

in August 1958, and it was these latter machines that provided the much-modified airframe that was ultimately developed into the many Iroquois variants listed below.

HU-1:
Designations given to nine preproduction aircraft procured beginning in June 1959 (and the basis for the 'Huey' nickname by which the entire Iroquois series is universally known). Each HU-1 was powered by a single 700 shp Lycoming T53-L-1A turbine, and each used the two-bladed rotor/stabilizer-bar combination that would be characteristic of all succeeding Huey variants. All nine HU-1s were redesignated UH-1 in 1962.

HU-1A:
First production Iroquois model, 182 of which were delivered beginning in late 1959. The first fourteen of these aircraft had the same T53-L-1A turbine as the HU-1, but the remaining examples were powered by the 960 shp T53-L-5 derated to 770 shp. The HU-1A was the first Huey variant to see combat, the HU-1A-equipped Utility Tactical Transport Company (UTTC) arriving in Vietnam in October 1962 to supplement the activities of the CH-21 units that had been operating in-country since December 1961. Some of the HU-1A aircraft operated in Vietnam by the UTTC were field-modified for use as armed escorts through the addition of various combinations of machine guns and rocket pods. All HU-1A aircraft were redesignated UH-1A under the 1962 Tri-Service system.

TH-1A:
Fourteen of the first 182 production HU-1A aircraft were allocated this designation following their 1962 conversion into instrument flight trainers. All were based at the Army Aviation Center and School at Fort Rucker, Alabama.

XH-1A:
The Army's initial experiences with helicopter operations in Vietnam pointed out quite forcefully the need for a heavily-armed gunship version of the UH-1. The Army had, in fact, been conducting armament trials with various types of helicopters since the early 1950s and this research, coupled with the knowledge gained through the operation in Vietnam of field-modified armed helicopters, allowed the fairly rapid development of the XH-1A weapons testbed. This aircraft, a standard UH-1A modifed for its research role, was experimentally fitted with a wide variety of weapons and gunnery control systems, many of which were later adopted for operational use.

YHU-1B:
Designation given to four prototype aircraft incorporating the 960 shp T53-L-5 engine, increased chord main rotor blades, enlarged rear cabin able to accommodate eight troops or three stretchers, weapons attachment points, pre-installed wiring for

gunnery control systems, and other detail changes. The development of this variant began in 1959, and all four examples were evaluated by the Army during 1960. One of the machines was subsequently returned to Bell for conversion into a high-speed compound research helicopter, generally known today by the company designation Model 533. With the sponsorship of the Army Transportation Research Command this aircraft (serial 56-6723) was fitted with a modified rotor mast inside a redesigned fairing, a modified vertical tail unit, and extensive streamlining. These changes resulted in level flight speeds of over 170 mph, and a maximum of 180 mph was recorded during shallow dives. The machine was subsequently equipped with two 920 lb st J69-T-9 turbojet engines, one fixed to either side of the cargo cabin, as well as with two stub wings. Other engines were also experimentally fitted, and the Model 533 ultimately achieved speeds in excess of 300 mph.

HU-1B:
Production aircraft incorporating those modifications introduced on the YHU-1B. Later examples were powered by an 1100 shp T53-L-11 engine in place of the T53-L-5. The Army took delivery of 1014 HU-1Bs between March 1961 and December 1965; the type was redesignated UH-1B in 1962. The first UH-1Bs, eight gunships and seventeen 'slicks' (lightly-armed transports), arrived in South Vietnam in May 1963.

NUH-1B:
Designation applied to a single UH-1B (serial 64-18261) used for special electronics tests beginning in mid-1963. This aircraft was eventually returned to normal service as a standard UH-1B.

This machine, 60-3547, was the second of four YHU-1B pre-production aircraft. These helicopters retained the T53-L-5 engines of late-model HU-1As, but differed in having increased chord main rotor blades, a larger rear cabin, and the ability to carry weapons. *(Bell Helicopter)*

UH-1C:
Production aircraft essentially identical to the late-model T53-L-11-equipped UH-1B, but with an improved main rotor system and increased fuel capacity. A total of 767 examples were procured between 1965 and 1967.

YUH-1D:
Prototype based on Bell's commercial Model 405. This aircraft was powered by the same T53-L-11 engine as the UH-1C and late model UH-1Bs, but had an enlarged cabin capable of accommodating twelve troops or six stretchers. The first of an eventual seven YUH-1D prototypes flew for the first time in August 1961.

UH-1D:
Production version of the YUH-1D. The first of an eventual 2008 examples was delivered to the Army in August 1963.

UH-1H:
Production aircraft, based on the UH-1D, incorporating a 1400 shp T53-L-13 engine. The Army began taking delivery of this variant in 1968, and has since acquired over 5000 examples (many of them upgraded UH-1Ds). At least four UH-1H aircraft were modified for field evaluation of the Army's proposed Standoff Target Acquisition System (SOTAS); modifications included the addition of extensive mission-related electronic systems, the installation of a twelve-foot long, plank-shaped rotating antenna beneath the main cabin, retractable skid-type landing gear needed to allow the unrestricted in-flight rotation of the plank antenna, and the fitting of extensive and highly sophisticated electronic countermeasures (ECM) equipment intended to increase the machine's chances of survival over the modern electronic battlefield. The four SOTAS Hueys apparently retained their original designations throughout the test period, and were evidently returned to standard UH-1H configuration after the UH-60 Blackhawk (q.v.) was chosen to continue the SOTAS tests during the late 1970s.

EH-1H:
Electronic warfare version of the standard UH-1H. Developed specifically for use with the AN/ALQ-151 QUICK FIX signals location, classification, and disruption system, the first EH-1H is thought to have made its first post-conversion flight in 1972. The Army placed orders for five EH-1H aircraft in 1979, and at least three had actually been delivered by April 1981. The current status of the EH-1H programme and the actual number of aircraft in service are unknown, however, for the Army subsequently placed orders for the more capable EH-60 Blackhawk.

VH-1H:
Designation applied (apparently unofficially) to several UH-1H aircraft modified for use as staff transports for senior Army and

political leaders. Used primarily in the Washington, DC, area, these machines have plush VIP interiors and, in some cases, sport high-visibility external markings indicating their special status. Those aircraft remaining in service are gradually being replaced in the VIP transport role by similarly modified VH-60A Blackhawks.

UH-1M:
Designation given in 1968 to thirty-six UH-1C aircraft modified for use in the Army's Iroquois Night Fighter and Tracker (INFANT) project in Vietnam. The INFANT system was developed by the Hughes Aircraft Company with the sponsorship of the Army's Southeast Asia Night Operations (SEA NITEOPS) programme office, and used low light-level television (LLLTV) equipment and infrared searchlights to detect enemy activity during the hours of darkness. The UH-1Cs were fitted with uprated 1400 shp T53-L-13 engines and were configured to carry both the detection devices and the accompanying slaved XM-21 (or similar) weapon system. The first UH-1M arrived in Vietnam in October 1969, and the type remained in service for the duration of American participation in the conflict. The surviving UH-1Ms were put into storage in the United States following the American withdrawal from Vietnam, and several are known to have been transferred to the Government of El Salvador during the early 1980s. As far as can be determined the machines supplied to El Salvador are not equipped with the INFANT system, though they were nonetheless specifically referred to as UH-1Ms by the U.S. Government when the transfer was announced.

UH-1V:
As of mid-1985 at least 220 standard UH-1H machines had been converted for use as dedicated aeromedical evacuation aircraft

The quintessential utility helicopter; a UH-1H (71-20048) in flight. Essentially identical to the earlier UH-1D, the -H model Huey retains its predecessor's elongated cabin but is equipped with the more powerful T53-L-13 engine. Though ultimately intended for replacement by the UH-60, the UH-1H is certain to remain in Army service well into the next century. *(Bell Helicopter)*

under a programme administered by the Army Electronics Command. These UH-1Vs are equipped with advanced avionics optimized for all-weather, low-level flight, and carry sophisticated on-board life-support systems and high-speed rescue hoists.

The capable UH-1 family of helicopters has provided sterling service to the Army in a variety of roles for almost thirty years. Current Army plans call for the type to remain in service until completely supplanted by the UH-60 Blackhawk sometime in the late 1990s.

TECHNICAL DATA *(All versions, except where noted)*

Engine:
One 825 shp Lycoming XT53 turbine (XH/YH-40)
One 700 shp Lycoming T53-L-1A turbine (UH-1 and early-model UH-1A)
One 960 shp Lycoming T53-L-5 turbine (UH/TH/HX-1A, YUH-1B, early-model UH-1B)
One 960 shp Lycoming T53-L-5 turbine, plus two 920 lb st Continental J69-T-9 turbojets or two 3300 lb st Pratt & Whitney JT12-A3 turbojets (Model 533)
One 1100 shp Lycoming T53-L-11 turbine (UH/NUH-1B, UH-1C, YUH/UH-1D)
One 1400 shp Lycoming T53-L-13 turbine (UH/EH/VH-1H, UH-1M/1V)

Dimensions:
Main rotor diameter: 44 ft
48 ft (all -1D and -1H variants)

Fuselage length: 42 ft 7 in
44 ft 6 in (all -1D and -1H variants)

Height (to top of main rotor hub): 14 ft 7 in

Weight (empty/gross, in lbs):
4370/5800 (XH/YH/40)
4523/8500 (All UH-1/1A and UH-1B variants)
5827/9500 (UH-1C)
4717/9500 (All UH-1D/H variants)
5110/9500 (UH-1M)

Performance:
Speed (cruising/maximum, in mph):
110/125 (XH/YH-40, UH-1/1A/1B)
128/135 (UH-1C)
127/145 (UH-1D/H & variants)
110/300+ (Model 533)
128/144 (UH-1M)

Service Ceiling: 16,900 ft (XH/YH-40, UH-1/1A/1B)
18,500 ft (all others)

Range:
190 miles (XH/YH-40)
220 miles (UH-1/1A/1B)
315 miles (UH-1C)
289 miles (UH-1D)
299 miles (UH-1H & variants)
332 miles (UH/1M)

Armament:
During the course of its long service life the Huey has carried a wide range of offensive and defensive armament, the exact composition of which depended largely on the individual aircraft's assigned mission. Machines used primarily for transport tasks usually have provision for one 7.62 mm M-60 machine gun in each main cabin door, while those aircraft (from YUH-1B onward) assigned to fire suppression, armed escort, or pure attack duties have carried various combinations of fixed and flexible .30 calibre, .50 calibre, or 7.62 mm machine guns (both single- and multi-barrelled), 20 mm cannon, 40 mm grenade launchers, 2.75 inch unguided rockets, or TOW or SS-11 anti-tank missiles.

Accommodation:
Two to three crew (all versions), plus:
six passengers or two stretchers (XH/YH-40, UH-1/1A)
eight passengers or three stretchers (UH-1B)
nine passengers or three stretchers (UH-1C/1M)
twelve to fifteen passengers or six stretchers (UH-1D/1H & variants)

BELL SK-5

Type: Air cushion assault and utility transport vehicle

Manufacturer: Bell Aerosystems Company, Fort Worth, Texas.

HISTORY

In 1967 the Army Aviation Material Command awarded Bell Aerosystems Company a contract for the production of three Model 7255 military air cushion vehicles (ACVs). These craft, license-built variants of the British Hovercraft Corporation's commercial Model SR.N5, were each powered by a single 1250 shp turbine engine providing both cushion lift and propulsion. All three vehicles were essentially identical in design and layout, but two were heavily armed and configured for the assault ACV (AACV) role while the third machine was lightly armed and intended for use as a transport ACV (TACV). The three ACVs were delivered to the Army in April 1968 and allocated the non-standard designation SK-5 and the aircraft serials 68-15902 through -15904.

The Army had procured the SK-5s specifically for operational evaluation in the wetlands of southeast Asia, and all three hovercraft were airlifted to Bien Hoa, South Vietnam, in May 1968. The ACVs were ultimately based at Dong Tam on Vietnam's southeast coast, and were operated during the

The sole TACV rests on its deflated skirt while undergoing routine maintenance at Dong Tam, South Vietnam, in July 1968. This machine could be distinguished from the two AACVs by its lack of heavy armament (note that there is no .50 cal MG in the turret just behind and to the right of the open bow door). The TACV later underwent cold weather testing in Michigan and Alaska before being disposed of. *(Bell Helicopter)*

evaluation period by a composite unit initially designated the Airboat Platoon, 3rd Brigade, 9th Infantry Division. The unit, which was later redesignated the 39th Cavalry Platoon, began operations from Dong Tam in June 1968. The three ACVs subsequently engaged in a variety of tasks, including troop transport, armed reconnaissance, and casualty evacuation. The hovercraft proved well-suited to operations on Vietnam's extensive wetlands, being capable of sustained operations over large tracts of land that were virtually inaccessible by any other means. However, the vehicles were also found to be prone to mechanical failure, and were extremely vulnerable to enemy fire when not operating in close proximity to friendly troops.

The Army's combat evaluation of the SK-5 ACV ended in September 1970 without having conclusively determined the type's military potential. The Army, faced with the need to develop other, more urgently needed conventional systems, assigned the ACV a low research and development priority and disposed of the two AACV-configured vehicles outright. The third SK-5 was returned to the U.S. for further testing, first at the Army's Cold Regions Research Laboratory in Michigan, and then in Alaska, and was ultimately declared surplus and disposed of sometime in 1973.

TECHNICAL DATA

Engine:
One 1250 shp General Electric 7LM-100 JP-102 turbine

Dimensions:

Length:	38 ft 10 in
Beam (skirt inflated):	23 ft 9 in
Height (skirt inflated):	15 ft 11 in

Weight (empty/gross, in lbs):
10,225/21,100

Performance:
Speed (cruising/maximum, in mph):
54/77

Range: 180 miles

Endurance (at cruising speed):
3.5 hours

Armament:
The AACVs were equipped with two turret-mounted .50 calibre Browning M-2 heavy machine guns, two 7.62 mm M-60 machine guns, and a single belt-fed M-5 40 mm grenade launcher. In addition, the weapons of embarked troops could be fired through the open cabin windows. The TACV carried two window-mounted 7.62 mm M-60 machine guns for self-defense.

Accommodation:
In the AACV role the SK-5 was normally manned by a commander/operator, two turret gunners, two window gunners, and a radar operator/navigator. In the TACV role the crew consisted of just the operator and navigator, with up to thirty troops carried inside the vehicle.

BELL AH-1 COBRA

Type: Single-engined attack helicopter

Manufacturer: Bell Helicopter Textron, Fort Worth, Texas.

HISTORY

In early 1962 the Tactical Requirements Mobility Board issued a report that constituted the Army's first official endorsement of the use of armed escort helicopters in modern airmobile warfare. The wisdom of this view was validated during the first years of American involvement in the Vietnam conflict when the need for a specialized fire suppression and armed escort helicopter became all too apparent. The 1962 introduction into Vietnam of heavily armed UH-1 Iroquois utility helicopters dedicated to the attack role helped alleviate the problem, but this was an interim measure at best and in early 1963 the Army allocated $4 million to research and development of a purpose-built attack helicopter.

By early 1965 the Army had finalized its requirements for what it termed the Advanced Aerial Fire Support System (AAFSS) helicopter and several firms had begun development of highly sophisticated prototype aircraft. But the anticipated long lead time required for the design, construction, and production of the AAFSS, coupled with the immediate need for an adequate gunship helicopter for service in Vietnam, prompted the Army in August 1965 to open a competition for an interim AAFSS

AH-1G 66-15292, an aircraft of the first production batch, is seen here during its 1967 assignment to the Cobra Transition School at Vung Tau, South Vietnam. The aircraft is configured for the light scout role, armed with two XM-18E1 miniguns (one on each inboard wing pylon) and two seven-round M-157 rocket launchers (on the outboard wing pylons) in addition to the 7.62 mm minigun and 40 mm grenade launcher carried in the chin turret. Note the 'bolt-on' armor fixed to the fuselage side directly beneath the pilot's position, as well as the streamlined blister (directly beneath the stub wing root on both sides of the fuselage) which carried the ammunition for the pylon-mounted miniguns. *(Bell Helicopter)*

The most visible difference between the standard AH-1G and the AH-1Q was the latter's nose-mounted stabilized TOW missile sight. As shown in this view of 70-16055, one of the eight pre-production AH-1Qs delivered to the Army in 1973, this interim antitank helicopter retained the AH-1G's M-28 chin turret. The first of eighty-five production AH-1Qs was delivered in 1975; all examples were ultimately upgraded to AH-1S (Modified) standard, a variant almost indentical in outward appearance to the AH-1Q. *(Bell Helicopter)*

machine. Five aircraft were considered: the Bell Model 209, Boeing-Vertol's modifed CH-47A Chinook, a gunship version of Kaman's naval UH-2 Seasprite, Piasecki's Model 16H, and the Sikorsky S-61.

The Bell entry in the Interim AAFSS competition was an innovative aircraft derived from the firm's earlier D245, D255, and Model 207 Sioux Scout designs. Like these predecessors, the Model 209 featured a streamlined, narrow-width fuselage that accommodated a two-man crew in tandem seats with the pilot above and behind the co-pilot/gunner. The aircraft had stub wings with integral ordnance-carrying hardpoints, and was armed with two 7.62 mm machine guns in a remotely-controlled chin turret. The Model 209 was powered by a single 1100 shp T53-L-11 shaft turbine engine and used the rotor system, transmission, tailboom, and major internal components of the durable UH-1 Iroquois.

The Boeing-Vertol and Piasecki entries were eliminated from the Interim AAFSS competition in October 1965, and the remaining three competitors began comparative flight testing the following month. The Model 209 was named the winner of the 'fly-off' and on 4 April 1966 Bell was awarded an Army contract for two YAH-1G prototypes (the G suffix indicating the Army's belief that the new gunship was a version of the standard H-1 Iroquois). These two machines (serials 66-15246 and -15247) were the first of over 1200 Cobras acquired by the Army, the several variants of which are outlined below.

AH-1G:
First production version, one hundred of which were ordered on 13 April 1966. Powered by the same 1400 shp T53-L-13 engine (derated to 1100 shp) as the YAH-1G and initially armed with a single 7.62 mm machine gun in a TAT-102A chin turret (though this was changed in later production examples to either two machine guns, two 40 mm grenade launchers, or one of each), plus up to seventy-six 2.75 inch rockets in pods carried on the stub wings. Deliveries began in May 1967 and the first Cobras reached Vietnam the following August. The Army eventually acquired a total of 1119 -G model aircraft.

JAH-1G:
Designation applied to a single AH-1G (serial 71-20985) of the last production block used by the Army as an advanced engineering testbed.

TH-1G:
Standard early production AH-1G aircraft used as crew trainers; all weapons and associated systems deleted and full dual flight controls added.

AH-1Q:
In early 1973 the Army took delivery of eight pre-production AH-1Q Cobras, which were standard AH-1G machines modified for use with the TOW antitank missile. This modification included the addition of a Sperry-Univac helmet sight subsystem, a nose-mounted gyro-stabilized TOW sight, supporting electronics, and provision for a single four-round TOW launch canister on each outboard wing pylon. The AH-1Q was considered an interim antitank helicopter and it retained the standard -G model chin turret armament as well as the ability to carry 2.75 inch rocket pods on both inboard wing pylons. The first of the eighty-five production -Q model Cobras was delivered in June 1975; it and all subsequent AH-1Qs were ultimately converted to AH-1S (Modified) configuration.

AH-1R:
Designation given to a small number of standard AH-1Gs experimentally fitted with the 1800 shp T53-L-703 engine. These machines were not TOW-capable, and all were eventually brought up to AH-1S (Modified) standard.

AH-1S:
The Army's continuing development of the Cobra led, by the mid-1970s, to the appearance of the more powerful, better armed, and more capable AH-1S (Modified), AH-1S (Production), AH-1S (ECAS), and AH-1S (Modernized):
    The AH-1S (Modified) was the first -S model sub-variant to appear, entering Army service in 1974. The 'Mod S' retained the nose-mounted stabilized TOW sight and helmet-mounted sight systems of the AH-1Q, but was powered by the same 1800 shp

T53-L-703 engine as the AH-1R. The AH-1S (Modified) was intended for use primarily in the antitank role, but retained the AH-1G chin turret for self-defense and fire suppression. All ninety-three AH-1Q aircraft were brought up to this standard, as were 197 AH-1Gs.

The success of the AH-1S (Modified) led the Army to award Bell a follow-on contract for one hundred new-construction aircraft, which were known as AH-1S (Production). These machines incorporated the T53-L-703 engine, TOW system, and detail changes pioneered in the 'Mod S', but also featured a new flat-plate cockpit canopy, new cockpit layout and instrumentation intended to enhance the aircraft's nap-of-the-earth (NOE) low-level flight capabilities, and an interim infrared (IR) signature-suppressor mounted over the engine exhaust. The first of 297 AH-1S (Production) machines was delivered in 1976.

The AH-1S Enhanced Cobra Armament System (ECAS) sub-variant retained the engine, IR signature-suppressor, flat-plate canopy, and NOE cockpit of the AH-1S (Production) version, but was not initially equipped to fire 2.75 inch rockets. This new-construction aircraft also incorporated several significant changes, including composite main rotor blades, a new chin turret

The first AH-1S (Production) Cobra, 76-22570, attempts to blend into the scenery during an early test flight. These new-built machines retained the M-28 chin turret and incorporated the uprated engine, TOW system and detail changes pioneered by the AH-1S (Modified), but featured a new seven-surface flat-plate canopy, improved cockpit layout, and updated instrumentation intended to enhance low-level flight capabilities. This variant was redesignated AH-1P in late 1988. *(Bell Helicopter)*

The most recent Cobra sub-variant, originally known as the AH-1S (Modernized) but redesignated AH-1F in late 1988, incorporates the chin-mounted 20 mm rotary cannon, improved main rotor blade, and detail changes embodied in the earlier ECAS version, but also boasts an improved fire control system utilizing a pilot HUD, new fire control computer, and air data sensor. In addition, the AH-1S (Mod)/AH-1F is equipped with the AN/APQ-144 IR jammer (the small, multi-faceted cylindrical object attached to the rear section of the engine fairing), an IR signature suppressor fixed to the engine exhaust, and other detail changes. *(Bell Helicopter)*

housing a three-barrelled 20 mm rotary cannon, and a new weapons management system. The Army procured a total of ninety-eight AH-1S (ECAS) machines between September 1978 and October 1979.

The final Cobra sub-variant developed was the AH-1S (Modernized), which included both new-construction machines and upgraded AH-1G models. The AH-1S (Modernized) incorporated all the features of the ECAS Cobra, but was additionally equipped with a new cockpit head-up display (HUD), an improved 2.75 inch rocket management system, a fire-control computer, a canopy-mounted air data sensor, a more efficient IR suppressor, and an IR jammer mounted atop the engine exhaust fairing. The Army took delivery of the first of a planned 515 examples of this sub-variant (both new-construction and rebuilds of earlier machines) in 1980.

In late 1988 the Army adopted new designations for the final three AH-1S variants. The AH-1S (Production), AH-1S (ECAS), and AH-1S (Modernized) thus became, respectively, the AH-1P, AH-1E, and AH-1F.

TH-1S:
AH-1S machines (of all variants) used as crew trainers at Fort Rucker. This designation can be expected to change to TH-1P/-1E/-1F to conform with the redesignation of AH-1S aircraft mentioned above.

TAH-1S:
This designation is carried by later-model AH-1S (and -1P/E/F) machines used to train crewmen for the AH-64 Apache attack helicopter.

TECHNICAL DATA *(All versions, except where noted)*

Engine:
One 1400 shp Lycoming T53-L-13 turboshaft
One 1800 shp Lycoming T53-L-703 turboshaft
(AH-1Q/R/S)

Dimensions:
Main rotor diameter: 44 ft
Fuselage length: 44 ft 7 in
45 ft 2 in (AH-1Q/R/S)
Height (to top of
main rotor hub): 13 ft 6 in

Weight (empty/gross, in lbs):
6073/9500
6479/10,000 (AH-1S)

Performance:
Speed (cruising/maximum, in mph):
130/172
140/175 (AH-1R)
125/141 (AH-1S)

Service Ceiling: 11,400 ft
12,200 ft (AH-1R/S)

Range: 357 miles
315 miles (AH-1R/S)

Armament: See text

Accommodation:
Two crew

BELL H-58 KIOWA

Type: Single-engined light observation helicopter

Manufacturer: Bell Helicopter Textron, Fort Worth, Texas.

HISTORY

The Army's selection of the Hughes YOH-6A Cayuse as winner of the 1963 Light Observation Helicopter (LOH) competition fortunately did not bring to a halt Bell's continuing development of its entry, the Model 206/YOH-4A. Indeed, the Model 206 was modified for commercial applications and became highly successful as the Model 206A JetRanger. In 1968 the Army, desperately in need of a light scout helicopter with a greater useful load than the OH-6A, reopened the LOH competition and ultimately selected the Model 206A as the 'Lot 2' winner. The aircraft was designated the OH-58 Kiowa, and four variants have since seen service with the Army:

OH-58A:
Initial production version, similar in general layout to the earlier YOH-4A (q.v.) but with a redesigned, more streamlined nose, increased cabin seating, and 317 shp T63-A-700 engine of the

An OH-58A of the first production batch, 68-16695, is seen here during a 1969 field training exercise. Note that the fairing for the tail rotor linkage (seen along the top of the tailboom) has been removed; this was a fairly common practice with early model Kiowas, and was intended to make inspection and maintenance of the vital linkage easier. This particular machine is equipped with the door-mounted XM-27 7.62 mm minigun system, just visible outboard of the portside passenger door. *(Bell Helicopter)*

Though it incorporates a variety of important internal changes, the only readily indentifiable outward difference between the OH-58C and the earlier -A model Kiowa is the former's flat-plate windshield (shown here on OH-58C 69-16214). *(Bell Helicopter)*

Model 206A. The OH-58A was fitted with a larger diameter rotor than that found on the commercial machine, and had provision for an XM-27 7.62 mm minigun system in the aft portside passenger door. The Army procured 2200 examples of this variant beginning in May 1969, and the first OH-58A units deployed to Vietnam shortly thereafter. During the course of the conflict in Southeast Asia the Kiowa served ably in such roles as staff transport, light utility, and armed scout.

OH-58C:
Following the end of American participation in the Vietnam conflict the Army once again turned its attention toward Europe and the strengthening of its forces there against the possibility of a conventional war initiated by the Warsaw Pact nations. This reorientation of national defense priorities required the Army to develop, among many other weapons systems, an advanced scout helicopter (ASH) capable of surviving over the modern battlefield while locating and designating targets for more heavily armed attack helicopters. The period of time needed to fully develop an adequate ASH was anticipated to be quite long, however, and in November 1975 the Department of the Army approved a staff proposal advocating the modification of existing OH-58A Kiowas for use as interim scout aircraft. The resultant new variant, designated OH-58C, incorporated a more powerful 420 shp T63-A-720 engine equipped with the Black Hole infrared (IR) signature suppression system, a new low-glare flat plate windshield, improved cockpit instrumentation, additional armor plating, and the AN/APR-39 (V) 1 radar warning receiver. In 1976 the Army placed an order for an initial 585 conversions, and the first OH-58C was delivered in August 1979.

OH-58D:
In 1979 the Department of the Army adopted the Advanced Helicopter Improvement Programme (AHIP) as the most cost-effective method of developing the much-needed aeroscout

helicopter, and in September 1981 the Bell Model 406 was selected the winner of the AHIP design competition. The Bell proposal called for the conversion of existing OH-58A aircraft to OH-58D AHIP-standard all-weather target acquisition and designation platforms through the installation of uprated T703-AD-720 engines, four-bladed main rotors, improved tail rotors and transmissions, mast-mounted observation and target designation systems, revised avionics and electronics, and the ability to carry Stinger anti-aircraft missiles modified for air-to-air use. The programme was approved by Congress in late-1980 and, despite subsequent reductions in funding, the AHIP remains alive. The first production OH-58D was delivered in March 1986, and the Army hopes to acquire a total of 578 examples by 1991.

The OH-58D retains the bulged windshield of the OH-58A, but differs in several other important respects. As seen here, the -D model Kiowa's most prominent features are its redesigned rotor mast fairing and the characteristic mast-mounted sight. The gyro-stabilized and vibration-isolated sight, jointly developed by McDonnell-Douglas Astronautics and the Northrop Corporation's Electro-Mechanical Division, houses a telescopic TV camera for daylight observation, a forward-looking infrared system, and a laser rangefinder/target designator. The sight is independent of the rotor's movement, and can be aimed by either the pilot or co-pilot. *(Bell Helicopter)*

AH-58D:

In September 1987 the Army asked Bell Helicopter to develop a heavily-armed OH-58D variant capable of undertaking autonomous attack missions in addition to acquiring and designating targets for the AH-64 Apache. The first modified machine was delivered in December 1987, and by mid-January 1988 the Army had received seven out of an initial batch of fifteen (all drawn from the first 135 OH-58Ds delivered). The aircraft, officially known as Armed OH-58Ds but widely referred to within the Army as AH-58D Warriors, can carry four Hellfire anti-tank missiles, eight Stingers, two 7-round pods of 2.75 inch rockets, and two 7.62 mm or .50 calibre machine guns. Target acquisition and weapons aiming are done using the mast-mounted sight, which allows target engagement both at night and in bad weather. The Armed OH-58Ds are also thought to be fitted with radar warning receivers, infrared signature suppressors, and chaff and flare dispensers. All of the initial fifteen aircraft are assigned to D Company, 1st Battalion, 159th Aviation Brigade, 18th Airborne Corps at Fort Bragg, North Carolina. This unit deployed several Warriors to the Persian Gulf in mid-1988 as part of the U.S. oil tanker escort effort and, flying from Navy-operated barges equipped as special operations support bases, the Warriors are thought to have seen extensive action against Iranian assault boats attempting to attack U.S. and neutral shipping. And in early 1990 the Army announced a sweeping programme to convert a significant number of existing OH-58D machines to AH-58D standards over the following four years. This is seen as a relatively inexpensive way to bolster the armed helicopter force in a time of increasingly tight defense budgets.

TECHNICAL DATA (All versions, except where noted)

Engine:
One 317 shp Allison T63-A-700 turboshaft (OH-58A)
One 420 shp Allison T63-A-720 turboshaft (OH-58C)
One 650 shp Allison T703-AD-720 turboshaft (OH-58D)

Dimensions:

Main rotor diameter:	35 ft 4 in (OH-58A/C)
	35 ft 0 in (OH-58D)
Fuselage length:	40 ft 11 in
Height (to top of	
main rotor hub):	9 ft 5 in (OH-58A/C)
	8 ft 6 in (OH-58D)

Weight (empty/gross, in lbs):
1583/3000 (O-58A)
1600/3200 (OH-58C)
2825/4500 (OH-58D, estimated)

Performance:
Speed (cruising/maximum, in mph):
117/138 (OH-58A)
120/140 (OH-58C)
138/149 (OH-58D, estimated)

Service ceiling:
19,000 ft (OH-58A)
18,900 ft (OH-58C)
12,000 ft (OH-58D, estimated)

Range:
299 miles (OH-58A)
356 miles (OH-58C)
345 miles (OH-58D, estimated)

Armament:
Provision for one XM-27 minigun in OH-58A/C, though Kiowas operated in Vietnam often sported various non-standard combinations of fixed and flexible machine guns in addition to the minigun. The OH-58D can carry two twin-tube Stinger missile launchers, while the Armed OH-58D variant can be equipped with Hellfire and Stinger missiles, 2.75 inch rocket pods, and .50 calibre or 7.62 mm machine guns.

Accommodation:
One to two crew, three to four passengers (OH-58A/C)
2 crew (OH-58D).

BELL H-63

Type: Twin-engined attack helicopter prototype

Manufacturer: Bell Helicopter Textron, Fort Worth, Texas.

HISTORY

In November 1972 the Army solicited design proposals for a new Advanced Attack Helicopter (AAH) intended for the all-weather anti-armor role. The Army's specifications required that the new aircraft be powered by twin General Electric T700 turboshaft engines and armed with up to sixteen Hellfire or TOW anti-tank missiles in addition to a single 30 mm cannon. Preliminary design proposals were submitted by Boeing-Vertol, Bell, Hughes, Lockheed, and Sikorsky, and in June 1973 Bell and Hughes were selected as finalists and were each awarded contracts for the construction of two prototype aircraft.

Bell's entry in the AAH competition carried the company model number 409 and the military designation YAH-63, and was based largely on the firm's earlier, privately-developed Model 309 King Cobra. Like the Model 309 the YAH-63 seated its two man crew in tandem within a narrow fuselage, though the Bell design teamed reversed the generally accepted seating arrangement by putting the pilot in front in order to improve the aircraft's low-level 'nap-of-the-earth' (NOE) flight capabilities. In accordance with the Army's specifications the YAH-63 was powered by the same 1536 shp GE T700-GE-700 engines as those used in the competing Hughes YAH-64 (q.v.) and, also like the Hughes aircraft, was intended to carry its anti-tank ordnance load on short stub wings fixed to either side of the fuselage

The first YAH-63 prototype hovers above the taxiway at Fort Worth. This aircraft was extensively damaged in a June 1975 crash, but was repaired in time to take part in the Army-sponsored fly-off against the Hughes YAH-64. Note the tail skid fixed to the bottom of the tail rotor guard. *(Bell Helicopter)*

below the engine air intakes. The Bell AAH entry carried its three-barreled XM-188 30 mm cannon in a small chin turret just below the nose, immediately forward of a stabilized TOW sight. The YAH-63 had wheeled tricycle landing gear and a distinctive 'T'-tail, and retained the two-bladed, wide-chord main rotor characteristic of nearly all Bell helicopter designs.

The first prototype YAH-63 (serial 73-22246) made its maiden flight on 1 October 1975, but crashed during a test flight the following June. The aircraft was repaired and, along with the second prototype (73-22247), entered the official Army 'fly-off' against the YAH-64. On 10 December 1976 the Hughes machine was selected as the winning AAH design, and both YAH-63 prototypes were subsequently returned to Bell for disposal.

TECHNICAL DATA

Engines:
Two 1536 shp General Electric T700-GE-700 turboshafts

Dimensions:
Main rotor diameter:	51 ft
Tail rotor diameter:	9 ft 6 in
Wingspan:	17 ft 2 in
Fuselage length:	52 ft 5 in
Height (to top of main rotor hub):	12 ft 2 in

Weight (empty/gross, in lbs):
9800/15,000

Performance:
Speed (cruising/maximum, in mph):
167/202

Service Ceiling: 29,000 ft

Range: 515 miles

Armament:
One XM-188 30 mm rotary cannon in chin turret. Wing hardpoints could carry up to sixteen Hellfire or TOW anti-tank missiles, or up to seventy-six 2.75 inch unguided rockets in four pods, or up to four auxiliary fuel tanks, or various combinations of all of the above.

Accommodation:
Pilot and co-pilot/gunner.

BELL V-15

Type: Twin-engined VTOL
research aircraft

Manufacturer: Bell Helicopter
Textron, Fort Worth, Texas.

HISTORY

In May 1973 the Army's Air Mobility Research and Development Laboratory and NASA's Ames Research Center jointly awarded Bell Helicopter a contract for the construction and testing of two twin-engined, tilting-rotor VTOL research aircraft. Bell had long been a leader in tilt-rotor technology and the Model 301 design developed in response to the Army/NASA requirement drew heavily on knowledge gained from the earlier XV-3 convertiplane (q.v.). The first XV-15 (NASA serial 702) made its maiden hovering flight in May 1977, and was joined by the second example (NASA 703) in April 1979.

Like the earlier XV-3, the XV-15 derived both its vertical lift and forward propulsion from two wingtip-mounted tilting rotors. These were pointed directly upward for vertical takeoff and landing, and rotated to the horizontal position for forward flight. In the XV-3, however, both rotors were driven by a single piston engine mounted in the aircraft's central fuselage, whereas the XV-15's two 1550 shp powerplants were wingtip-mounted and each entire engine and rotor assembly tilted as a unit. The XV-15's two crew members sat side-by-side in a fully enclosed cockpit, and up to nine passengers could be accomodated in the rear cabin.

The second XV-15, NASA serial 703, is seen here making the transition from hovering to forward flight. In the photo above the craft is still in the hover mode with engine pods canted almost directly upward and landing gear still extended. In the top shot overleaf the gear has been retracted and the engine pods are rotating through forty-five degrees, and in the bottom photo the engines are fully horizontal and the craft is in normal forward flight. *(Bell Helicopter)*

The Army conducted extensive testing of the XV-15 in conjunction with NASA, and evaluated the aircraft's vulnerability to ground fire and its suitability for use as an electronic warfare platform. The Navy joined the XV-15 test programme in 1980, and in 1983 awarded Bell and Boeing-Vertol a contract for the joint design of an advanced XV-15 meant to fulfill the Joint Services' Advanced Vertical Lift Aircraft (JVX) requirement. The Navy ultimately placed orders on behalf of the Marine Corps for production versions of the improved V-22 Osprey design, though at the time this volume went to press the entire V-22 programme had been cancelled as a result of US defense budget reductions.

TECHNICAL DATA

Engines:
Two 1550 shp Avco-Lycoming LTC1K-4K turboshafts

Dimensions:
Wingspan (over engine nacelles):	35 ft 2 in
Wing Area:	169 sq ft
Rotor diameter (each):	25 ft
Fuselage length:	41 ft
Height (engine nacelles vertical):	15 ft 5 in

Weight (empty/gross, in lbs):
9570/15,000

Performance:
Speed (cruising/maximum, in mph):	230/382
Service Ceiling:	29,000 ft
Range:	512 miles
Armament:	None
Accommodation:	Two crew plus up to nine passengers

BELL D292 ACAP

Type: Composite airframe
research helicopter

Manufacturer: Bell Helicopter
Textron, Fort Worth, Texas.

HISTORY

In February 1981 the Army's Applied Technology Laboratory announced that Bell Helicopter and the Sikorsky Aircraft Division of United Technologies had both been awarded contracts for the design, construction, and initial flight testing of composite airframe research helicopters as part of the Advanced Composite Airframe Programme (ACAP). The programme's primary goal is the development of an all-composite helicopter fuselage some twenty-two per cent lighter and seventeen per cent cheaper to build, per production airframe, than conventional machines, yet which will still fulfill all existing military requirements for reliability, ease of maintenance, tolerance to crash and battle damage, and reduced radar signature. Bell and Sikorsky were each awarded contracts for the production of three machines; a tool-proof vehicle, a static test vehicle, and a flight test vehicle. Bell's ACAP machine, which carries the company model number D292, made its first flight in August 1985. By mid-January 1986 the aircraft had completed twelve of its projected fifty flight test hours.

The D292 was based on Bell's commercial Model 222 twin-turbine light helicopter and used that machine's 684 shp Avco Lycoming engines, transmission, and two-bladed main and tail rotors. The ACAP's tailboom, vertical fin, and rotor pylon are almost identical in appearance to those of the 222, though the D292's entire elongated pod-and-boom airframe is constructed of glass-reinforced plastic (GRP), graphite, and Kevlar. The use

The D292 lifts off on its first flght, August 1985. The aircraft uses the engines, transmission, and main and tail rotors of the Bell commercial Model 222, though its airframe is constructed almost entirely of composites. *(Bell Helicopter)*

of a particular composite material for a specific aircraft component is determined by the strength, flexibility or other primary characteristic required of that component. The D292's basic load-bearing structure is thus constructed primarily of graphite or graphite/epoxy, while the flooring and most of the craft's exterior 'skin' is made of a more ballistically-tolerant Kevlar/epoxy or glassfiber/epoxy blend. The seats for the helicopter's two crew members and two passengers are of Kevlar/epoxy and are designed to absorb the high vertical loads of a forty-foot-per-second crash landing, as are the legs of the craft's non-retracting tailwheel landing gear.

Detailed information regarding the D292's performance compared with the Sikorsky S-75 ACAP (q.v.) was not available at the time this book went to press, though it may be assumed that the future of the Bell machine in U.S. military service will be determined by the type's overall performance in all phases of the evaluation. It is also quite probable that the composite airframe materials and building techniques used by Bell and Sikorsky in the development of their respective ACAP machines will be incorporated into the design of the Army's LHX advanced technology helicopter, and almost certainly into the designs of future civil aircraft produced by both firms.

TECHNICAL DATA

Engines:
Two 684 shp Avco Lycoming LTS 101-750C-1 turboshafts

Dimensions:

Main rotor diameter:	42 ft
Tail rotor diameter:	6 ft 10.5 in
Fuselage length:	40 ft 5 ft
Height (to top of main rotor hub):	11 ft 2 in

Weight (empty/gross, in lbs):
5800 (approximately)/7,525

Performance:
Information not available at press time

Armament: None

Accommodation:
Crew of two, plus up to two passengers

BOEING L-15 SCOUT

Type: Single-engined liaison and observation aircraft

Manufacturer: Boeing Aircraft Company, Wichita, Kansas.

HISTORY

In late 1946 the Army awarded Boeing's Wichita Division a contract for the production of two prototype Model 451 single-engined two-place light liaison and observation aircraft. The first XL-15, as the type was designated, made its maiden flight on 13 July 1947.

The innovative XL-15 was powered by a single 125 hp Lycoming engine and featured a high wing and single tailboom supporting twin endplate rudders. The cabin offered an exceptional all-round view through numerous windows, the largest of which covered the rear-facing observer's position.

The second XL-15 prototype in flight. The machine's permanently extended, full-span 'flaperons' are just visible, as is the top portion of the rear-facing observer's window. The ten YL-15 service test aircraft differed from the prototypes only in having slightly larger rudders and somewhat different instrumentation. *(Boeing)*

Large permanently extended full-span 'flaperons' gave the machine excellent low-speed flying characteristics, and the entire aircraft could be rapidly dismantled for easy transportation.

The two XL-15 prototypes (serials 46-520 and -521) were followed by ten YL-15 service test and evaluation aircraft (47-423 through -432), the latter being delivered to the Army in late 1948 and early 1949. The YL-15s were essentially identical to the two prototypes, differing only in having slightly larger rudders and somewhat altered instrumentation, and were evaluated on floats as well as on their wheeled landing gear. After extensive testing the Army decided not to procure the type, and in late 1949 cancelled existing orders for forty-seven production L-15s. All remaining XL- and YL-15 aircraft were subsequently turned over to the U.S. Department of the Interior for use in Alaska.

TECHNICAL DATA

Engines:
One 125 hp Lycoming 0-290-7

Dimensions:
Wingspan:	40 ft
Wing area:	269 sq ft
Fuselage length:	25 ft 3 ft
Height:	8 ft 8 in

Weight (gross, in lbs):
2216

Performance:
Speed (cruising/maximum, in mph): 86/112

Service ceiling: 12,500 ft

Range: 217 miles

Armament: None

Accommodation:
Pilot and observer

BOEING-VERTOL H-47 CHINOOK

Type: Twin-engined assault transport helicopter

Manufacturer: Boeing-Vertol Company, Morton, Pennsylvania.

HISTORY

The CH-47 Chinook originated as the Vertol Model 114 of 1958, a larger and more capable follow-on development of Vertol's earlier Model 107 twin-engined assault transport helicopter. The Model 107 was evaluated in 1959 as the YCH-1 (q.v.) but found to be somewhat small for the Army's needs, and the service was quick to transfer its interest to the heftier Model 114. Five prototypes were ordered in June 1959 with the designation YHC-1B and the serials 59-4982 to -4986, and the type made its first flight in September 1961.

The common origin of the YHC-1A and YHC-1B was evident in the general layout of each aircraft, for both were powered by twin turbine engines driving tandem rotors mounted at either end of a ramp-equipped, box-like fuselage. There the resemblance between the two machines ended, however, for the YHC-1B was more than twice as long and nearly twice as heavy as the YHC-1A. The smaller craft carried its two 1050 shp T58 turboshaft engines internally at the base of the aft rotor pylon, whereas

A CH-47A Chinook of the fifth production batch lifts a pontoon bridge section into place. Early production -A model machines were powered by two 2200 shp engines, while later examples were fitted with two 2650 shp units. *(Boeing Helicopters)*

View from below of one of four ACH-47A gunships modified for operational evaluation in Southeast Asia during the mid-1960s. The machine seen here is armed with three .50 calibre heavy machine guns, a minigun pod, and a 19-cell launcher for 2.75 inch rockets. *(Boeing Helicopters)*

the YHC-1B's two 1940 shp T55 powerplants were mounted externally, one on either side of the rear pylon. Both aircraft were crewed by a pilot, co-pilot, and crew chief, though the YHC-1B could lift twice as many troops as its smaller predecessor.

The Army was well pleased with the YHC-1B prototypes (which were redesignated YHC-47A in 1962), and in late 1961 placed orders with the renamed Boeing-Vertol Division for the first of more than 700 production Chinooks of the following variants:

HC-1B:
Initial designation for first production model, changed to CH-47A in 1962. A total of 349 examples was delivered beginning in 1961. Early production aircraft were powered by two 2200 shp T55-L-5 engines, whereas late model machines had the 2650 shp T55-L-7.

ACH-47A:
Gunship version of the standard -A model Chinook. Four aircraft (serials 64-13145, -13149, -13151, and -13154) were modified in 1965 for operational evaluation in Southeast Asia. Modifications

included the removal of all cargo-handling equipment, cabin soundproofing, and all but five troop seats, and the addition of 2000 pounds of armor plating and installation of weapons pylons on each side of the aircraft outboard of the front wheels. Provision was made for extensive armament of one 20 mm cannon, up to five 7.62 mm M-60 or .50 calibre M-2 machine guns, two pylon-mounted XM-128 19-round pods of 2.75 inch rockets, a single chin-mounted 40 mm grenade launcher, and a variety of hand-held small arms. Three of the four ACH-47A machines were deployed to Vietnam in June 1966 and served primarily with the 1st Cavalry Division. The advent of the much more suitable AH-1 Cobra gunship and the loss in action of two of the less manoeuvrable and more vulnerable modified Chinooks ensured that the ACH-47A concept did not progress past the evaluation stage.

JCH-47A:
Designation given to the second production HC-1B/CH-47A (60-3449) when used for temporary flight testing.

YCH-47B:
The third prototype YCH-47A (59-4984) was so designated after being equipped with two 2850 shp T55-L-7C engines, upgraded avionics, modified rotor blades, and other detail changes. The machine was the prototype for the -B model Chinook, and flew for the first time in October 1966.

The -B model Chinook, the first production example of which is seen here lifting a two and one half ton truck, differed from the -A model in having two 2850 shp engines, modified rotor blades, and upgraded avionics. *(Boeing-Helicopters)*

Externally almost indistinguishable from the CH-47A and B, the -C model Chinook is capable of lifting a load nearly equal to the CH-47A's gross weight. *(Boeing Helicopters)*

CH-47B:
Production aircraft incorporating the improvements pioneered on the YCH-47B. A total of 108 examples was delivered beginning in May 1967.

CH-47C:
Production aircraft introduced in early 1968. Outwardly similar to the CH-47B, the -C model is powered by two 3750 shp T55-L-11C engines and features strengthened dynamic components, increased internal fuel tankage, and other detail changes. The -C model's gross weight is nearly 18,000 pounds higher than that of the original CH-47A's 33,000 pounds, and the -C is capable of lifting a load very nearly equal to the -A model's gross weight. The Army acquired a total of 270 Boeing-built CH-47Cs plus, beginning in 1985, eleven nearly identical aircraft built in Italy by Augusta. These latter machines were originally constructed for the Imperial Iranian Air Force, but were purchased by the Army after the Iranian revolution, designated CH-47C, and transferred to the Pennsylvania Army National Guard.

CH-47D:
Most recent Chinook variant produced, based on upgraded CH-47A, B, and C model aircraft. The CH-47D was designed to have the same performance as the CH-47C but be more mechanically reliable, easier to maintain, and cheaper to operate. The upgrading process includes the installation of two 4500 shp T55-L-712 engines, improved fiberglass rotor blades, upgraded

transmission and drive system, new hydraulics, and improved electrical and flight control systems. The first CH-47D (an improved -A) was rolled out in March 1979 and deliveries of a planned 436 machines began in early 1982.

MH-47D:
Designation applied to several CH-47D aircraft modified for special operations support missions and assigned to the special warfare-dedicated 160th Aviation Battalion at Fort Campbell, Kentucky. These helicopters are reportedly equipped with forward-looking infrared radar (FLIR), increased fuel tankage, sophisticated inertial navigation and satellite-assisted global positioning systems, extensive ECM suites, chaff and flare dispensers, cockpit instrumentation compatible with night vision goggles and, according to some knowledgeable sources, a fixed aerial refuelling probe. The MH-47D is apparently intended as a stopgap special operations aircraft that will eventually be replaced by the MH-47E.

MH-47E:
In late 1987 the Army awarded Boeing Helicopters an $81 million contract for the development of a prototype MH-47E

Most recent of the Chinook variants, the CH-47D is intended to have the same performance as the -C model, but with improved reliability and lower operating costs. *(Boeing Helicopters)*

special warfare support helicopter. Intended for clandestine, deep penetration missions, the MH-47E will have an unrefuelled combat range of some 3700 km, uprated T55-L-714 engines, upgraded 'glass' cockpit with new avionics and multiple CRT displays, Omega and Global Positioning navigation systems, extensive ECM equipment, chaff and flare dispensers, a non-retractable in-flight refuelling probe, an advanced fuel system, a high-speed rescue hoist, increased troop seating, and heavier defensive armament. Options to the original prototype-development contract could result in the delivery of an initial seventeen production machines (converted from earlier-model Chinook airframes) beginning in December 1990.

TECHNICAL DATA (All versions, except where noted)

Engines:

Two 1940 shp Lycoming T55-L-3 turboshafts (YCH-47A)

Two 2200 shp T55-1-5 or 2650 shp T55-L-7 turboshafts (ACH/CH/JCH-47A)

Two 2850 shp T55-L-7C turboshafts (YCH/CH-47B)

Two 4500 shp T55-L-712 turboshafts (CH-47D)

Dimensions:

Rotor diameter (each): 59 ft 1 in
60 ft (YCH/CH-47B, CH-47C/D)

Fuselage length: 51 ft

Height (to top of aft rotor hub): 18 ft 6 in

Weight (empty/gross, in lbs):

17,913/33,000 (YCH/CH/JCH-47A)
22,000/31,000 (ACH-47A)
19,375/40,000 (YCH/CH-47B)
20,547/46,000 (CH-47C)
22,784/53,500 (CH-47D)

Performance:

Speed (cruising/maximum, in mph):
164/178 (YCH/CH/JCH-47A)
155/168 (ACH-47A)
177/196 (YCH/CH-47B)
165/190 (CH-47C)
160/185 (CH-47D)

Service ceiling:
9500 FT (YCH/CH/JCH-47A)
16,300 ft (YCH/CH-47B)
19,000 ft (CH-47C/D)

Range:
115 miles (YCH/CH/JCH-47A)
351 miles (YCH/CH-47B)
245 miles (CH-47C/D)

Armament:
See text for ACH-47A. Other variants normally have provision for two 7.62 mm machine guns, one mounted in each waist window.

Accommodation:
Two to three crew, all versions except ACH-47A, which had seven to nine crew. All versions except ACH-47A able to carry from twenty-two to fifty troops depending on operational needs.

BOEING-VERTOL H-61

Type: Twin-engined utility
helicopter prototype

Manufacturer: Boeing-Vertol
Company, Morton,
Pennsylvania.

HISTORY

Army experience with assault transport helicopters in Vietnam led, during the early 1970s, to the formulation of a requirement for a new Utility Tactical Transport Aircraft System (UTTAS) helicopter intended to eventually replace the UH-1 Iroquois in the assault transport, general utility, and aeromedical evacuation roles. The UTTAS specification issued in January 1972 called for a simple, robust, and mechanically reliable aircraft capable of lifting an entire eleven-man infantry squad — or an equivalent weight in cargo — to medium altitudes at a minimum cruising speed of 201 mph. All designs proposed in response to the specification were required to use two General Electric T700-GE-700 turboshaft engines, and were to have wheeled landing gear, duplicate or heavily armored critical mechanical components, manual rotor blade folding, and only minimal avionics. In August 1972 Boeing-Vertol and Sikorsky were selected as finalists in the UTTAS competition, and each firm was awarded a contract for the construction and initial flight testing of three prototype aircraft.

One of three YUH-61 prototypes evaluated by the Army makes a low pass for the camera. The YUH-61 was somewhat smaller and some 1200 pounds lighter than the competing Sikorsky YUH-60. *(Boeing Helicopters)*

Boeing-Vertol's UTTAS entry carried the company model number 237, and the first of the three prototypes contracted for by the Army made its maiden flight in November 1974. The YUH-61A, as the Army designated the Boeing-Vertol machine, featured a four-bladed hingeless main rotor made of composite materials, had built-in work platforms that allowed easy access to all critical mechanical components, and was somewhat smaller and some 1200 pounds lighter than Sikorsky's competing YUH-60A.

All three YUH-61A prototypes (serials 73-21656 through -21658) were delivered to the Army in March 1976, and the UTTAS 'fly-off' was conducted over the next eight months. In December 1976 Sikorsky's entry was named the winner of the competition, and all three YUH-61As were returned to Boeing-Vertol shortly thereafter. The firm subsequently entered a 'navalized' version of the Model 237 in the Navy's LAMPS II competition for a ship-based multi-purpose helicopter, but again lost out to the Sikorsky H-60 (q.v.) and eventually ceased further development of the type.

TECHNICAL DATA

Engines:
Two 1500 shp General Electric T700-G-700 turboshafts

Dimensions:

Main rotor diameter:	49 ft
Tail rotor diameter:	11 ft 3.6 in
Fuselage length:	52 ft 6 in
Height (to top of main rotor hub):	15 ft 6 in

Weight (empty/gross, in lbs):
9750/19,700

Performance:
Speed (cruising/maximum, in mph): 167/178

Service Ceiling: 14,000 ft

Range: 370 miles

Armament:
Provision for two window-mounted M-60 7.62 mm machine guns.

Accommodation:
Three crew, plus up to twenty troops or seven stretchers.

BRANTLY HO-3

Type: Single-engined
    observation helicopter
    prototype

Manufacturer: Brantly
Helicopter Corporation,
Philadelphia, Pennsylvania.

HISTORY

In 1949 the Army procured five examples of the Brantly Model B-2 light helicopter for evaluation in the observation role. The type, which had first flown in February 1953, was a small and simple piston-powered aircraft originally intended for the projected 'personal helicopter' market envisaged during the early 1950s. The five machines obtained by the Army (serials 58-1492 through -1496) were designated YHO-3 and tested at both Fort Rucker and the Naval Air Test Center at Patuxant River, Maryland. The aircraft was ultimately judged to be too small to be of practical military use, however, and all five examples were eventually returned to the manufacturer.

The Army's decision not to adopt the YHO-3 did not mean that the type would not eventually see Army service, however, for in early 1986 the Army began taking delivery of the first of an as yet undisclosed number of newly manufactured Hynes Helicopters H-5T versions. Hynes, which obtained manufacturing rights for several Brantly helicopter designs when the latter firm

This photo clearly illustrates the YHO-3's small size and distinctive 'ice cream cone' shape. Note that a plexiglas bubble has been fitted to the cockpit framing directly above each crewman's head. *(Hynes Helicopters)*

Hynes H-5T remotely-piloted target variant of the Brantly B-2. Note the fiberglass forward section intended to make the craft resemble a Soviet Mi-24 Hind helicopter gunship. *(Hynes Helicopters)*

went out of business, developed the H-5T variant of the earlier Model B-2 as a remotely-piloted reconnaissance platform and gunnery target. Those machines purchased by the Army are thought to all be targets, and many are known to have been given fiberglass bodies closely resembling in outline, if not size, the Soviet Mi-24 Hind-D helicopter gunship.

TECHNICAL DATA

Engine:
One 180 hp Lycoming VO-360-A1A piston

Dimensions:

Main rotor diameter:	23 ft 8 in
Tail rotor diameter:	3 ft 9 in
Fuselage length:	21 ft 9 in
Height (to top of main rotor hub):	6 ft 11 in

Weight (empty/gross, in lbs):
980/1670

Performance:
Speed (cruising/maximum, in mph): 90/100

Service Ceiling: 9000 ft

Range: 300 miles

Armament: None.

Accommodation:
Pilot and observer.

CESSNA U-20

Type: Single-engined
liaison and light cargo
transport aircraft

Manufacturer: Cessna Aircraft
Corporation, Wichita, Kansas.

HISTORY

In 1949 the Army purchased, through an Air Force-administered contract, fifteen examples of Cessna's commercial Model 195 high-wing cabin monoplane for evaluation in the light cargo transport, liaison, and search and rescue roles. The Army found the rugged and dependable Cessna to be ideally suited to its intended tasks, and ultimately purchased eighty-three aircraft in three variants:

LC-126A:
Designation allocated to the fifteen evaluation aircraft (serials 49-1947 to -1960 and 49-2773) upon the Army's decision to procure the type in quantity. These machines were each

A U-20C in flight. This variant, used primarily as an instrument flight trainer, was virtually identical in appearance to the earlier LC-126A and LC-126B/U-20B. *(Robert J. Pickett)*

powered by a single 300 hp Jacobs R-755-11 radial engine, seated up to five persons in addition to the pilot, and served primarily as light cargo transports and liaison aircraft.

LC-126B:
Five machines (serials 50-1249 to -1253) purchased by the Army in 1950 for use by the Army National Guard. These aircraft were almost identical to the LC-126A, and at least three of the five remained in service in 1962 and were redesignated U-20B.

LC-126C:
In 1952 the Army began taking delivery of the first of sixty-three aircraft that had been modified for use as instrument flight trainers. These machines (serials 51-6958 through -6315) were redesignated U-20C in 1962.

TECHNICAL DATA *(All versions, except where noted)*

Engine:
One 300 hp Jacobs R-755-11 radial

Dimensions:
Wingpsan:	36 ft 2 in
Length:	27 ft 4 in
Height:	8 ft 4 in

Weight (empty/gross, in lbs):
2250/3350

Performance:
Speed (cruising/maximum, in mph):
140/180

Service Ceiling: 19,800 ft

Range: 900 miles

Armament: None.

Accommodation:
Pilot and up to five passengers (LC-126A/B).
Instructor and three students (LC-126C).

CESSNA O-1 BIRD DOG

Type: Single-engined
observation and
liaison aircraft

Manufacturer: Cessna Aircraft
Corporation, Wichita, Kansas.

HISTORY

The Army's long association with the Cessna Bird Dog began as the result of a design competition held during the period April-June 1950. The competition itself was a result of the Army's increasingly urgent need for a modern fixed-wing, two-place observation and liaison aircraft to replace the obsolescent World War II-vintage types still in service at that time. A rigorous evaluation showed the high-winged Cessna Model 305A to be exceptionally well-qualified for the job, for its performance far exceeded the Army's original requirements as well as the abilities of the other competing designs. The Model 305A was duly declared the winner of the competition, and the first production Bird Dog was delivered in December 1950. The Army ultimately procured nearly 3000 aircraft in the following variants:

L-19A:
First production version, 2222 of which were acquired. This variant was powered by a 213 hp Continental engine. All surviving examples were redesignated 0-1A in 1962.

L-19A-IT:
Designations given to the last sixty-six L-19A machines built after they had been modified for use as instrument flight trainers. Modifications included the installation of full instrument panels and blind flying curtains in the rear cockpit.

TL-19A:
Dual control trainer modification of the standard L-19A. The exact number of aircraft so modified is unknown, but is thought to have totalled no more than ten examples.

The simple but highly capable L-19A, was the first Bird Dog variant procured by the Army. *(Robert J. Pickett)*

The sole XL-19B in flight shortly before setting a world light aircraft altitude record in 1953. The machine was powered by a 210 shp Boeing XT50 turboprop engine, the exhaust for which can be seen just behind and below the propeller. *(Robert J. Pickett)*

XL-19B:
Designation allocated to a single L-19A (serial 52-1804) experimentally fitted with a 210 shp Boeing XT50-BO-1 turboprop engine. This aircraft flew for the first time in November 1952, and in 1953 set a world light aircraft altitude record of 37,063 feet.

XL-19C:
Two standard -A model Bird Dogs (52-6311 and -6312) fitted in 1954 with 210 shp Continental (Turbomeca) XT51-T-1 Artouste turboprop engines.

TL-19D:
Production version of the commercial Model 305B used by the Army as an instrument flight trainer. Similar to the L-19A, but equipped with dual instrument panels and powered by a 210 hp 0-470-15 engine driving a constant-speed propeller. The Army purchased 310 examples beginning in 1956. In 1962 surviving machines were redesignated TO-1D.

L-19E:
In 1958 the Army began taking delivery of the first of some 450 L-19Es, which were based on the commercial Model 305C and incorporated a strengthened airframe and other detail changes. These aircraft became O-1Es in 1962.

TL-19E:
Army records indicate that some twenty L-19E aircraft were modified for use as trainers through the addition of full flight

controls in the rear cockpit. These machines were redesignated TO-1Es under the 1962 Tri-Service designation system.

O-1F:
Early Army combat experience in Vietnam pointed out quite forcefully the need for a fixed-wing Forward Air Control (FAC) aircraft to replace the OH-13 Sioux and OH-23 Raven helicopters initially used in that role. The two ageing helicopters were quickly found to be totally unsuited for observation work in the 'hot and high' conditions routinely encountered in Southeast Asia, and both the Army and USAF therefore fell back on the much more capable O-1. The Bird Dog's performance was excellent in comparison to that of the Sioux and the Raven, and the Cessna also had a far better maintenance record and considerably lower operating costs. The Army, for its part, decided to use the O-1 in the FAC role until a more suitable light helicopter could be introduced into service, and therefore procured limited numbers of O-1F and O-1G Bird Dogs on loan from the USAF. The O-1F was essentially a standard TO-1D that had been converted first to USAF O-1D FAC configuration through the deletion of its dual controls, and had later been further modified through the addition of underwing hardpoints and a VHF radio. Most O-1F aircraft operated by the Army were returned to the Air Force or turned over to the South Vietnamese following the November 1966 introduction into Vietnam service of the Hughes OH-6 Cayuse observation helicopter. However, some examples of the O-1F remained in the Army inventory through the mid-1970s.

O-1G:
Essentially a standard O-1A converted for USAF FAC use in the

The impressive performance of the XL-19B led the Army to experiment further with turboprop-powered Bird Dogs, the result being the XL-19C. This photo shows one of the two L-19As converted to XL-19C standard through the addition of a 210 shp Continental (Turbomeca) XT51 engine. *(Robert J. Pickett)*

Though the stenciling on its side identifies this machine as an O-1D, it is in fact more accurately described as an O-1F. Built in 1955 as a TL-19D instrument trainer, the aircraft was converted to USAF O-1D standard for use as a stopgap FAC platform in Vietnam pending arrival in that country of the Hughes OH-6 Cayuse. Visible modifications made to this machine include the addition of underwing hardpoints for target marking munitions and installation of wingtip-mounted VHF radio antennae. The high-visibility markings quickly gave way to a more subdued paint scheme once the aircraft entered combat in Southeast Asia. *(Robert J. Pickett)*

same way as the O-1F. As mentioned above, some examples of this type were loaned to the Army for FAC use in Vietnam pending the arrival in that country of the Hughes OH-6. A few examples of the O-1G remained in the Army inventory until as late as 1974.

TECHNICAL DATA *(All versions, except where noted)*

Engine:
One 213 hp Continental O-470-11 piston
One 210 shp Boeing XT50-BO-1 turboshaft (XL-19B)
One 210 shp Continental (Turbomeca) XT51-T-1 turboshaft (XL-19C)
One 210 hp Continental O-470-15 piston (TO-1D, O-1F)

Dimensions:
Wingpsan: 36 ft
Wing area: 174 sq ft
Fuselage length: 25 ft 10 in
27 ft 8 in (XL-19B)
27 ft 10 in (XL-19C)
Height: 7 ft 4 in

Weight (empty/gross, in lbs):
1614/2100
1680/2200 (XL-19B)
1685/2200 (XL-19C)
1614/2400 (TO-1D, O-1F)

Performance:
Speed (cruising/maximum, in mph):
100/135
135/150 (XL-19B/C)

Service Ceiling: 18,500 ft
37,063 ft (XL-19B)

Range: 550-625 miles

Armament:
O-1 aircraft used in the FAC role were normally equipped with wing-mounted launchers for target-designation rockets, and some were known to carry observer-operated light automatic weapons for self-defense. Non-FAC aircraft were not normally armed.

Accommodation:
Pilot and one passenger/observer.

CESSNA T-37

Type: Twin-engined jet
trainer

Manufacturer: Cessna Aircraft
Corporation, Wichita, Kansas.

HISTORY

During the late 1950s the Army Aviation Test Board and the Aviation Combat Developments Agency (ACDA) began to jointly explore the feasibility of using Army-operated fixed-wing jet aircraft in the artillery adjustment, tactical reconnaissance, and ground attack roles. Operational necessity dictated that any such aircraft be easy to maintain under field conditions and capable of operating from unimproved forward air strips, and these prerequisites indicated that any jet procured for Army use would have to be simple and relatively small, yet at the same time be of robust construction and able to offer a performance significantly better than that of the various piston-engined machines then in Army service. Cessna's diminutive T-37 twin-engined primary trainer admirably fulfilled all these requirements,

Temporarily in Army markings, the three Project LONG ARM T-37s fly a tight formation over rural Alabama during 1958. *(Robert J. Pickett)*

and in early 1958 three examples borrowed from the Air Force were sent to Fort Rucker to begin a one year Army evaluation programme dubbed Project LONG ARM.

The Cessna Model 318 had been adopted by the Air Force as the T-37 after winning a 1953 USAF-sponsored design competition for a new primary jet trainer. The first of two prototype XT-37s had made its maiden flight in early 1954, and the first eleven production T-37As had entered USAF service in 1955. The three aircraft evaluated by the Army were all -A model machines of the fourth production batch, and carried the serial numbers 56-3464 to -3466. The T-37, widely if unofficially known as the 'Tweetybird', was characterized by low-set, non-swept wings, side-by-side crew seats, and a broad forward fuselage. The type was equipped with ejection seats for both crewmen, and its cockpit instruments and controls were identical to those found in frontline USAF aircraft. The T-37A was powered by two Continental J69 turbojets, one buried in each wing root, and was quite manoeuvrable and relatively easy to fly.

The Army's evaluation of the T-37 found the aircraft to be ideally suited for Army use and both the Aviation Board and the ACDA recommended quantity procurement of the type. However, mounting Air Force opposition to Army ownership and operation of fixed-wing jet aircraft eventually forced the Army to abandon the planned T-37 acquisition and all three machines used in the Project LONG ARM tests were returned to the Air Force in early 1959. The T-37 evaluation was not a complete loss, however, for it provided the precedent for the Army's later testing of the Northrop N-156, Fiat G.91, and Douglas A4D (q.v.).

TECHNICAL DATA

Engines:
Two 920 lb st Continental J9-T-9 turbojets

Dimensions:

Wingspan:	33 ft 10 in
Wing Area:	184 sq ft
Fuselage length:	29 ft 4 in
Height:	9ft 5in

Weight (empty/gross, in lbs):
3850/6600

Performance:
Speed (cruising/maximum, in mph): 368/408

Service Ceiling:	39,200 ft
Range:	796 miles
Armament:	None

Accommodation:
Two crew.

CESSNA H-41 SENECA

Type: Single-engined light
utility and observation
helicopter

Manufacturer: Cessna Aircraft
Corporation, Wichita, Kansas.

HISTORY

Shortly after its 1952 acquisition of the Seibel Helicopter Company, Cessna undertook development of an innovative light helicopter it designated the CH-1. The aircraft made its maiden flight in 1954, and in 1957 the Army purchased ten examples of the advanced commercial model CH-1B for test and evaluation. These machines, serials 56-4236 through -4245, were allocated the designation YH-41.

The YH-41 was of all-metal construction and provided seating for a pilot and up to three passengers in a cabin closely resembling that of one of Cessna's light fixed-wing aircraft. The Seneca* was powered by a single nose-mounted 260 hp supercharged Continental piston engine driving the two-bladed main and anti-torque rotors via a shaft which passed between the two forward seats.

The Army's evaluation of the YH-41 showed it to be an excellent high altitude performer, though the type's limited

The YH-41's nose-mounted piston engine drove the main and tail rotors via a drive shaft which passed between the pilot and co-pilot. This particular machine is 56-4237, the second YH-41. *(Robert J. Pickett)*

payload and rather complex maintenance requirements precluded its large scale procurement by the Army. The ten YH-41s were eventually relegated to miscellaneous flight test duties, most having to do with high-altitude helicopter operations, and in 1962 the surviving aircraft were redesignated NH-41As.

---

* The Senecas were an American Indian people of what is now western New York state.

TECHNICAL DATA

Engine:
One supercharged 260 hp Continental FSO-526 piston

Dimensions:
Main rotor diameter: 35 ft
Tail rotor diameter: 7 ft
Fuselage length: 32 ft 8 in
Height (to top of
rotor hub): 8 ft 5 in

Weight (empty/gross, in lbs):
2050/3100

Performance:
Speed (cruising/maximum, in mph):
105/122

Service Ceiling: 12,250 ft

Range: 270 miles

Armament: None

Accommodation:
Pilot and up to three passengers.

CESSNA U-3

Type: Twin-engined light
utility transport

Manufacturer: Cessna Aircraft
Corporation, Wichita, Kansas.

HISTORY

Cessna introduced its Model 310 light twin-engined cabin monoplane in 1954, and three years later the machine was named winner of a USAF competition for a new liaison and utility transport aircraft. The Air Force subsequently purchased 160 L-27As 'off-the-shelf', and in 1960 ordered thirty-five more advanced L-27B machines capable of all-weather operations. The Army's long association with the 'Blue Canoe' (the universal, if unofficial, nickname given to the aircraft because of the distinctive blue colour schemes carried by USAF VIP transport versions) began in 1960 with the acceptance of the first of an eventual twenty-five ex-Air Force L-27As. In addition, the Army also assumed ownership of at least thirteen L-27Bs transferred from USAF stocks. Under the 1962 Tri-Service designation system the L-27A and L-27B became, respectively, the U-3A and U-3B.

An immaculate U-3A (58-2166) of the Virginia Army National Guard photographed at Byrd Field, Virginia, in April 1976. The -B model Blue Canoe differs in having an all-weather flight capability, a swept vertical stabilizer, more powerful engines, seating for an additional passenger, and an extra rear cabin window on each side of the fuselage. Both models are equipped with permanently-attached wingtip fuel tanks. (Jim Sullivan)

The U-3 is a conventional all-metal, low-wing, twin-engined cabin monoplane with retractable tricycle landing gear. The -A variant, which Cessna designated the Model 310B, is characterized by a non-swept tail unit, twin 240 hp engines, and accommodation for a pilot and up to four passengers. The U-3B, initially known as the Model 310E and later the 310M, differs from the U-3A in having a sharply-swept vertical tail, more powerful 260 hp engines, seating for up to six persons in addition to the pilot, an added rear window on either side of the cabin, more sophisticated instrumentation and communications equipment, and an all-weather flight capability. Both variants are equipped with permanently-attached fifty U.S. gallon wingtip fuel tanks.

The Cessna U-3 has seen extensive Army service in the general utility and staff transport roles, and has also been used as an electronics testbed and an air-route survey platform. Though eventually replaced in the Air Force inventory by more advanced types the U-3 remains in limited service with the Army's reserve components. As far as can be determined, by the summer of 1986 approximately ten U-3As and at least eight U-3Bs were still operational with either the National Guard or Army Reserve.

TECHNICAL DATA *(Both versions, except where noted)*

Engines:
Two 240 hp Continental O-470-M (U-3A)
Two 260 hp Continental IO-470-D (U-3B)

Dimensions:
Wingspan (over
 tip tanks): 36 ft (U-3A)
  37 ft 6 in (U-3B)
Wing area: 175 sq ft
Fuselage length: 27 ft 1 in (U-3A)
  29 ft 7 in (U-3B)
Height: 10 ft 5 in (U-3A)
  9 ft 11.25 in (U-3B)

Weight (empty/gross, in lbs):
2900/4700 (U-3A)
3062/5100 (U-3B)

Performance:
Speed (cruising/maximum, in mph):
 213/232 (U-3A)
 223/240 (U-3B)

Service Ceiling: 20,500 ft (U-3A)
  21,500 ft (U-3B)

Range: 850 miles (U-3A)
  1110 miles (U-3B)

Armament: None

Accommodation:
Pilot and up to four passengers (U-3A).
Pilot and up to five passengers (U-3B).

CESSNA T-41 MESCALERO

Type: Single-engined trainer
and liaison airplance

Manufacturer: Cessna Aircraft
Corporation, Wichita, Kansas.

HISTORY

In mid-1966 the Army ordered 255 examples of Cessna's Model R-172E single-engined, high-wing cabin monoplane for use as primary flight trainers. The aircraft were designated T-41B Mescaleros*, and were basically similar to the T-41A machines already in service with the Air Force. The first six T-41Bs (serials 67-15000 to -15005) entered service in November 1966, and all the remaining machines had been delivered by March 1967.

The first of 255 T-41B Mescaleros acquired by the Army. Some seventy-seven Mescaleros, including this one, remained in Army service at the time of writing. *(Robert J. Pickett)*

The T-41B differed from the USAF's T-41A in having a more powerful 210 hp engine, constant speed propeller, a strengthened fuselage, and more advanced avionics. The majority of Army Mescaleros have been used as primary flight trainers, though many have also served in the general liaison role. Those examples currently remaining in the Army inventory, some seventy-seven aircraft in late 1988, continue to be used primarily as trainers.

---

* The Mescaleros were an Apache people of Texas and New Mexico.

TECHNICAL DATA *(Both versions, except where noted)*

Engine:
One 210 hp Continental IO-360-D piston

Dimensions:
Wingspan: 35 ft 9.5 in
Wing area: 174 sq ft
Fuselage length: 26 ft 6 in
Height: 8 ft 11 in

Weight (empty/gross, in lbs):
1255/2400

Performance:
Speed (cruising/maximum, in mph):
115/153

Service Ceiling: 17,500 ft

Range: 600 miles

Armament: None

Accommodation:
One instructor and one student in trainer role.
Pilot and up to three passengers in utility/liaison role.

CHRYSLER VZ-6

Type: Single-engined VTOL
research vehicle

Manufacturer: Chrysler
Corporation, Detroit,
Michigan.

HISTORY

In 1956 the Army solicited proposals for a light aerial utility vehicle that would, it was hoped, combine the versatility and ease of operation of the ubiquitous Jeep with the ability to overfly particularly hazardous or difficult terrain. Army planners envisaged a simple and robust craft capable of both hovering and low-altitude forward flight at moderate speeds, with the ability to carry a 1000 pound payload for several hours at a 'cruising altitude' of between five and twelve feet. Several firms submitted design proposals, and in early 1957 contracts for prototype development were awarded to Chrysler, Curtiss-Wright, and Piasecki.

Chrysler's entry in the 'flying Jeep' competition was a single-place craft that used one 500 hp reciprocating engine to drive two ducted propellers. The engine was located in the center of

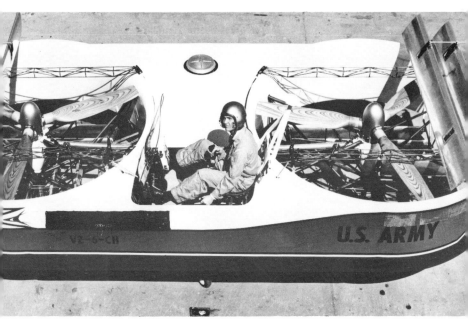

The first of the Army's two VZ-6s, 58-5506, prior to delivery. The machine's general layout was quite similar to that of the Piasecki VZ-8; both featured fore and aft lift fans with pilot and engine in between. The sectioned vanes attached to the duct tops controlled direction of travel by deflection of the slipstream. *(U.S. Army Transportation Corps Museum)*

the rectangular-shaped vehicle, next to the off-set pilot's position, with one ducted fan forward and one aft. Rubber skirts around the outside of the vehicle's bottom edge helped sustain the fan-generated lift, while forward propulsion resulted from lowering the craft's nose and using duct-mounted vanes to deflect some of the propellers' slipstream to the rear.

The Army took delivery of two Chrysler VZ-6 prototypes (serials 58-5506 and -5507) in late 1958, and tethered flight testing began in early 1959. At a gross weight of some 2400 pounds the VZ-6 was overweight and underpowered, and both examples additionally suffered from severe lateral stability problems. Indeed, during the course of the first non-tethered 'flight' the first prototype flipped completely over. The pilot escaped without serious injury but the craft itself was damaged beyond economical repair. Rather than subsidize further costly design modifications the Army chose to terminate the VZ-6's development, and both prototypes were disposed of in 1960.

TECHNICAL DATA

Engine:
One 500 hp Lycoming piston

Dimensions:
Propeller diameter: 8 ft 6 in
Vehicle overall length: 21 ft 6 in
Height (to top of
  pilot's seat):   5 ft 2 in

Weight:
2400 lbs (gross)

Performance:
Data not available

Accommodation: Pilot only.

CONSOLIDATED-VULTEE L-13

Type: Single-engined liaison and observation airplane

Manufacturer: Consolidated-Vultee Corporation, Wayne, Indiana.

HISTORY

Toward the end of the Second World War Consolidated-Vultee produced a new single-engined, high-wing cabin monoplane intended for general liaison and battlefield observation tasks. Two examples (45-58708 and -58709) were evaluated by the Army in 1945 with the designation XL-13, but the type was judged to be unsuitable and was not procured in quantity at that time. The Air Force did subsequently adopt the L-13, however, with the first of some 300 -A model aircraft entering USAF service in 1947. These machines were powered by 250 hp Franklin O-425-9 engines in place of the 245 hp O-425-5 power-plants used in the XL-15 prototypes, could accommodate five passengers in addition to the pilot, and had folding outer wing panels and tail units.

Shortly after the outbreak of the Korean War the Army, urgently in need of liaison and observation aircraft, acquired the first of an eventual forty-three L-13As from USAF stocks. The only modifications made to these machines in Army service

The L-13's characteristic tail unit is shown to good advantage in this shot of 46-068, the first production -A model machine. *(U.S. Army Transportation Corps Museum)*

91

were the elimination of the wing- and tail-folding capability and the installation of Army-standard communications and navigation equipment. The majority of Army L-13As were assigned to aviation units in the United States in order to free other, more capable, aircraft for service in Korea, and the type had virtually disappeared from the Army inventory by 1954. The Air Force later converted twenty-eight -A model aircraft to L-13B standard through the addition of skis and other cold weather gear, but this variant was not adopted for Army use.

TECHNICAL DATA *(All versions, except where noted)*

Engine:
One 245 hp Franklin O-425-5 piston (XL-13)
One 250 hp Franklin O-425-9 piston (L-13A)

Dimensions:
Wingspan: 40 ft 6 in
Fuselage length: 31 ft 9 in
Height: 7 ft 2 in

Weight (empty/gross, in lbs):
2050/3500

Performance:
Speed (cruising/maximum, in mph): 106/115

Service Ceiling: 15,000 ft

Range: 488 miles

Armament: None

Accommodation:
Pilot and up to five passengers, or pilot and two stretchers.

CURTISS-WRIGHT VZ-7

Type: Single-engined VTOL
research aircraft

Manufacturer: Santa Barbara
Division of Curtiss-Wright
Corporation, Santa Barbara,
California.

HISTORY

Like the Chrysler VZ-6 and Piasecki VZ-8 (q.v.), the Curtiss-Wright VZ-7 was developed in response to an Army Transportation Corps requirement for a 'flying jeep' type light VTOL utility vehicle. Curtiss-Wright's Santa Barbara Division (formerly the Aerophysics Development Corporation) was awarded an Army contract in 1957 for the development and initial flight testing of two prototype aircraft. These vehicles (serials 58-5508 and -5509) were delivered to the Army in mid-1958.

The VZ-7 was of exceedingly simple design, essentially consisting of a rectangular central airframe to which four vertically-mounted propellers were attached in a square pattern. The central fuselage carried the pilot's seat, flight controls, fuel and lubricant tanks, and the craft's single 425 shp Turbomeca

The first VZ-7, 58-5508, in hovering flight. The machine's single shaft turbine engine was carried on the rear portion of the rectangular central keel and drove four propellers, two of which are visible here, via extension shafts. *(U.S. Army)*

93

Artouste IIB shaft turbine engine. Both prototypes originally had ducted fans, though both engines were eventually modified to operate with unshrouded propellers. The VZ-7's control system was also very simple; directional movement was controlled by varying the thrust of each individual propeller, with additional yaw control provided by moveable vanes fixed over the engine exhaust.

Both VZ-7 examples performed adequately during the builder's initial flight test programme, and both did reasonably well when evaluated by the Army. The craft were capable of hovering and forward flight and proved relatively stable and easy to operate. However, the design proved consistently incapable of meeting the altitude and speed requirements specified by the Army and both examples were subsequently withdrawn from service and returned to the manufacturer in mid-1960.

TECHNICAL DATA

Engine:
One 425 shp Turbomeca Artouste IIB turboshaft

Dimensions:

Span (over propeller units):	16 ft
Propeller diameter:	6 ft 6 in
Fuselage length:	17 ft
Height (to top of pilot's seat):	9 ft 4 in

Weight (empty/gross, in lbs):
1700/2100

Performance:
Speed (cruising/maximum, in mph): 25/32

Service Ceiling: 200 ft (approximately)

Range: Not determined

Armament: None

Accommodation:
Normally pilot only, though the second prototype was sometimes fitted with a second seat for use by an observer.

CURTISS-WRIGHT MODEL 2500

Type: Twin-engined ground effect research vehicle

Manufacturer: Curtiss-Wright Corporation, Woodbridge, New Jersey.

HISTORY

In early 1960 the Army Transportation Research Command purchased two Curtiss-Wright Model 2500 Air Car ground effect machines (GEMs) 'off-the-shelf' for engineering and operational evaluation as part of an ongoing investigation into the military potential of air-cushioned vehicles. The acquisition of the two Air Cars followed by only a few months the Army's decision to help fund the development of Princeton University's Model X-3 GEM (q.v.), and was intended to ascertain the relative values of the Model 2500's plenum-chamber lift system as compared with the annular-jet system of the Princeton X-3.

Curtiss-Wright had developed the Air Car as a four-passenger commercial vehicle and hoped that it would be accepted by the public as a sort of air-cushioned equivalent of the family car. In order to increase the machine's outward resemblance to an automobile Curtiss-Wright's designers gave the Model 2500 such car-like features as dual headlights, tail lights, turn indicators, rudimentary bumpers, and a convertible top. The overall visual effect was rather peculiar, but despite its eccentric appearance the Air Car was essentially straightforward in construction. The machine was built of welded steel tubing covered by moulded sheet metal, and was powered by two 180 hp Lycoming engines mounted one forward and one aft of the passenger compartment. Each engine was used to drive, via reduction gears, a single four-bladed lift fan placed within a plenum chamber. The two chambers created an air cushion some ten to fifteen inches thick, and forward propulsion was supplied by air bled off from

Curtiss-Wright's attempts to make the Air Car look as much as possible like a family car show to good advantage in this photo of the Army's first Model 2500. Forward propulsion was provided by expelling bleed air through two sets of exhaust louvers, the starboard pair of which are seen here fore and aft of the passenger door. *(U.S. Army Transportation Corps Museum)*

The second Air Car crossing a water obstacle during the operational evaluation. Though fairly manoeuvrable the Model 2500 was not really capable of all-terrain operation. *(U.S. Army Transportation Corps Museum)*

the chambers and expelled at low velocity through two sets of louvers on each side of the vehicle.

The Air Car was fairly manoeuvrable and could reach speeds of up to 38 mph, yet it was not really capable of all-terrain operation and never really caught on commercially. The Army's two vehicles (which were neither type-classified nor allocated serial numbers) did provide much useful information on plenum chamber air-cushioned vehicle theory and operation, however, and it was with some reluctance that they were finally returned to Curtiss-Wright at the end of the sixty-day evaluation.

TECHNICAL DATA

Engines:
Two 180 hp Lycoming VO-360-A1A

Dimensions:
Diameter of lift fans:	4 ft 7 in
Body length:	21 ft
Width:	8 ft
Height (to top of windshield):	6 ft 1 in

Weight (loaded, in lbs):
2770

Performance:
Speed (cruising/maximum, in mph):
20/38
Normal operating height above ground
10-12 in

Armament: None

Accommodation:
Operator and up to three passengers.

DE HAVILLAND U-6 BEAVER

Type: Single-engined liaison and utility transport airplane

Manufacturer: De Havilland Aircraft of Canada, Downsview, Ontario.

HISTORY

The de Havilland commercial Model DHC-2 was intended from the beginning to be used primarily in the rugged bush country of northern Canada, and its design therefore incorporated many features — widetrack landing gear, ease of maintenance under field conditions, excellent STOL characteristics, and so on — that were also highly desirable in a military liaison and transport aircraft. The U.S. Army was understandably interested in the DHC-2, and monitored the machine's progress from its first flight in 1947 onward. However, U.S. political opposition to the purchase of foreign-built military aircraft prevented the Army's acquisition of the DHC-2 for several years. Indeed, it was not until 1950 that Congress, finally made aware of the Army's desperate need for modern aircraft for use in Korea, relented and authorised the Army's purchase of two DHC-2s for evaluation. These initial YL-20 Beavers (serials 51-5110 and -5111) were eventually joined in Army service by 654 production aircraft of the following variants:

L-20A:
First production version, which differed from the commercial DHC-2 only in having Army-standard navigation and communications equipment. A total of 648 examples was acquired, with delivery beginning in 1952 (this being the largest fixed-wing

An early production model L-20A/U-6A in flight. The Army procured 648 examples of this variant, which could carry up to seven persons, or one stretcher and attendant, in addition to the pilot. This machine sports the red and white high-visibility 'Arctic' paint scheme common to aircraft operated in extreme cold weather areas. *(De Havilland-Canada)*

order placed by the post-WWII Army up to that time). Surviving L-20As were redesignated U-6A in 1962.

L-20B:
Essentially similar to the L-20A, though with minor equipment changes. Six examples (53-7780 through -7785) were procured; survivors became U-6B in 1962.

TU-6A:
Post-1962 designation applied to several U-6A aircraft fitted with full dual controls and used as crew trainers.

The de Havilland Beaver saw extensive service with the Army, including combat duty in both Korea and Vietnam. The type was operated on wheels, skis, and floats, and formed the backbone of Army aviation operations in the key transitional period between 1955 and 1965.

TECHNICAL DATA *(All versions, except where noted)*

Engine:
One 450 hp Pratt & Whitney R-985-AN-1 radial (YL-20)
One 450 hp Pratt & Whitney R-985-AN-1, -AN-3, -AN-39, or -AN-39A radial (U-6A/B, TU-6A)

Dimensions:
Wingspan: 48 ft
Wing area: 250 sq ft
Fuselage length: 30 ft 4 in
Height (on wheeled
landing gear): 9 ft

Weight (empty/gross, in lbs):
3000/5100

Performance:
Speed (cruising/maximum, in mph):
125/163

Service Ceiling: 20,000 ft

Range: 690 miles

Armament:
None normally fitted, though Beavers operated in Vietnam were occasionally seen with door-mounted 7.62 mm M-60 machine guns.

Accommodation:
One pilot, plus up to seven passengers or one stretcher and one attendant (YL-20, U-6A/B).
One instructor pilot and up to three students (TU-6A).

DE HAVILLAND U-1 OTTER

Type: Single-engined medium   Manufacturer: De Havilland
STOL transport   Aircraft of Canada,
                              Downsview, Ontario.

HISTORY

In 1951 de Havilland of Canada introduced the commercial Model DHC-3 STOL utility aircraft as a larger and more powerful follow-on to the very successful DHC-2 Beaver. The U.S. Army evaluated a single DHC-3 company demonstrator aircraft at Fort Bragg, North Carolina, in mid-1953, and in March 1955 purchased six production examples 'off-the-shelf' for extensive service testing. These six aircraft (serials 55-2973 to -2978) were initially given the interim designation YC-137, though this was changed to YU-1 prior to delivery.

The Army was well pleased with the YU-1, and in 1956 accepted the first of an eventual 184 U-1A production examples. At the time of its adoption by the Army the Otter was the largest and heaviest single-engined utility aircraft in the world. The Army put the Otter's many strengths to good use, using it in conjunction with helicopters to move troops, supplies, casualties, and VIPs in nearly every theater of Army operations. The U-1A could be operated on floats and skis in addition to normal wheeled landing gear and this, coupled with the type's excellent STOL capabilities, gave it a versatility unmatched by most other fixed-wing utility aircraft then in use. The Otter was one of the first types of Army aircraft to be deployed to South Vietnam (in February 1962), and saw extensive service during that conflict in the transport, communications, observation, liaison, casualty evacuation, and special operations support roles. In addition, a

This machine, 55-2977, was one of the six commercial model DHC-3s purchased 'off-the-shelf' for service testing in 1955. The Army ultimately acquired 184 essentially identical U-1A production examples. At the time of its adoption by the Army the Otter was the largest and heaviest single-engined utility aircraft in the world. *(Peter M. Bowers Collection)*

number of U-1As were modified for use as electronic warfare support aircraft with the designation RU-1A. The Army also operated a handful of U-1B variants, which were ex-Navy aircraft equipped with slightly different avionics.

The Otter's versatility ensured that the type remained in frontline Army service well past the point at which most other fixed-wing utility aircraft had been retired in favor of helicopters. Indeed, records indicate that the last U-1A was not withdrawn from active Army service until 1974, and several examples remained in use with the Reserve and National Guard for several additional years.

TECHNICAL DATA *(All versions, except where noted)*

Engine:
One 600 hp Pratt & Whitney R-1340-59 radial

Dimensions:
Wingspan:	58 ft
Wing area:	375 sq ft
Fuselage length:	41 ft 10 in
Height:	12 ft 7 in

Weight (empty/gross, in lbs):
4431/8000

Performance:
Speed (cruising/maximum, in mph): 138/153

Service Ceiling: 17,400 ft

Range: 945 miles

Armament:
None normally fitted.

Accommodation:
Two crew and up to nine passengers.

DE HAVILLAND C-7 CARIBOU

Type: Twin-engined STOL
tactical transport

Manufacturer: De Havilland
Aircraft of Canada,
Downsview, Ontario.

HISTORY

In 1955 de Havilland of Canada began design work on a twin-engined, STOL-capable utility transport intended as a 'big brother' to the existing DHC-2 Beaver and DHC-3 Otter. The U.S. Army was from the beginning intended by de Havilland to be the primary user of the new DHC-4, and the company's design team therefore went to great lengths to produce a machine specifically tailored to meet the Army's stringent requirements. This corporate foresight quickly paid off, for in 1957 the Army ordered five prototypes for service evaluation. The first civil model DHC-4 made its maiden flight in July 1958 and the first YAC-1, as the Army designated the type, made its debut in March of the following year. The five YAC-1s (57-3079 to -3083) were delivered beginning in October 1959, and in early 1960 the Army awarded de Havilland the first of several contracts for the construction of AC-1 production aircraft. The Army ultimately acquired fifty-six AC-1A machines and 103 of the slightly heavier AC-1B model. In 1962 the designations of these aircraft were changed to, respectively, CV-2A and CV-2B.

The rugged and reliable CV-2 Caribou was powered by two 1450 hp engines and could haul nearly four tons of cargo or up to forty passengers into and out of the roughest forward air fields. The machine's body-width rear cargo door was designed to allow vehicles up to three tons to drive onto and off the aircraft, and could be lowered in flight to allow the air-dropping of men, vehicles and supplies. The Army capitalized on the Caribou's unique talents by quickly making it the backbone of aerial resupply activities in the United States and, from June 1962 onward, in Southeast Asia.

The CV-2 was ideally suited to service in Vietnam and the surrounding areas, and was used to haul every conceivable type of cargo in all weathers. However, the Caribou's success as a tactical transport in Vietnam ultimately helped rekindle the long-simmering Army-Air Force dispute over which service should operate large fixed-wing transport aircraft in support of Army operations. The Caribou had from the beginning exceeded the weight limit tacitly recognized by the Army and Air Force as the dividing line between their respective fixed-wing 'spheres of influence', and the Air Force was eventually able to show that the CV-2 could be even more valuable if its operations were totally integrated with those of the Tactical Air Command's C-123s and C-130s. In late 1966 the Army and Air Force Chiefs of Staff therefore negotiated an agreement under which all CV-2 aircraft would be turned over to the Air Force; in return, the

A fine air-to-air study of YAC-1 57-3082 (ex-Canadian civil registration CF-LKG-X) one of five commercial DHC-4s ordered by the Army in 1957 for service evaluation. Production Caribous differed only in having minor equipment changes and higher gross weights. This particular machine sports the high-visibility 'Arctic' paint scheme of gloss white fuselage with gloss red tail and wing tips. *(De Havilland Canada)*

Army would be allowed to keep its OV-1 Mohawk (q.v) battlefield reconnaissance machines and would be given a free hand in developing its helicopter force*. The agreement went into effect on 1 January 1967, at which time all CV-2A and CV-2B aircraft were officially added to the Air Force inventory with the designations C-7A and C-7B, respectively.

The 1966 Army-Air Force agreement did not mean the total disappearance of the Caribou from Army service, however. Several C-7A and C-7B aircraft engaged in particularly important tasks at the time the agreement went into effect were allowed to remain in the Army inventory with the understanding that they would be transferred to the Air Force upon completion of their special duties. In addition, some twenty Caribous of both variants found their way back into Army service in the years following the agreement. Almost all of these latter machines

---

* The agreement did not inhibit the Air Force's later, highly vocal opposition to the AH-56A Cheyenne attack helicopter, opposition which ultimately helped bring about the termination of the Cheyenne programme.

were used to transport outsize cargos between Army installations to which the Air Force could not or would not dispatch suitable transport aircraft, though several C-7s were also used to support the Army's parachute demonstration team until replaced by Fokker F-27 Mk 400M aircraft (q.v.) in 1985-86. As of mid-1988 at least thirteen Caribou remained in service with the Army and Army National Guard, several being used as VIP transports with the designation VC-7A. These aircraft are to be replaced by ten Shorts C-23 Sherpas (q.v.) ordered by the Army in October 1988.

TECHNICAL DATA *(Both versions, except where noted)*

Engines:
Two 1450 hp Pratt & Whitney R-2000-7M2 radials

Dimensions:

Wingspan:	95 ft 7.5 in
Wing area:	912 sq ft
Fuselage length:	72 ft 7 in
Height:	31 ft 9 in

Weight (empty/gross, in lbs):
16,920/26,000 (CV-2A)
16,920/28,500 (CV-2B)

Performance:
Speed (cruising/maximum, in mph):
182/216 (CV-2A)
170/205 (CV-2B)

Service Ceiling: 27,500 ft

Range: 1400 miles

Armament: None

Accommodation:
Pilot, co-pilot, crew chief and load master; plus thirty-two to forty passengers or fourteen stretchers and eight passengers.

DE HAVILLAND V-7 BUFFALO

Type: Twin-engined STOL
tactical transport

Manufacturer: De Havilland
Aircraft of Canada,
Downsview, Ontario.

HISTORY

In May 1962 the Army issued a request for proposals (RFP) for a STOL-capable tactical transport larger and able to carry heavier loads than the CV-2 Caribou then entering service. Some twenty-five aircraft companies replied to the RFP, and in early 1963 the Army selected de Havilland of Canada's DHC-5 Buffalo for operational evaluation. The first of four YAC-2 prototypes (serials 63-13686 to -13689) made its maiden flight in April 1964, and all four aircraft were delivered to the Army in April 1965. The type had been redesignated YCV-7 during construction; this was changed to CV-7A upon completion of the service tests.

The CV-7 Buffalo outwardly resembled the earlier Caribou, having as it did the same twin engine, high wing, and squared-fuselage layout. However, the Buffalo was powered by two 2850 shp General Electric T64 turbine engines in place of the Caribou's twin pistons, and was easily differentiated from the earlier aircraft by its high 'T' tail. The CV-7 could lift a load nearly twice that of the Caribou, yet its high-lift wing with double-slotted flaps and spoilers gave it STOL capabilities significantly better than those of the CV-2.

The CV-7 Buffalo was potentially the most capable aircraft in the Army's inventory, but the 1966 Army-Air Force agreement

The first of four Buffalo prototypes acquired by the Army, YCV-7 63-13686, in flight shortly after delivery in April 1965. Though generally similar in appearance to the earlier Caribou, the Buffalo was a vastly more capable transport aircraft and offered better STOL performance than its predecessor. *(De Havilland Canada)*

regarding the allocation of large fixed-wing transport aircraft prevented the utilisation of that potential. In accordance with the agreement all four Army C-7s were transferred to the Air Force on 1 January 1967, at which time the type's designation was changed to C-8.

TECHNICAL DATA

Engines:
Two 2850 shp General Electric T64-10 turboprops

Dimensions:
Wingspan: 96 ft
Fuselage length: 77 ft 3 in
Height: 28 ft 7 in

Weight (empty/maximum, in lbs):
22,864/41,000

Performance:
Speed (cruising/maximum, in mph):
253/287

Service Ceiling: 31,000 ft

Range: 529 miles (with
                        maximum payload)

Armament: None

Accommodation:
Crew of two to four; up to forty-one passengers or twenty-four stretchers and six attendants.

DE HAVILLAND V-18

Type: Twin-engined STOL
utility transport

Manufacturer: De Havilland
Aircraft of Canada,
Downsview, Ontario.

HISTORY

In the early 1970s the Alaska Army National Guard identified a need for a STOL-capable administrative, logistical and personnel transport aircraft able to operate throughout western and northern Alaska on a year-round basis. Given the varying topography and demanding weather conditions found in these areas, the Army preferred a twin-engined machine capable of operating with skis and floats as well as wheeled landing gear. Several designs were evaluated, and in 1976 the Army selected de Havilland of Canada's DHC-6 Series 300 Twin Otter as the best qualified aircraft.

The Alaska Army National Guard's first two Twin Otters (76-22565 and -22566) during manufacturer's trials just prior to delivery. Note the high-flotation landing gear and high-visibility paint schemes. *(De Havilland Canada)*

De Havilland had begun design work on the DHC-6 in January 1964, intending the machine to be a larger and more capable follow-on to the immensely successful DHC-3 Otter. A high-wing, twin-turboprop aircraft with fixed tricycle landing gear, the Twin Otter more than lived up to its designers' expectations and was eventually built in three basic versions. The first of these was the Series 100, which was powered by two 580 ehp PT6A-20 engines, followed by the Series 200 with increased luggage space, and the Series 300 with the more powerful PT6A-27 turboprops. The Series 300 aircraft selected by the Army differed from their civilian counterparts primarily in having increased fuel tankage, high-flotation wheeled landing gear with provision for skis and floats, military-standard avionics and communications equipment, slightly modified cabin interiors, and the shorter, more rounded noses characteristic of float-equipped civilian Twin Otters.

The first two UV-18As (76-22565 and 76-22566) entered service with the Alaska Guard in 1976. These were joined by a further two (79-23255 and -23256) in FY 1979, and by a final two (82-23835 and -23836) in FY 1982. As of early 1989 all six aircraft were in service with the Alaska Guard's 207th Arctic Reconnaissance Group.

TECHNICAL DATA

Engines:
Two 652 ehp Pratt & Whitney of Canada PT6A-27 turboprops

Dimensions:

Wingspan:	65 ft
Wing area:	420 sq ft
Fuselage length:	49 ft 6 in
Height:	19 ft 6 in (without floats)

Weight (empty/maximum, in lbs):
7415/12,500

Performance:
Speed (cruising/maximum, in mph): 185/225

Service Ceiling: 26,700 ft

Range: 892 miles

Armament: None

Accommodation:
Crew of two to three; plus up to eighteen passengers or eight stretchers and three attendants.

DE LACKNER HZ-1

Type: Single-engined VTOL
research vehicle

Manufacturer: De Lackner
Helicopter Company, Mount
Vernon, New York.

HISTORY

The De Lackner model DH-4 Aerocycle flying platform was the first of several one-man flying machines the Army evaluated during the late 1950s and early 1960s, and was certainly one of the more innovative of these various 'individual lift devices'. Developed by De Lackner as a private venture and originally named the Heli-Vector, the DH-4 first flew in January 1955. The Army ordered twelve examples 'off-the-shelf' shortly thereafter, and assigned them the serial numbers 56-6928 through -6939. The aircraft was initially designated YHO-2 (a designation which was later also applied to five Hughes H-55 helicopter prototypes, q.v.), though this was subsequently changed to HZ-1.

Like the somewhat similar Hiller VZ-1 Pawnee (q.v.), the Aerocycle carried its single pilot and 43 hp engine on a circular platform located just above two belt-driven, contra-rotating

The first of twelve HZ-1s procured by the Army for evaluation, 56-6928, is seen here during a pre-delivery factory test flight. Note the bicycle-like handlebar controls and air bag landing gear. The total lack of protective enclosure around the contra-rotating propellers unnerved more than a few prospective pilots. *(U.S. Army Transportation Corps Museum)*.

fifteen-foot propellers. The engine throttle and a few basic instruments were attached to bicycle-type handlebars fixed to a three-foot tall pedestal atop the main platform. The pilot stood to the rear of the pedestal and was secured to it by safety belts, and guided his craft by simply leaning in the desired direction of travel. The machine's landing gear initially consisted of a single large air bag placed directly beneath the propellers and augmented by four smaller air bags fixed to outrigger bars, though this system was ultimately abandoned in favor of helicopter-type metal skids. The HZ-1 was surprisingly stable despite its rather ungainly appearance, and its top speed of more than 70 mph made it considerably faster than most of the other unconventional one-man flying machines evaluated by the Army.

The Army's research into 'individual lifting devices' was intended to explore the feasibility of increasing the mobility of selected ground combat units by providing their members with inexpensive, safe, and easily operated personal aircraft. The Aerocycle was especially successful in the ease of operation category, for during the service tests soldiers required only about twenty minutes of instruction before flying the aircraft. However, the 'individual lifting device' concept was eventually deemed to be impractical in the light of then-current Army tactical doctrine and was abandoned, and the De Lackner Aerocycle thus became no more than an interesting footnote in the history of Army aviation.

TECHNICAL DATA

Engine:
One 43 hp Kiekhaefer Mercury Mark 55 outboard motor

Dimensions:
Propeller diameter: 15 ft
Height (bottom of main air bag to top of handlebars: 7 ft

Weight (empty/gross, in lbs):
172/457

Performance:
Speed (cruising/maximum, in mph): 55/75

Service Ceiling: 5000ft

Range: 15 miles

Armament: None

Accommodation:
Pilot only.

DOAK VZ-4

Type: Single-engined VTOL testbed   Manufacturer: Doak Aircraft Company, Torrance California.

HISTORY

The Doak Model 16 ducted-fan research vehicle was yet another participant in the Army-sponsored programme to develop a utility and observation aircraft combining the VTOL capabilities of a helicopter with the higher speed and greater manoeuvrability of a conventional fixed-wing airplane. The Model 16 was developed under an Army Transportation Research and Engineering Command contract and made its first flight in February 1958. The single prototype was put through extensive pre-delivery flight testing and therefore was not officially accepted by the Army until September 1959. Upon acceptance the craft, which had already been allocated the serial number 56-9642, was given the designation VZ-4.

Despite its rather fragile appearance the VZ-4 was a robust and fairly capable aircraft. The fuselage was constructed of welded steel tubing covered by moulded plastic, while the wings and tail were metal-skinned. The aircraft was designed to accommodate a pilot and observer sitting in tandem, though as far as can be determined the observer's seat was never actually installed in the prototype. A single 1000 shp Lycoming T53-L-1 turbine mounted in the fuselage just aft of the cockpit drove two

The sole VZ-4, 56-9642, begins its maiden hovering flight in February 1958. The scoop-like air intake for the machine's single T53 turbine engine can be seen just aft of the rear canopy. *(U.S. Army Transportation Corps Museum)*

ducted-fan airscrews, one fixed within each rotating wingtip fan assembly. The fans were set in the vertical position for takeoff and landing, and were rotated into the horizontal plane for normal forward flight. Some additional directional stability was provided by routing the turbine exhaust through a set of hinged louvers mounted in the aircraft's tail.

The VZ-4 was the end product of Doak's many years of research and development in the VTOL field, and the aircraft proved reasonably useful in exploring the military potential of non-helicopter VTOL vehicles. After some three years of joint testing by the Army and NASA the sole VZ-4 was withdrawn from the Army inventory and subsequently operated solely by NASA.

TECHNICAL DATA

Engine:
Originally an 840 shp Lycoming YT53 turbine, though this was replaced by a 1000 shp Lycoming T53-L-1 shortly after the beginning of flight testing

Dimensions:
Wingspan (over fan assemblies):	25 ft 7 in
Wing area:	96 sq ft
Fuselage length:	32 ft
Height:	10 ft 1 in

Weight (empty/gross, in lbs):
2400/3300

Performance:
Speed (cruising/maximum, in mph): 175/230

Service Ceiling: 12,000 ft

Hover Ceiling: 6000 ft

Range: 250 miles

Armament: None

Accommodation:
Pilot and observer.

DOMAN H-31

Type: Single-engined utility
 helicopter

Manufacturer: Doman
Helicopter Company,
Danbury, Connecticut.

HISTORY

In the spring of 1953 Doman Helicopters introduced their Model
LZ-5 eight-place utility aircraft, the second of the firm's designs
to incorporate a novel non-articulated, sealed rigid rotor system.
The Army purchased two aircraft (serials 52-5779 and -5780) in
late 1953 for service test and evaluation with the designation
YH-31. The type's unique rotor system was found to provide
only a slight increase in performance over that of other, more

The second YH-31, 52-5780, hovers above the Doman company ramp
during a pre-delivery check flight. The type's fuselage cargo area was
relatively spacious and its sealed rigid rotor system was innovative and
technically quite advanced, but the YH-31 was ultimately judged to be quite
unsuitable for widespread Army use. Both examples were subsequently
used as VIP transports in the Washington, DC, area. *(American Helicopter
Society)*

conventional systems, and was also judged to be more difficult to maintain under field conditions. There was therefore no further YH-31 procurement, and the two service test machines were ultimately converted into VH-31 VIP transports and used in the Washington, DC area until their 1958 withdrawal from the Army inventory.

TECHNICAL DATA

Engine:
One 400 hp Lycoming SO-580-A1A, SO-580-B, or SO-580-D piston (each YH-31 prototype was successively fitted with each engine type).

Dimensions:

Main rotor diameter:	48 ft 4 in
Tail rotor diameter:	4 ft 8 in
Fuselage length:	37 ft 10 in
Height (to top of main rotor hub):	10 ft 3 in

Weight (empty/gross, in lbs):
2860/5200

Performance:
Speed (cruising/maximum, in mph): 78/104

Service Ceiling: 11,500 ft

Range: 240 miles

Armament: None

Accommodation:
One pilot and up to seven passengers or one pilot, two crew, and two stretchers.

DOUGLAS C-47 SKYTRAIN

Type: Twin-engined medium cargo and personnel transport

Manufacturer: Douglas Aircraft Company, El Segundo, California.

HISTORY

The military derivatives of the famed Douglas DC-3 commercial airliner form what is without doubt the best known and most widely used family of medium cargo and troop transport aircraft yet built. The C-47, the most numerous military variant, has served in the navies and air forces of more than fifty nations and has participated in virtually every declared and covert conflict waged on this planet since the early days of the Second World War.

That the C-47 would eventually appear in the post-World War II Army's aircraft inventory was, in a sense, inevitable. The 1947 creation of the U.S. Air Force left the Army without a single aircraft capable of carrying a significant outsize cargo load or more than twelve passengers, and in the years immediately following the separation of the services the USAF was often unable or unwilling to provide large enough aircraft upon the Army's request. The obvious solution to this problem was for the Army to operate its own medium transport aircraft, but the Air Force was extremely reluctant to sanction the required

Eight of the approximately thirty-six Skytrains operated by the Army were of the C-47E variant illustrated here. Originally built for the USAAF as C-47As, the -E model Skytrains were fitted with specialized electronic equipment and used by the USAAF, USAF and, ultimately, the Army, in the airways check role. The Army retired its last C-47 in 1982. *(Harry Gann)*

exception to the 5000-pound gross weight limitation when the Army proposed its plan. However, the Air Force's inability to consistently provide required on-call transport aircraft support ultimately forced it to agree to the Army's proposal. The C-47 was chosen for Army use for several reasons: there were plenty immediately available; the type was robust and well-suited to the sort of rough field conditions often encountered by Army aircraft; and, almost certainly, because senior Air Force leaders felt that the Army's operation of an elderly and (apparently) obsolescent type would not seriously detract from the Air Force's image.

The first C-47 aircraft were transferred from the Air Force to the Army in the early 1950s, and during the following two decades the latter service operated some thirty-six C-47s. The majority of these Skytrains (twenty-one) were ex-USN R4D variants, while the remainder were former USAF examples. The Army-operated aircraft were of the following models:

C-47A:
Two ex-USAF aircraft (serials 43-15070 and -15982), each powered by two 1200 hp Pratt & Whitney R-1830-92 radials. The -A model was the most numerous C-47 variant and was equipped with a port-side cargo door and strengthened fuselage floor.

VC-47A:
The Army operated a single ex-USAF example (43-15700) of this VIP transport version, which was essentially a standard C-47A with a plush executive interior.

C-47B:
The C-47B was designed specifically for high-altitude operations in the World War II China-Burma-India theater, and was equipped with two 1200 hp R-1830-90C engines fitted with two-stage blowers. The three examples operated by the Army (serials 43-48980, -49241, and -49281) were all ex-USAF machines, and all apparently retained the modified engines.

NC-47B:
Designation applied to a single ex-USAF C-47B (43-16277) modified by the Army for electronics testing duties. This machine is sometimes referred to, incorrectly, as an NC-47J.

C-47E:
During the Second World War Pan American Airways modified eight -A and -B model Skytrains to C-47E standard for USAAF use as airways check aircraft. The machines were each powered by two 1290 hp R-2000-4 engines, and were fitted with extensive arrays of electronic navigation and communications equipment. All eight examples were transferred by the USAF to the Army beginning in 1954, and some of them continued to be operated in the airways check role following the transfer.

C-47H:
Post-1962 designation applied to Navy R4D-5 aircraft, which were essentially identical to the C-47A. Ten of these -H model aircraft were transferred from the Navy to the Army between October 1963 and April 1966.

NC-47H:
Designation given to a single ex-Navy C-47H modified for permanent testing duties.

TC-47H:
In 1962 Navy R4D-5R personnel transports were redesignated TC-47H; the Army acquired one example (BuNo 17181) in the mid-1960s.

C-47J:
Post-1962 designation applied to Navy R4D-6 aircraft. The Army operated seven examples of this variant, which was identical to the C-47B.

TC-47K:
Designation allocated to Navy R4D-7 navigational trainers after 1962. These aircraft were essentially identical to USAAF/USAF TC-47B trainers, differing only in the types of electronic training aids fitted. The Army operated two TC-47Ks (BuNos 99827 and 99848), though it is unclear if the machines were actually used in the navigational training role.

The C-47 Skytrain served the post-World War II Army long and well in a variety of roles. Indeed, the Army was the last of the U.S. military services to operate the venerable 'Gooney Bird', with the last Army Skytrain (ex-Navy C-47H BuNo 12436) being retired to the Army Aviation Museum at Fort Rucker in 1982.

TECHNICAL DATA (All versions, except where noted)

Engines:
Two 1200 hp Pratt & Whitney R-1830-92 radials
(C/VC-47A, C/NC/TC-47H)
Two 1200 hp Pratt & Whitney R-1839-90C radials
(C/NC-47B, C-47J, TC-47K)
Two 1290 hp Pratt & Whitney R-2000-4 radials (C-47E)

Dimensions:
Wingspan:	95 ft 6 in
Wing area:	987 sq ft
Fuselage length:	63 ft 9 in
Height:	17 ft

Weight (empty/gross, in lbs):
17,700/26,000 (C/VC/NC/TC-47A/H)
18,135/26,000 (C/NC/TC-47B/J/K)

Performance:
Speed (cruising/maximum, in mph):
160/230

Service Ceiling: 24,000 ft (C/VC/NC/TC-47A/H)
26,000 ft (C/NC/TC-47B/J/K)
31,000 ft (C-47E)

Range: 1600 miles

Armament: None

Accommodation:
Two to three crew, plus twenty-one to forty troops in troop transport configuration, twelve to fifteen passengers in VIP transport role, or 6000 to 7100 pounds of cargo.

DOUGLAS C-54 SKYMASTER

Type: Four-engined heavy transport

Manufacturer: Douglas Aircraft Company, El Segundo, California.

HISTORY

Though the Army's acquisition of C-47 Skytrain (q.v.) aircraft provided a much-needed ability to transport cargo and passenger loads that were beyond the capabilities of then-current helicopters, there remained the occasional need to move a particularly large or unwieldy piece of cargo quickly from one place to another. The USAF's inability to consistently provide the required transport prompted the Army to seek a suitable aircraft for its own use. In the late 1950s, after extensive inter-service negotiations, the Air Force agreed to supply the Army with a single Douglas C-54 Skymaster.

The aircraft transferred to the Army, serial 42-72656, was a C-54D that had been built at Douglas Aircraft's Chicago, Illinois, plant during the Second World War. The -D model was the most common C-54 variant, and could carry up to forty-four passengers in airline-type seats, up to fifty troops in jump seats, or up to 32,000 pounds of cargo. The Army's C-54 was used primarily to transport missile components and other outsized loads, and its port-side cargo door was fitted with a twin-boom loading hoist. The aircraft was eventually supplanted in service by the de Havilland Caribou, and was finally withdrawn from the Army inventory sometime in the early 1960s.

TECHNICAL DATA

Engines:
Four 1350 hp Pratt & Whitney R-2000-11 Twin Wasp radials

Dimensions:
Wingspan:	117 ft 6 in
Wing area:	1460 sq ft
Fuselage length:	93 ft 10 in
Height:	27 ft 6 in

Weight (empty/gross, in lbs):
38,000/72,000

Performance:
Speed (cruising/maximum, in mph): 210/265

Service Ceiling: 22,350 ft

Range: 3100 miles

Armament: None

Accommodation:
Two to five crew, forty-four to fifty passengers.

The Army's sole Skymaster, a C-54D acquired from the Air Force, was used primarily to transport missile components. *(Harry Gann)*

DOUGLAS A4D SKYHAWK

Type: Single-engined light
attack aircraft

Manufacturer: Douglas
Aircraft Company, El
Segundo, California.

HISTORY

The Air Force's success in blocking Army acquisition of the Cessna T-37 (q.v.) following the type's 1957 evaluation at Fort Rucker did not lessen the Army's determination to continue its search for a suitable jet-powered, fixed-wing forward air control (FAC) and tactical reconnaissance platform. The USAF had continued to insist that it alone should be responsible for operating such aircraft in support of Army forces and was therefore understandably chagrined when, in 1961, the Army decided to test not one, but three, types of high-performance jet in a competitive 'fly-off'. The machines chosen for evaluation were the Fiat G.91 (q.v.), the Northrop N-156 lightweight fighter prototype (q.v.), and the Douglas A4D (later A-4) Skyhawk.

The Skyhawk, brainchild of Douglas' prolific designer Edward A. Heinemann, was developed during the early 1950s as a jet-powered replacement for the propeller-driven Douglas AD (later A-1) Skyraider then in Navy and Marine Corps service. Heinemann had long advocated the development of attack aircraft smaller, lighter, less expensive, and more capable than those machines that had appeared in the immediate post-World War II period, and he incorporated all his innovative design concepts into the A4D. The Skyhawk, which first flew in June 1954, was a

The dual-wheeled main landing gear fitted to both Skyhawks evaluated by the Army is clearly visible in this photo of the second aircraft, believed to be Navy BuNo 148490. Special 'bulged' doors were installed to cover the modified landing gear; those for the left main gear are just discernible on the underside of the left wing, immediately inboard of the outer droptank. *(Harry Gann)*

diminutive craft with a wingspan of just 27.5 ft and a maximum loaded weight of less than 15,000 pounds. Yet the airplane was capable of speeds in excess of 650 mph and could carry more than 5000 pounds of offensive ordnance. The first A4D-1 production aircraft began joining frontline Navy and Marine Corps units in 1955, and by 1960 the majority of U.S. naval attack squadrons were equipped with some variant of the basic Skyhawk.

The Army chose to evaluate the A4D primarily because the type's simplicity of design, rugged construction, and proven ground attack capabilities were all qualities much to be desired in an Army FAC and tactical reconnaissance aircraft. The Skyhawk variant chosen for Army testing, the A4D-2N, was especially attractive, for it had been specifically developed for low-level attack at night and in bad weather. The two A4D-2N machines borrowed from the Navy (one of which was BuNo 148483) were slightly modified for the Army tests; each was fitted with high-flotation, dual-wheeled main landing gear instead of the normal single-wheeled units, and each was equipped with a drag parachute in a canister fixed beneath the rear fuselage. Both machines retained their normal Navy markings and color schemes for the duration of Army evaluation.

The Army's overall opinion of the Skyhawk was very favourable. The craft proved itself to be an exemplary ground attack machine with excellent low-altitude handling characteristics. This opinion ultimately proved to be of only academic interest, however, for the Army's subsequent decision to accede to USAF pressure and abandon the quest for fixed-wing jet aircraft led in late 1961 to the cancellation of further planned Skyhawk testing. Soon thereafter both A4D-2N aircraft were returned to stock configuration and given back to the Navy.

TECHNICAL DATA

Engine:
One 7000 lb st Wright J65-W-16A turbojet

Dimensions:
Wingspan: 27 ft 6 in
Wing area: 260 sq ft
Fuselage length: 40 ft 2 in
Height: 15 ft 2 in

Weight (empty/gross, in lbs):
9850/24,500

Performance:
Speed (cruising/maximum, in mph): 410/673

Service Ceiling: 38,000 ft
Range: 2520 miles

Armament:
Two internal 20 mm cannon and up to 5000 pounds of external stores.

Accommodation:
Pilot only.

FAIRCHILD VZ-5

Type: Single-engined V/STOL
research aircraft

Manufacturer: Fairchild
Engine & Airplane
Corporation, Hagerstown,
Maryland.

HISTORY

Like most of the V/STOL prototypes evaluated by the Army in
the late 1950s and early 1960s the Fairchild Model M-224-1 was
an innovative but rather odd-looking craft. The airplane's
deflected-slipstream lift system was based on broad full-span
flaps which drooped nearly five feet from the shoulder-mounted
main wing when fully deployed. A single T58 turbine engine
buried in the fuselage was used to drive the four small
propellers mounted on the wing leading edges, with short or
vertical takeoffs and landings being accomplished by deploying
the flaps and thereby deflecting the prop wash almost directly
downward. The single-seat M-224 was of welded steel tube
construction with fabric covering, had a sixteen-foot tall, strut-
braced 'T' tail, and was fitted with non-retractable tricycle
landing gear. The fact that the M-224's normal takeoff attitude
had the machine resting on its tail skid with its nose pointing
skyward at a forty-five-degree angle did nothing to improve its
looks.

The sole VZ-5 on Fairchild's company airfield prior to being handed over to
the Army for evaluation. Note the high 'T' tail, four propellers, and endplates
for the huge full-span flaps. *(U.S. Army Transportation Corps Museum)*

Its strange appearance not withstanding, the M-224 proved to be a capable V/STOL performer. The single example made its first flight in November 1959, and was officially handed over to the Army in early 1960. The craft was designated VZ-5 and allocated the serial number 56-6940, and was jointly operated by Army and NASA crews throughout its three-year test programme.

TECHNICAL DATA

Engine:
One 1024 shp General Electric YT58-GE-2 shaft turbine

Dimensions:
Wingspan:	32 ft 9 in
Wing area (with flaps fully deployed):	191 sq ft
Fuselage length:	33 ft 8 in
Height:	16 ft 10 in

Weight (empty/gross, in lbs):
3382/3976

Performance:
Speed (cruising/maximum, in mph): 140/184
Other data not available

Armament: None

Accommodation:
Normally pilot only, though on several occasions an observer was carried in a small seat installed just behind the pilot's seat.

FIAT G.91

Type: Single-engined
tactical fighter
and reconnaissance
aircraft

Manufacturer: Societa Per
Azioni FIAT, Turin, Italy
(G.91R-1).
Dornier GmbH,
Friedrichshafen, West
Germany (G.91R-3).

HISTORY

Like the Douglas A4D-2N Skyhawk and Northrop N-156 (q.v.), the Fiat G.91 was evaluated by the Army in 1961 as a possible forward air control (FAC) and tactical reconnaissance platform. Originally developed in response to a NATO requirement for an easily maintained light tactical fighter able to operate from unimproved forward airfields, the G.91 was a simple and robust aircraft capable of carrying a significant weapons load at high subsonic speeds. The type made its first flight in August 1956 and was eventually adopted for service by the Italian, Greek, and West German Air Forces.

The G.91 attracted U.S. Army attention primarily because those features that led to its adoption by NATO — simplicity, ease of maintenance, and the ability to operate from primitive forward airstrips — were precisely the qualities the Army desired in its proposed FAC and tactical reconnaissance aircraft. In late 1960 the Army arranged to 'borrow' two West German machines, both of which were transported to the U.S. aboard a USAF C-124 Globemaster. The aircraft were accompanied by Italian Air Force test pilot Riccardo Bignamini, who had flight

The muzzles of two of the machine's four .50 calibre machine guns are clearly visible in this close-up view of the G.91R-1, as are the forward and starboard ports for two of the aircraft's three nose-mounted Vinten reconnaissance cameras. Italian test pilot Riccardo Bignamini was killed when this machine crashed during Army evaluation. *(Aeritalia)*

The German-built G.91R-3 was virtually identical in appearance to the G.91R-1, the only obvious visual difference being the replacement of the latter's four machine guns by two 30 mm DEFA cannon. Note that both aircraft carried bright yellow test markings over their standard Luftwaffe camouflage. *(Aeritalia)*

tested the first G.91 prototype, and by several Luftwaffe pilots and mechanics. While under evaluation at Fort Rucker the two aircraft sported Army markings, but retained their three-color Luftwaffe camouflage and carried their constructor's numbers (c/ns) in place of standard U.S. military serial numbers. One of the machines (Luftwaffe code BD+102, c/n 0052) was an Italian-built G.91R-1 armed reconnaissance version, while the other aircraft (EC+105, c/n 0065) was a slightly different German-built G.91R-3 variant.

The Army's G.91 evaluation team found the type to be easy to fly, relatively simple to maintain under field conditions, and more than capable of fulfilling the FAC and reconnaissance roles envisaged for it. However, the crash of the G.91R-1 and the resultant death of Riccardo Bignamini brought the evaluation process to an early conclusion. This setback was soon followed by the Army's decision to acquiesce to Air Force pressure and renounce all plans to acquire and operate fixed-wing tactical jet aircraft. The surviving G.91 was therefore returned to the Luftwaffe in early 1962.

TECHNICAL DATA *(Both versions, except where noted)*

Engine:
One 5000 lb st Bristol Orpheus 803 turbojet

Dimensions:

Wingspan:	28 ft 1 in
Wing area:	177 sq ft
Fuselage length:	33 ft 9 in
Height:	13 ft 2 in

Weight (empty/gross, in lbs):
7250/12,500 (G.91R-1)
7550/12,500 (G.91R-3)

Performance:
Speed (cruising/maximum, in mph):
403/650

Service Ceiling: 40,000 ft

Range: 1150 miles

Armament:
Four .50 calibre Browning machine guns (G.91R-1) or two 30 mm DEFA cannon (G.91R-3), plus two underwing pylons capable of carrying various combinations of bombs, napalm canisters, AS.20 or AS.30 missiles, or pods of two inch or 2.75 inch unguided rockets

Accommodation:
Pilot only.

FOKKER F-27

Type: Twin-engined medium utility transport

Manufacturer: Fokker Aircraft BV, Amsterdam, Holland.

HISTORY

In late 1984 the Army announced its intention to replace the five ageing de Havilland C-7A Caribous (q.v.) used by the Fort Bragg-based Golden Knights parachute demonstration team with newer and more capable aircraft. The C-7As, among the few such machines remaining in Army service, had formed the backbone of the Golden Knights' aviation section since 1975 but were no longer considered capable of providing adequate support for the team's hectic domestic and international touring schedule. In November 1985 the Army leased two Fokker F-27 Mk 400M twin-engined medium transports for interim use by the Golden Knights pending the final selection of a Caribou replacement aircraft. The two Fokkers were delivered to Fort Bragg in December 1985 bearing the serial numbers 85-1607 and -1608 and the Golden Knights' distinctive black and gold livery. The Army chose not to type-classify the machines, and they are thus officially referred to by their commercial designation.

The Mk 400M is a 'militarized' version of Fokker's immensely successful F-27 Friendship medium-range airliner, which first flew in 1955, and shares that machine's high-wing, twin-engined layout and characteristic high-set fin and tailplane. The Mk 400M aircraft acquired for the Golden Knights are each powered by twin Rolls-Royce Dart Mk 551 turboprops driving four-bladed

One of the Army's two F-27 Mk 400M aircraft prepares to drop members of the Golden Knights parachute demonstration team. Each machine can accommodate up to forty-eight parachutists, and the large dispatch doors on either side of the fuselage (seen here in the open position) allow all jumpers to exit the aircraft in a matter of seconds. *(Fokker)*

constant-speed propellers, and each aircraft is capable of carrying two underwing auxiliary fuel tanks that extend the craft's range to over 2700 miles. Each machine can accommodate up to forty-eight parachutists in folding canvas seats, and large dispatch doors on either side of each aircraft's rear fuselage allow all jumpers to exit the aircraft in a matter of seconds.

The Golden Knights unit is divided into two parachute demonstration teams, two competition teams, an aviation section, and a headquarters group. Both demonstration teams travel an average of 280 days out of each year, and the acquisition of the two F-27s has, as expected, given the teams more flexibility in performing their shows, while at the same time reducing the travel time between performance sites. The more than satisfactory service provided by the two leased F-27s obviously gave the type a definite advantage during the final competitive selection of the team's new aircraft, which in October 1988 resulted in the Army's outright purchase of both machines.

TECHNICAL DATA

Engines:
Two 2330 ehp Rolls-Royce Dart Mk 551 turboprops

Dimensions:

Wingspan:	95 ft 2 in
Wing area:	753.5 sq ft
Fuselage length:	77 ft 3.5 in
Height:	27 ft 11 in

Weight (empty/gross, in lbs):
24,720/45,900

Performance:
Speed (cruising/maximum, in mph): 298/325

Service Ceiling: 30,000 ft

Range: 2727 miles

Armament: None

Accommodation:
Crew of two to three, plus up to forty-eight parachutists.

GRUMMAN V-1 MOHAWK

Type: Twin-engined tactical reconnaissance and EW aircraft

Manufacturer: Grumman Aircraft Corporation, Bethpage, New York.

HISTORY

The immensely successful OV-1 family of aircraft evolved from the Grumman Model G-134, which in March 1957 was named the winner of a joint Army and Marine Corps competition for an all-weather battlefield surveillance airplane capable of carrying wing-mounted stores. The Marine Corps' withdrawal from the programme soon after the selection of the G-134 did nothing to dampen the Army's enthusiasm for the design, and Grumman was soon awarded a contract for nine YAO-1A examples (serials 57-6463 through -6467 and 57-6538 through -6541) for service test and evaluation. These machines were each powered by two 960 shp T53-L-3 turboprops, housed two crewmen side-by-side under a maximum-visibility 'bug eye' canopy, and had two wing hardpoints capable of carrying a total of 2700 pounds of ordnance, auxiliary fuel tanks, or mission-related electronic equipment. The first YAO-1A made its maiden flight in April 1959, and shortly thereafter the Army placed orders for the first of some 250 production aircraft of several variants:

AO-1A:

First production version, fitted with a KA-30 or KA-61 wide angle camera and intended primarily for tactical photo-reconnaissance. The first of sixty-four examples (serials 59-2603 to -2620, 60-3720 to -3744, and 63-13114 to -13134) was accepted by the Army in September 1960. The AO-1As (all of which were redesignated OV-1A in 1962) were built with 960 shp T53-L-3 engines, though most were later upgraded with more powerful

The AO-1 was originally intended to have a high 'T' tail, as shown on this Grumman engineering mockup, though this had been exchanged for the characteristic 'triple tail' prior to the type's first flight. *(Grumman)*

YAO-1A 57-6463 in flight. This machine, the first of nine service test aircraft delivered to the Army, first flew in April 1959. Note the almost complete absence of the extensive antenna arrays that would quickly become one of the Mohawk's most obvious characteristics. *(Grumman)*

1150 shp T53-L-7 or T53-L-13 series powerplants. The aircraft could be fitted with two additional underwing pylons, which increased it's stores capacity by 1000 pounds, and featured three upward-firing photographic flare ejectors in the fuselage. The AO-1A/OV-1A was the first production aircraft accepted for Army-wide use to be powered by turbine engines, and the first equipped with crew ejection seats.

JOV-1A:
Designation given to several standard OV-1A machines configured for ground attack duty in Vietnam in 1964 and 1965. These aircraft each had six underwing hardpoints, and carried various combinations of podded .30 and .50 calibre machine guns, 2.75 inch folding fin aerial rocket (FFAR) pods, light bombs, and auxiliary fuel tanks. The armed Mohawks were operated primarily by the 73rd Aerial Surveillance Company and proved to be fairly successful in the ground attack role, though USAF opposition to the Army's 'unauthorized' use of fixed-wing attack aircraft eventually forced the abandonment of the armed Mohawk programme.

AO-1B:
Second production version, distinguished from the -A model by the addition of a long rectangular AN/APS-94 Side-looking Airborne Radar (SLAR) pod under the forward fuselage, a six-foot increase in wingspan, and the deletion of dual flight controls and fuselage-mounted speed brakes. Early -B model aircraft were powered by T53-L-7 engines, while later production examples had the uprated T53-L-15s. Two AO-1As (63-13118 and -13119) were converted to -B model standard, and an additional ninety AO-1Bs were new-build. The first -B model Mohawk was delivered to the Army in April 1961, and in 1962 all examples were redesignated OV-1B under the Tri-Service designation scheme.

AO-1C:
Third production version, essentially identical to the basic -A model Mohawk but with a UAS-4 infrared mapping sensor mounted in the central fuselage and without dual flight controls. Late-production aircraft were built with T53-L-15 engines, which were ultimately retrofitted to all -C models, amd most machines had sealed wing leading-edge slats. A total of 129 were built, the first being handed over to the Army in October 1961. The AO-1C was redesignated OV-1C in 1962.

YOV-1D:
Official, if not widely recognized, designation applied to four pre-production OV-1C aircraft (67-18898, -18899, -18902, and -18904) adapted in 1968 to use three cameras and either the SLAR pod or infrared mapping sensor.

OV-1D:
Production model incorporating features pioneered in the YOV-1D testbeds and intended for the battlefield surveillance and target-acquisition roles. Some thirty-seven examples were new-built, and all were powered by either T53-L-15 or T53-L-701 engines. This variant's sensors include the AN/UPD-7 radar surveillance system, AN/AAS-24 infrared scanners, and KS-60 reconnaissance cameras. Approximately 110 OV-1B and OV-1C aircraft have been upgraded to OV-1D standard.

The first production OV-1A (foreground) in formation with the first production OV-1B. The OV-1A was intended primarily for tactical photo-reconnaissance, and was the first turbine-powered production aircraft to be accepted for Army-wide use. The OV-1B differed from the -A model in having a slightly larger wing span, more powerful engines (in later production aircraft) and, most obviously, in having the AN/APS-94 SLAR pod fixed beneath the fuselage. *(Grumman)*

The first YOV-1D prototype in flight. This machine was built as an OV-1C, but was one of four aircraft converted to YOV-1D standard through the addition of a third reconnaissance camera, the improved AN/AAS-24 infrared surveillance system, and the installation of the ADR-6 radiological surveillance system. The addition of these upgraded systems combined in one airframe all the visual, photographic, radar, and infrared surveillance abilities of the three previous Mohawk models. *(Grumman)*

The Army is believed to possess some thirty-six RV-1D electronic intelligence aircraft, all of which are conversions from earlier OV-1B and OV-1C airframes. The RV-1D is, as this photo shows, almost identical in outward appearance to the earlier Mohawk variants. This particular aircraft, a converted OV-1C assigned to the 73rd Military Intelligence Company in Stuttgart, Germany, has its removable SLAR pod fitted and is finished in the overall light gray paint scheme applied to Army tactical aircraft in Europe and Korea. *(Grumman)*

RV-1C:
Designation applied to an unknown number of standard OV-1C Mohawks converted into interim electronic intelligence (ELINT)-gathering platforms during the mid-1970s. The major modification made to these airplanes under the Quick Look I programme seems to have been the addition of the AN/APQ-142 radar emissions location and classification system, the major elements of which were housed in two squared pods carried one on either side of the machine's outboard stores pylons. The RV-1C is thought to have been developed as a stopgap measure, and the few examples of the type are believed to have been withdrawn from service during the early 1980s.

RV-1D:
An ELINT aircraft developed from the OV-1B under the Quick Look II programme, the RV-1D is believed to be equipped with the AN/ALQ-133 tactical ELINT system, the AN/ASN-86 inertial navigation system, and on-board data processing and realtime transmission equipment. It is thought that the Army currently operates approximately thirty-six RV-1Ds, with one example known to have been shot down over Central America in 1984.

TECHNICAL DATA *(All versions, except where noted)*

Engines:
Two 960 shp Avco-Lycoming T53-L-3 turboprops (YOV-1A)
Two T53-L-3 or 1150 shp T53-L-7 or T53-L-15 (OV-1B/C, RV-1C)
Two T53-L-7 or T53-L-15 (YOV-1D)
Two T53-L-15 or T53-L-701 (OV-1D, RV-1D)

Dimensions:
Wingspan: 42 ft
47 ft 11 in (OV-1B/D, RV-1D)
Wing area: 330 sq ft
360 sq ft (OV-1B/D, RV-1D)
Fuselage length: 41 ft
Height: 12 ft 8 in

Weight (empty/gross, in lbs):
9937/12,672
11,070/17,020 (OV-1B)
10,450/16,685 (OV-1C, YOV-1D)
12,054/18,450 (OV-1D)
RV-1C/D, unknown

Performance:
Speed (cruising/maximum, in mph): 207/325

Service Ceiling: 33,000 ft

Range (without external tanks): 1230-1530 miles

Armament:
None normally fitted (see text for JOV-1A details).

Accommodation:
Two crew (pilot and co-pilot/systems operator in YOV/OV/JOV-1A, pilot and systems operator in all others).

GRUMMAN GULFSTREAM I and II

Type: Twin-engined VIP
      transport

Manufacturer: Grumman
Aircraft Corporation,
Bethpage, NY.

HISTORY

Under the terms of its 1947 'division-of-duties' agreement with the Air Force, the Army was — and is — prohibited from owning and operating fixed-wing, jet-powered attack and reconnaissance aircraft. Though the Army stretched the boundaries of this prohibition to the limits in the late 1950s and early 1960s in order to evaluate the Cessna T-37, Douglas A-4, Fiat G-91, Northrop N-156, Hawker-Siddeley XV-6, and Lockheed XV-4 (all of which see), no serious attempt has ever been made to acquire tactical jets. Jet-powered transport machines are another matter, however, for over the past two decades the Army has owned and operated, albeit without fanfare, at least four Gulfstream business jets-turned-VIP aircraft*; two early Grumman-built examples, and two later Gulfstream IV/C-20 aircraft built by Gulfstream Aerospace (q.v.).

The prototype Grumman Gulfstream I twin-turboprop light executive transport flew for the first time in August 1958, and received its FAA Type Approval the following year. The elegant machine's excellent performance and relatively long range quickly made it popular with regional airlines and air-minded

Virtually identical (except in colour scheme) to this Coast Guard VC-4A VIP transport, the Corps of Engineers' Gulfstream I 'Castle One' was acquired in 1961 and served for two decades. *(Grumman)*

131

The Corps of Engineers is active in many parts of the world, including some areas where the sight of a U.S. military aircraft might attract unwanted attention, so the agency's Gulfstream II maintains a politically discrete low-profile by carrying a non-military colour scheme and civil registration. *(U.S. Army Corps of Engineers)*

corporate executives, and ultimately attracted the attention of the Army Corps of Engineers. The Corps, responsible for public engineering projects throughout the United States and its overseas territories in addition to overseeing conventional military engineering within the Army, had long believed that commercial airlines of the Air Force's special VIP transport unit could not adequately meet the specialized domestic and international travel requirements of the Corps' senior commanders. The agency, which is authorized to purchase and operate its own aircraft under special Congressional legislation passed in 1954, was thus in the market for a dedicated VIP transport and in 1961 purchased a production Gulfstream I.

This machine was operated in civil markings and differed from regular commercial aircraft only in having additional military-standard communications and navigation equipment. The Gulfstream I (dubbed 'Castle One' after the Corps' insignia) was based at Andrews Air Force Base, Maryland, and ably served the Corps of Engineers until replaced by a turbofan-powered Gulfstream II in 1981.

The Gulfstream II, a logical and equally elegant successor to the Gulfstream I, flew for the first time in October 1966. Offering both a better performance and longer range than its predecessor, the Gulfstream II treated business and corporate flyers to a level of technical sophistication and creature comfort not readily available in other contemporary 'bizjets'. The Corps of Engineers, which had been seeking an aircraft better able to fly the long over-water routes often travelled by the agency's senior commanders, found the Gulfstream II quite attractive. However, the purchase of a suitable (second-hand) example was not completed until 1981, using funds authorized the previous year in the Energy and Water Development Appropriations Act. The Corps' aircraft, also known as 'Castle One', is finished in an attractive three-colour paint scheme and carries the civil registration N831GA. Also based at Andrews, it is used to support the Corps' activities throughout the U.S. and in sixteen foreign countries.

---

* The Army has acquired at least one additional Gulfstream I — and a Gates Learjet — through the U.S. Government's Confiscated/Excess Aircraft Programme (C/EAP). These machines are apparently used in anti-smuggling efforts, though detailed information about Army aircraft acquired through C/EAP is classified.

TECHNICAL DATA

Engines:
Two 2210 eshp Rolls-Royce Dart 529-8 turboprops (G-I)
Two 11,400 lb st Rolls-Royce Spey Mk 511-8 turbofans (G-II)

Dimensions:

Wingspan:	78 ft 6 in (G-I)	
	68 ft 10 in	
Wing area:	610 sq ft (G-I)	
	793.5 sq ft	
Fuselage length:	63 ft 9 in (G-I)	
	79 ft 11 in	
Height:	22 ft 9 in (G-I)	
	24 ft 6 in	

Weight (empty/gross, in lbs):
21,900/35,100 (G-I)
38,000/57,500

Performance:
Speed (cruising/maximum, in mph):
288/348 (G-I)
515/585

Service Ceiling: 33,600 ft (G-I)
43,000 ft

Range: 2540 miles (G-I)
3460 miles

Armament: None

Accommodation:
Two crew, ten to fourteen passengers (G-I)
Three crew, nineteen passengers.

GULFSTREAM C-20

Type: Twin-engined VIP transport

Manufacturer: Gulfstream Aerospace Corporation, Savannah, Georgia.

HISTORY

The Army's acquisition of two Gulfstream Aerospace C-20E aircraft was the result of a 1986 Department of Defense decision to provide both the Army and the Navy with VIP transports comparable to the eleven C-20A and -B machines already in service with the USAF. The Army had not previously expressed an overt interest in acquiring the 'militarized' version of the Gulfstream III, but was nonetheless delighted with the opportunity to free itself from dependence on the USAF's often overworked VIP transport fleet and thus did not resist DoD's initiative. The $40 million necessary for the purchase of the two aircraft, the establishment of a contract maintenance programme, and the training of the Army crews was duly allocated in the FY 1987 U.S. Defense Budget, and both aircraft were accepted by the Army in June 1988.

The C-20s operated by the Army, Navy, and Air Force are derivatives of the standard commercial Gulfstream III business jet. A direct development of the Grumman Gulfstream II (q.v.)*, the III retains that earlier machine's engines and general layout, but incorporates redesigned wings of greater span, a slightly longer fuselage, greater internal fuel capacity, and more capable avionics. The Gulfstream III's distinctive winglets allow the craft to operate with higher takeoff weights than its predecessor, as

The first of the two C-20Es acquired, 87-0139, is seen here at Gulfstream Aerospace's Savannah, Georgia, headquarters just after being handed over to the Army. The machine's characteristic winglets allow greater take-off weights, faster operating speeds, higher cruising altitudes, and increased fuel efficiency. *(U.S. Army)*

134

well as increasing fuel efficiency, operating speed, and cruising altitude. The type first entered U.S. military service in 1983, when the Air Force leased three C-20A machines. These aircraft were subsequently purchased outright, and in 1986 were joined in USAF service by an additional C-20A and seven C-20Bs equipped with more advanced avionics gear and slightly modified seating layouts. The Army machines differ from the USAF and Navy aircraft only in their seating arrangement and the type of communications equipment installed.

The Army's C-20s are operated by the Army Priority Air Transport Detachment out of Andrews Air Force Base, Maryland, and fly both within the continental U.S. and abroad. The machines carry the serial numbers 87-0139 and -0140, sport the attractive two-tone high-gloss paint scheme and 'UNITED STATES OF AMERICA' logo common to U.S. military VIP transport aircraft, and carry discrete 'U.S. ARMY' stencils on each wing. Training of the Army crews was carried out at Gulfstream's Savannah, Georgia, facility, and the company continues to provide maintenance and refresher training support under contract to the Army.

---

* In September 1978 that portion of the Grumman Corporation responsible for the development and production of the Gulfstream family of aircraft was sold to American Jet Industries, Inc, subsequently becoming the Gulfstream American Corporation. The firm was ultimately renamed Gulfstream Aerospace Corporation, and in 1985 became a subsidiary of Chrysler Corporation.

TECHNICAL DATA

Engines:
Two 11,400 lb st Rolls-Royce Spey Mk 511-8 turbofans

Dimensions:

Wingspan:	77 ft 10 in
Winglet height:	5ft 4 in
Wing area:	934.5 sq ft
Fuselage length:	74 ft 4 in
Height:	24 ft 4 in

Weight (empty/gross, in lbs):
32,000/69,700

Performance:
Speed (cruising/maximum, in mph): 509/580

Service Ceiling: 45,000 ft

Range: 4200 miles

Armament: None

Accommodation:
Two to three crew, plus up to nineteen passengers.

HAWKER SIDDELEY V-6 KESTREL

Type: Single-engined V/STOL tactical fighter

Manufacturer: Hawker Siddeley Aviation, Ltd, Kinston-Upon-Thames, England.

HISTORY

In 1957 Hawker Aircraft began development of the Model P.1127 V/STOL tactical fighter as a private venture undertaken in collaboration with the Bristol Siddeley Engines Company. The Kestrel, as the P.1127 was ultimately named, was an innovative aircraft that derived both vertical lift and forward thrust from engine exhaust vectored through two pairs of fuselage-mounted rotating nozzles. The machine's V/STOL capability was intended to facilitate operations from dispersed and unprepared sites, thereby freeing the Kestrel from reliance on fixed bases and thus increasing its chances of survival in combat. The British Government ordered six P.1127 prototypes in 1959, and the first tethered hovering flights began in October of the following year. The Kestrel's first transitions from hovering flight, and back, occurred in September 1961.

The second of three American-owned aircraft of the original Tripartite Kestrel Evaluation Squadron nears touchdown at West Raynham early in the test programme. This machine carried the British serial XS689 during the multinational evaluations in England, but was assigned the U.S. military serial 64-18263 upon arrival at Edwards AFB. Note the unique Tripartite Squadron fin flash on the vertical stabilizer. *(British Aerospace)*

136

The U.S. Defense Department showed a great interest in the P.1127 from the type's inception, going so far as to financially support Bristol Siddeley's development of the Kestrel's Pegasus engine. In 1962 this interest in the Hawker 'jump jet' led the United States to join Great Britain and West Germany in the joint purchase of nine P.1127s. These aircraft were used to equip a Tripartite Kestrel Evaluation Squadron officially formed at RAF West Raynham, Norfolk, on 1 April 1965. The U.S. contributed four pilots to the multinational unit; one each from the Navy and Air Force and, significantly, two from the Army.

The presence in the Tripartite Squadron of the Army pilots, Lieutenant Colonel Lou Solt and Major Al Johnson, was a concrete indication of the Army's intense interest in the Kestrel. Unlike the Fiat G.91, Douglas A-4, and other fixed-wing jet aircraft the Army considered for the close-support/armed tactical reconnaissance role, the P.1127 offered a V/STOL capability that would allow it to be deployed to forward areas virtually alongside the troops it was intended to support. The Army, locked in its continuing battle with the Air Force over which service should provide close air support for Army units, saw the Kestrel's forward deployment capability — independent of the Air Force's increasingly elaborate fixed air bases — as a positive argument in support of its case. Not only would Army-operated Kestrels be able to react quickly to requests for close air support — far more quickly than Air Force aircraft tied to distant runways and vulnerable fixed support facilities — but they could also be flown, maintained, and protected entirely by Army personnel.

The Tripartite Squadron was disbanded upon the January 1966 conclusion of the multinational Kestrel evaluation, at which time the three American-owned aircraft were shipped to the United States for further tri-service testing. These three machines were eventually joined in the U.S. by the three former West German aircraft — the Federal Republic having decided to abandon the P.1127 in favor of indigenous V/STOL designs — as well as by one of the British examples. All seven Kestrels were allocated the designation XV-6A and assigned U.S. military serials (64-18262 through -18268), though the former British P.1127 actually retained its RAF serial (XS695). The aircraft were extensively test flown by Navy, Air Force, and Army personnel but, despite glowing evaluations made by the pilots, each of the services ultimately declined to place production orders for additional examples. The USAF and Navy were already committed to the purchase of other, more conventional aircraft, and neither service felt the P.1127's unique V/STOL capabilities would be of more than marginal operational value (a notion totally invalidated by the outstanding combat record compiled during the 1982 Falklands War by the Kestrel's very capable descendants, the RAF Harrier and Royal Navy Sea Harrier)*. The Army, for its part, eventually lost its battle with the Air Force over which service would provide fixed-wing close air support for Army units and, as a result, was compelled to abandon its intended procurement of the P.1127. The seven U.S. Kestrels were ultimately withdrawn from service and disposed of in the late 1960s.

---

* The U.S. Marine Corps maintained an active interest in the P.1127 despite the Navy's decision not to procure the type for itself, and ultimately acquired large numbers of the more advanced Anglo-American Kestrel variant, the British Aerospace-McDonnell Douglas AV-8A Harrier (with planned large-scale procurement of the even more advanced AV-8B).

TECHNICAL DATA

Engine:
One 15,500 lb st Bristol Siddeley Pegasus turbofan

Dimensions:

Wingspan:	22 ft 11 in
Wing area:	230 sq ft
Fuselage length:	42 ft 6 in
Height:	10 ft 9 in

Weight (empty/gross, in lbs):
10,180/17,500

Performance:
Speed (cruising/maximum, in mph): 524/750

Service Ceiling: 45,000 ft

Range: 1245 miles

Armament:
None fitted to evaluation aircraft

Accommodation:
Pilot only.

HELIO U-10 COURIER

Type: Single-engined STOL utility and liaison aircraft

Manufacturer: Helio Aircraft Corporation, Bedford, Massachusetts.

HISTORY

In the late 1940s aeronautical engineers Otto Koppen and Lynn Bollinger set out to design and build a single-engined light airplane that would offer unsurpassed short takeoff and landing (STOL) performance, excellent low-speed flight characteristics, and a relatively high cruising speed. The flight testing of a Piper Vagabond modified for use as a proof-of-concept vehicle began in April 1949, and construction of the first Helio-Four production aircraft began at the end of that year. The Helio-Four was extensively modified during the course of construction, primarily to increase its potential military value, and the design ultimately evolved into the much more sophisticated commercial Helio Courier.

This float-equipped U-10B, photographed at Bad Tolz, Germany, in July 1966, was among the first of some twenty Couriers acquired by the Army beginning in 1953. The aircraft were used almost entirely for special warfare operations, and this particular machine is fitted with loudspeakers (just aft of the cabin door) for psychological warfare activities. Note the overall gray colour scheme and extended leading edge slats. *(George Fischbach via Peter M. Bowers)*

An innovative craft whose unique high-lift flap system and full-span leading edge slats provided almost uncanny STOL performance, the Helio Courier quite naturally attracted the Army's immediate and continued interest. In 1952 a single commercial model H-391 Courier was procured 'off-the-shelf' for Army evaluation with the designation YL-24 and the serial number 52-2540. This all-metal, high-wing cabin monoplane was powered by a single 260 hp Lycoming piston engine and could accommodate three persons in addition to the pilot. The Army was quite impressed by the YL-24, but budgetary restraints resulting from the need to purchase large numbers of helicopters and more orthodox fixed-wing aircraft for service in Korea precluded an immediate Army order for additional Couriers.

The decision not to acquire the Helio Courier during the Korean War period did not signal a loss of interest in the type; indeed, the Army continued to closely monitor the aircraft's evolutionary development and was particularly interested in the USAF's 1953 purchase of three L-28A (commercial Model H-295) Super Couriers. These aircraft were followed into Air Force service by an additional twenty-six -A model machines, all of which were redesignated U-10A in 1962. The Air Force went on to procure fifty-seven examples of the longer range U-10B and thirty-six of the still further improved U-10D, and it was the early operational successes enjoyed by these USAF U-10s in Vietnam that ultimately induced the Army to purchase the Helio Courier, albeit in relatively small numbers. Starting in 1963 the Army procured more than twenty U-10A, B, and D aircraft, the majority of which were used to support covert Special Forces operations in Vietnam and, after the end of the American involvement in Southeast Asia, in other world trouble spots. The type was gradually supplanted in frontline service by more advanced fixed- and rotary-wing aircraft, though as late as mid-1985 at least five U-10s remained active with Special Forces units in the Reserve Components.

TECHNICAL DATA (All versions, except where noted)

Engine:
One 260 hp Lycoming GO-435-C2B2-G piston (YL-24)
One 295 hp Lycoming GO-480-G1D6 piston (U-10A/B/D)

Dimensions:

Wingspan:	39 ft
Wing area:	231 sq ft
Fuselage length:	31 ft
Height:	8 ft 10 in

Weight (empty/gross, in lbs):
1800/3000 (YL-24)
2037/3400 (U-10A)
2080/3485 (U-10B)
2095/3600 (U-10D)

Performance:
Speed (cruising/maximum, in mph):
150/175 (YL-24)
150/185 (U-10A/B/D)

Service Ceiling: 20,500 ft

Range: 600 miles (YL-24, U-10A)
710 miles (U-10B/D)

Armament:
None normally fitted

Accommodation:
One pilot (all versions), plus three (YL-24), four (U-10A/B), or five (U-10D) passengers.

HILLER H-23 RAVEN

Type: Single-engined
   observation, training,
   and utility helicopter

Manufacturer: Hiller
Helicopter Company, Palo
Alto, California.

HISTORY

In 1948 the young aircraft designer Stanley Hiller developed the commercial Model 360 light helicopter as a test bed for his innovative 'Rotor-Matic' control system. This system, which used a hanging control column and small servo rotors mounted diagonally below the main rotor, provided excellent directional stability and for the first time allowed 'hands-off' helicopter flight. The Model 360 was refined into the Hiller commercial UH-12A (a company, not military, designation), a three-place, open-cockpit craft powered by a 200 hp Franklin engine. In the fall of 1950 the Army purchased a single UH-12A for evaluation and allocated the machine the desigation YH-23A. This aircraft (serial 50-1254) differed from the standard commercial UH-12A in having only two seats, and was powered by a 178 hp Franklin engine. The type's successful performance during the evaluation led the Army to order one hundred production examples in October 1950, the largest single helicopter order placed by the Army up to that time. The nearly 1800 Ravens ultimately procured by the Army were of the following variants:

The Army operated nearly 1800 Ravens of seven variants between 1950 and 1971, and the type served in roles ranging from aircrew trainer to flying ambulance. The machine shown here is an OH-23G dual control trainer (serial 61-3122), 793 examples of which were acquired beginning in early 1962. *(U.S. Army Transportation Corps Museum)*

H-23A:
First production model, one hundred of which were delivered beginning in early 1951. The H-23A was essentially identical to the YH-23A, with the same powerplant, seating for two, and skid-type landing gear. Most H-23As were delivered to the Army in air ambulance configuration with one totally enclosed exterior stretcher pannier mounted on either side of the cabin. This variant saw extensive service during the Korean War in both the casualty evacuation and general utility roles.

H-23B:
Generally similar to the H-23A, the -B model Raven differed from its predecessor in having a 200 hp Franklin (or, in some later model machines, a 250 hp Lycoming) engine, a combination skid and wheel landing gear, and various detail changes. The H-23B could also be fitted with stretcher panniers, though the majority of the 273 machines procured by the Army between 1952 and 1956 were not so equipped. More than half of all -B model aircraft were used as basic helicopter flight trainers at Fort Wolters, Texas. All surviving examples were redesignated OH-23B in 1962.

H-23C:
Military version of the commercial Model UH-12C. This variant differed from the H-23B in having seating for three under a one-piece plexiglass canopy, as well as in having metal, rather than wooden, rotor blades. The Army purchased 145 examples beginning in 1956, and those remaining in service in 1962 were redesignated OH-23C.

H-23D:
This Raven variant differed from earlier versions in having a completely new rotor and transmission system, as well as numerous design changes intended to increase by some sixty percent the number of hours that could be flown between airframe overhauls. In addition, the H-23D was powered by a 250 hp Lycoming engine rather than the 200 hp Franklin powerplants used in the H-23B and early model H-23Cs. The Army procured a total of 438 -D model Ravens, delivery of which began in 1956. The H-23D, which was redesignated OH-23D in 1962, was the Army's primary basic helicopter trainer until supplanted in that role by the Hughes TH-55 (q.v.) in the mid-1960s.

H-23F:
A military version of the commercial Model 12E-4, the H-23F was a four-place aircraft ordered by the Army in early 1962 specifically for use in Central and South America with the Army element of the Inter-American Geodetic Survey. All twenty-two machines acquired by the Army were powered by the 305 hp Lycoming VO-540-A1B engine, had extended cabin sections,

and sported inverted-vee tailplanes on the boom just forward of the tail rotor. Though ordered with the H-23F designation most of these aircraft were delivered as OH-23Fs.

H-23G:
Essentially a three-place, dual control version of the H-23F, the -G model was powered by the same 305 hp Lycoming engine. The Army procured 793 examples of this variant beginning in early 1962, and most were delivered with the Tri-Service designtion OH-23G.

The H-23 Raven served the Army well in a variety of roles, and saw extensive combat duty in both Korea and Vietnam. The last H-23 in the regular Army, a -D model trainer (serial 57-3007) that had logged more than 100,000 accident-free miles at Fort Wolters, was retired from active duty and transferred to the Army Reserve in 1971.

TECHNICAL DATA *(All versions, except where noted)*

Engine:

One 178 hp Franklin O-335-4 piston (YH/H/OH-23A)

One 200 hp Franklin O-335-6 piston (early model H/OH-23B)

One 250 hp Lycoming VO-435-23B piston (late model H/OH-23B, all H/OH-23C,D)

One 305 hp Lycoming VO-540-A1B piston (H/OH-23F,G)

Dimensions:

Main rotor diameter:	35 ft 5 in
Tail rotor diameter:	4 ft 4 in
Fuselage length:	27 ft 9 in (YH/H/OH-23A,B,C,D)
	29 ft 10 in (H/OH-23F)
	28 ft 6 in (H/OH-23G)
Height (to top of main rotor hub):	9 ft 9.5 in (YH/H/OH-23A,B,C,D,F)
	10 ft 2 in (H/OH-23G)

Weight (empty/gross, in lbs):

1816/2700 (YH/H/OH-23A,B,C,D)

1813/2800 (H/OH-23F)

1759/2800 (H/OH-23G)

Performance:

Speed (cruising/maximum, in mph):
78/82 (YH/H/OH-23A)
76/84 (H/OH-23B,C)
82/95 (H/OH-23D)
90/96 (H/OH-23F,G)

Service Ceiling: 13,200 ft
(YH/H/OH-23A,B,C,D)
15,200 ft
(H/OH-23F,G)

Range: 197 miles
(YH/H/OH-23A,B,C,D)
225 miles (H/OH-23F,G)

Armament:
None normally fitted, though machines used in Vietnam occasionally carried light automatic weapons mounted in the port-side cabin door.

Accommodation:
One pilot, one observer/student/passenger, plus provision for two external stretchers in air ambulance configuration (YH/H/OH-23A,B)

One pilot, two observers/students/passengers (H/OH-23C,D,G)

One pilot, three observers/passengers (H/OH-23F).

HILLER VZ-1 PAWNEE

Type: Multi-engined VTOL
research vehicle

Manufacturer: Hiller
Helicopter Company, Palo
Alto, California.

HISTORY

In late 1953 the U.S. Navy's Office of Naval Research (ONR), acting as technical direction agent for the Army, awarded Hiller Helicopters a contract for the development of a twin-engined ducted fan VTOL research vehicle of the 'flying platform' type. The craft was intended to explore both the practicality of the ducted fan as a propulsion unit for V/STOL aircraft and the potential military value of the flying platform as a tactical reconnaissance and transport vehicle. The first prototype of the Hiller machine was completed in September 1954 and given the interim, non-standard Navy designation YHO-1E. The vehicle

The second Pawnee, 56-6944, in flight. The third machine differed in having a much taller duct, a circular landing skid, and a seat for the pilot. *(U.S. Army Transportation Corps Museum)*

made its first non-tethered flight in February 1955, and shortly thereafter was redesignated VZ-1.

The first VZ-1 prototype bore a superficial resemblance to the contemporary De Lackner HZ-1 (q.v.) and, like that machine, carried its pilot and twin 40 hp engines on a small circular platform directly above two contra-rotating airscrews. Unlike those of the HZ-1, however, the Hiller machine's fans were mounted inside a five-foot diameter duct, beneath which were fitted eight moveable vanes used to improve the craft's lateral stability. The VZ-1's pilot stood upright just behind the narrow control pedestal, to which he was secured by safety belts, and held onto a set of bicycle-like handlebars fitted with a simple twist throttle and a propeller torque control. The flying platform was kinesthetically controlled; to initiate directional movement the pilot would simply lean in the desired direction and alter the craft's altitude by increasing or decreasing engine power.

The Army was favorably impressed by the VZ-1's performance during the initial ONR-managed flight test programme, and in November 1956 ordered a single modified example for service testing and operational evaluation. This second VZ-1 differed from the first example in having a third 40 hp engine, an eight-foot diameter duct without lower control vanes, and a simplified control pedestal. The second Pawnee (serial 56-6944) made its maiden flight in 1958, and the following year was joined in Army service by a third, further modified example. This third VZ-1 (serial 56-6945) had a duct of greatly increased height, a single circular landing skid instead of the three- and four-point wheeled landing gear of the earlier craft, conventional helicopter-type flight controls, and a seat for the pilot.

The VZ-1s provided a wealth of valuable information about VTOL flight in general and the value of the ducted fan in particular, but ultimately proved to be too ungainly, too heavy, too slow, and too mechanically delicate to be of any real value on the battlefield. Further development of the type was therefore suspended and all three types had been withdrawn from service by 1963.

TECHNICAL DATA *(All versions, except where noted)*

Engines:
Two 40 hp Nelson H-56 (first prototype)
Three 40 hp Nelson H-56 (second and third prototypes)

Dimensions:

Duct diameter:	5 ft (first prototype)
	8 ft (second and third prototypes)
Height to top of pedestal:	7 ft 5 in (first prototype)
	7 ft 10 in (second prototype)
Height to top of pilot's seat (third prototype):	9 ft 5 in

Weight (empty/gross, in lbs):
No figures available for first prototype
465/665 (second prototype)
565/765 (third prototype)

Performance:
Maximum speed:
15 mph (first prototype)
10 mph (second prototype)
No other data available

Armament:
None

Accommodation:
Pilot only.

HILLER H-32 HORNET

Type: Ramjet-powered light helicopter prototype

Manufacturer: Hiller Helicopter Company, Palo Alto, California.

HISTORY

Another of Stanley Hiller's innovative helicopter designs, the commercial Model HJ-1 Hornet was intended primarily for the civilian commuter market and first flew in 1950. The two-place craft was of exceedingly simple construction, consisting mainly of a reinforced steel tube framework overlaid with a skin of fiberglass and plastic laminate. The Hornet was powered by two Hiller 8RJ2B ramjets, one fixed to the end of each main rotor blade, with an auxiliary one horsepower gasoline engine being

The Hornet's diminutive size is well illustrated in this view of 55-4963, the first of an additional twelve YH-32s acquired by the Army in 1955 following successful initial trials of the first two prototypes. The YH-32 differed from the civil model HJ-1 only in having two small tail surfaces at the extreme end of the tailboom. *(Peter M. Bowers)*

used to spin the rotor blades up to the 50 rpm required prior to ignition of the ramjets.

The Army felt that the Hornet might have some military value as a light and easily maintained battlefield observation platform, and in 1952 ordered two examples for service test and evaluation. These YH-32s (serials 53-4663 and -4664), which were delivered in mid-1953, differed from the commercial Model HJ-1 only in having two small tailplanes attached to the aft end of the tailboom. A follow-on order for twelve additional examples was placed in 1955 in order to permit a more thorough evaluation of the type's military potential. These twelve aircraft (55-4963 through -4974) were all delivered by late 1956, but within a year the Army determined that the YH-32 was unsuitable and all fourteen Hornets were subsequently withdrawn from service.

TECHNICAL DATA (All versions)

Engines:
Two Hiller 8RJ2B ramjets, each of 38 lbs net thrust, plus one 1 hp auxiliary starter engine.

Dimensions:

Main rotor diameter:	23 ft
Tail rotor diameter:	2 ft 8 in
Fuselage length:	11 ft 4 in
Height (to top of main rotor hub):	8 ft

Weight (empty/gross, in lbs):
530/1080

Performance:
Speed (cruising/maximum, in mph): 69/80

Service Ceiling: 11,500 ft

Range: 280 miles

Armament: None

Accommodation:
Pilot and one observer/passenger.

HILLER H-5

Type: Single-engined light observation helicopter prototype

Manufacturer: Hiller Helicopter Company, Palo Alto, California.

HISTORY

The Hiller Model 1100 was developed in response to the Army's 1960 solicitation for a new turbine-powered light observation helicopter (LOH), and in 1961 was named a finalist in that hotly-contested competition along with the Bell Model 204 and the Hughes Model 369. Each firm was subsequently awarded a contract for the construction of five test and evaluation machines, with the Hiller aircraft receiving the designation YHO-5 and the serial numbers 62-4207 through -4211. The first YOH-5, as the type was redesignated under the 1962 Tri-Service system, first flew in January 1963 and by April 1964 all five examples had been delivered to the Army Aviation Test Board at Fort Rucker, Alabama.

The Hiller YOH-5's fairly conventional design featured the standard 'pod-and-boom' configuration, skid landing gear, and extensive cockpit glazing. Like all entrants in the LOH competition the YOH-5 was powered by a single 250 shp Allison T63-A-5 turboshaft, though the Hiller craft used the powerplant to drive the innovative 'L'-type high-lift, semi-rigid main rotor system. This consisted of two blades, each of aluminium honeycomb and stainless steel construction and each attached to the rotor

The first of five YOH-5s ordered by the Army, 62-4207 (the company-applied serial number on the tailboom is incorrect) is shown here just prior to delivery. Though not adopted by the Army the type went on to achieve considerable commercial success as the Fairchild-Hiller FH-100. *(U.S. Army)*

148

hub by a single drag strut and the main retention bolt. The system incorporated automatic stabilization augmentation, and the main blades could be unlocked and folded to the rear when not in use.

Both the YOH-5 and the Bell YOH-4 (q.v.) were judged to be more than able to fulfill the payload, speed, and range requirements set forth in the LOH type specifiation. However, neither Hiller nor Bell could match the ridiculously low cost-per-unit price offered by Hughes for the equally capable YOH-6 (q.v.) and, despite formal protests by Hiller, the Hughes design was named winner of the LOH competition in May 1965. The YOH-5 was subsequently developed as a civil helicopter and was marketed abroad as the Fairchild (Hiller) FH-1100.

TECHNICAL DATA

Engine:
One 250 shp Allison T63-A-5 turboshaft

Dimensions:
Main rotor diameter: 35 ft 6 in
Tail rotor diameter: 6 ft
Fuselage length: 29 ft 11.5 in
Height (to top of
    main rotor hub):   9 ft 3.5 in

Weight (empty/gross, in lbs):
1370/2530

Performance:
Speed (cruising/maximum, in mph):
    118/128

Service Ceiling: 17,200 ft

Range: 320 miles

Armament:
Provision for two XM-7 systems (each consisting of two linked 7.62 mm M-60 machine guns) or two XM-8 40 mm grenade launcher systems, or one of each, attached to main cabin door frames.

Accommodation:
Pilot, co-pilot/observer, and up to two passengers.

HUGHES V-9

Type: Twin-engined
    propulsion research
    vehicle

Manufacturer: Hughes
Helicopters, Culver City,
California.

HISTORY

In 1962 Hughes Helicopters was awarded an Army contract for the development and construction of a research helicopter utilizing a hot-cycle propulsion system. The resulting XV-9A (serial 64-15107) made its first flight in November 1964.

Though rather ungainly-looking the XV-9A was of essentially straightforward construction. Indeed, in order to save time and money in the building of what was certain to be the only vehicle of its type Hughes' engineers assembled the XV-9A using the cockpit of an OH-6A, the landing gear of a Sikorsky H-34, and a simple purpose-built cylindrical fuselage with a twin-rudder 'V' tail. It was, in fact, the XV-9A's experimental propulsion system that made the otherwise mundane craft unique. The system was built around two pod-mounted General Electric YT64-GE-6

The sole XV-9A departing Hughes Field on one of its first test flights. The machine's hot-cycle propulsion system ducted the exhaust from two modified YT64 engines directly through the rotor hub and expelled the gases at near-sonic speeds through vaned cascades in the rotor blade tips. (U.S. Army)

engines fitted to the ends of two high-set stub wings, one on either side of the fuselage directly below the main rotor hub. Each engine's turbine section had been removed, and hot exhaust gases were ducted directly through the rotor hub to be expelled at near-sonic speeds through vaned cascades in each of the three blade tips. Smaller exhaust ports on either side of the tail boom just forward of the rudders provided some additional directional stability.

The XV-9A's flight test programme was completed in August 1965, with a total of 19.1 hours having been flown. The hot-cycle propulsion system had proved to be overly complex and the aircraft itself had been plagued by stability problems; the Army therefore returned ownership of the XV-9A to Hughes and abandoned any further hot-cycle research.

TECHNICAL DATA

Engines:
Two 2850 shp General Electric YT64-GE-6 turbines modified to operate as gas generators

Dimensions:
Main rotor diameter: 55 ft
Fuselage length: 45 ft
Height (to top of rotor hub): 12 ft

Weight (empty/gross, in lbs):
8500/15,300

Performance:
Speed (cruising/maximum, in mph): 150/173

Service Ceiling: 11,500 ft

Range: 165 miles

Armament: None

Accommodation:
Pilot and co-pilot/flight engineer.

HUGHES H-55 OSAGE

Type: Single-engined primary helicopter trainer

Manufacturer: Hughes Helicopters, Culver City, California.

HISTORY

In 1955 the aviation division of Hughes Tool Company began development of the Model 269 light piston-engined helicopter in response to a growing commercial demand for simple, easily maintained rotary wing aircraft. The Model 269 was certainly simple, consisting essentially of a welded steel tube fuselage to which were attached a tube-type tailboom, twin landing skids, a two-seat enclosed cabin, and a four-cylinder piston engine driving a three-bladed, fully articulated main rotor and a two-bladed anti-torque tail rotor. Yet the Model 269 was not as frail as it looked, for it proved to be a robust and hardy craft capable of operating in a variety of demanding roles.

The Army became interested in the Model 269 primarily because the machine's rugged construction, ease of maintenance, and relatively low operating costs were attributes much to be

TH-55A 64-18126, a machine of the second production batch, in flight during June 1966. The Osage's simple but rugged construction made it an ideal primary helicopter trainer, and the type remained in service at Fort Rucker until mid-1988. (U.S. Army)

desired in a light observation helicopter. And it was with that role in mind that the Army purchased five Model 269 aircraft in 1958 for service test and evaluation. These five helicopters, designated YHO-2 and allocated the serial numbers 58-1324 through -1328, were found to be eminently suitable for their intended military role but budgetary constraints prevented any immediate acquisition of the type. The financial situation eased by 1964, however, and that year the Army selected the slightly modified Model 269A as its new primary helicopter trainer and subsequently ordered a total of 792 aircraft. The TH-55A, as the type was designated, continued to train Army helicopter pilots until June 1988, when the 139 surviving machines were replaced in the primary helicopter training role by the Bell UH-1 Iroquois.

TECHNICAL DATA

Engine:
One 180 hp Lycoming HIO-360-A1A (YHO-2)
One 180 hp Lycoming HIO-360-B1A (TH-55A)

Dimensions:
Main rotor diameter: 25 ft 3.5 in
Tail rotor diameter: 3 ft 4 in
Fuselage length: 22 ft 4 in
Height (to top of
rotor hub):   8 ft 3 in

Weight (empty/gross, in lbs):
1008/1850

Performance:
Speed (cruising/maximum, in mph):
66/86

Service Ceiling: 11,500 ft

Range: 204 miles

Armament: None

Accommodation:
Pilot and one student.

HUGHES H-6 CAYUSE

Type: Single-engined light
observation helicopter

Manufacturer: Hughes
Helicopters, Culver City,
California.

HISTORY

The Army's 1960 solicitation for a new light observation helicopter (LOH) touched off one of the most fiercely contested corporate competitions in American aviation history. Twelve companies submitted a total of twenty-two designs, one of which was the Model 369 offered by the (then) Aircraft Division of the Hughes Tool Company. In May 1961 the Hughes, Hiller, and Bell entrants were selected as finalists in the LOH competition and each firm was subsequently awarded an Army contract for the production of five test and evaluation aircraft. The Hughes machines were assigned the serial numbers 62-4212 through -4216 and the designation YHO-6, though the latter was changed to YOH-6 under the 1962 Tri-Service designation system. The maiden flight of the first YOH-6 occurred in February 1963, and all five examples were delivered to the Army Aviation Test Board at Fort Rucker over the following eight months. The LOH 'fly-off' between the YOH-6, Bell YOH-4 (q.v.), and Hiller YOH-5 (q.v.) lasted until late May 1965, at which time the Hughes design was named the winner.

The Army's selection of the YOH-6 as winner of the LOH contest was based more on economic realities than on any particularly outstanding attribute of the aircraft itself. This is not to say that the YOH-6 was not a capable performer, for its articulated rotor system, rugged construction, relative simplicity, mechanical reliability, and quite favourable power-to-weight ratio all helped make it the equal of the Bell and Hiller entries in all test categories. In the final analysis, however, it was Hughes'

Cayuse 65-12951, an OH-6A of the first production batch, was unofficially redesignated OH-6C after being experimentally equipped with an uprated Allison 250-C20 engine, five-bladed main rotor, modifed 'T'-tail, and other detail improvements. These changes were not adopted for general use on Army OH-6s, though they were later incorporated into Hughes' highly successful Model 500 series helicopters. *(McDonnell-Douglas Helicopters)*

The Army acquired a total of 1434 production Cayuses, all of which were OH-6As identical to the machine shown here. This particular aircraft, 67-16301, was photographed in 1971 while being used to train observation pilots for service in Vietnam. Note that the cabin doors have been removed, and that a multi-barrelled 7.62 mm minigun has been fixed outboard of the rear port-side door. *(U.S. Army)*

ability to offer the YOH-6 to the Army at a cost-per-unit price so far below that quoted by the other two finalists for their respective aircraft that ultimately decided the issue in Hughes' favour. Indeed, Hughes' price of $29,415 per bare airframe (no engine, instruments, or mission avionics) was so low that Hiller lodged a formal complaint with the Department of Defense (DoD) accusing Hughes of unethical business practices. This challenge was to no avail, however, for DoD judged Hughes' pricing policies to be perfectly legal and the selection of the YOH-6 as winner of the LOH competition was allowed to stand.

Within days of selecting the YOH-6 as its new LOH the Army awarded Hughes a multiyear contract for 714 production OH-6A aircraft. Follow-on orders for additional examples raised the total number of Cayuses delivered to the Army to 1434 by the time production ended in 1970. Though minor modifications were made to machines of the second and third production batches (built during 1967 and 1968-70, respectively) all Army Cayuses bore the OH-6A designation and all were basically identical. In operational service the Cayuse proved to be a rugged and dependable aircraft that was relatively easy to maintain under field conditions. These attributes were especially important in Vietnam, where between 1968 and 1973 the OH-6A flew more than two million combat hours in roles ranging from armed escort to photo-reconnaissance and aerial adjustment of artillery fire.

In the years immediately following the end of the Vietnam war the Army began replacing OH-6As in frontline service with the Bell OH-58 Kiowa (q.v.) aeroscout helicopter. Most surviving Cayuses, including some 420 machines damaged in Vietnam but later returned to flyable condition, were subsequently turned over to the reserve components. By 1984 a total of 350 OH-6As were in service with the Army National Guard, which plans to maintain the type as frontline equipment well into the 1990s. A fleet-wide upgrade programme intended to bring all National Guard Cayuses up to first-line status comparable to that of the regular Army's OH-58s is currently under consideration.

During the course of the 1983 American invasion of Grenada

it became apparent that the Army had acquired, at least in limited numbers, variants of the Hughes Model 500M-D Defender helicopter. On several occasions during Operation URGENT FURY Defenders were seen, and photographed, operating in support of Army and Navy special operations forces. Since that time Army-operated Defenders, known within the special operations community as 'Little Birds', are known to have participated in American attacks on Iranian gunboats in the Persian Gulf in the fall of 1987, and in the 1989 US invasion of Panama. Though the Army has never openly admitted its ownership or operation of the 500M-D the Defenders are thought to be assigned to the 160th Aviation Battalion, a special operations support unit based at Fort Campbell, Kentucky, that has become a key component of the United States' Special Operations Command.

A direct and highly evolved descendent of the OH-6A, the Defender first appeared in 1975 as a 'militarized' derivative of the commercial Model 500D. Both variants differ from the standard OH-6A in having the more powerful 420 shp Allison 250-C20B engine, an improved transmission, a slower-turning and thus quieter five-bladed main rotor, an extensively redesigned

The 500M-D Defender shown here is essentially similar to the aircraft used by Army special operations forces during Operation URGENT FURY and in support of U.S. forces in the Persian Gulf in 1987, though the Army machines used in Grenada were not fitted with the mast-mounted sight carried by this early prototype. The Defender is a direct descendent of the OH-6, but differs from the Cayuse in having a five-bladed main rotor, uprated engines, a redesigned tail unit, and a 'Black Hole' infrared signature suppression system. This installation redirects the engine exhaust through two small ducts mounted on either side of the rear fuselage, thus dramatically reducing the aircraft's infrared emissions and making it a much more difficult target for heat-seeking missiles. The Army's Defenders are thought to be designated either 'OH-8' or MH-6A'. *(MDHC)*

'T'-shaped tail with small end-plate fins, and greatly strengthened fuselage and landing gear. The 500M-D has, in addition, self-sealing fuel tanks, extensive armor protection for the crew and vital areas of the machine itself, the Hughes-developed 'Black Hole' infrared signature-reducing engine exhaust system, and provision for a wide variety of weapons and both active and passive reconnaissance systems.

Army procurement of the 500M-D is thought to have begun in 1980 or 1981, and the total number of aircraft in the inventory as of mid-1987 was approximately fifty. Of this number some thirty are thought to be configured for the light attack role, while the remainder are optimized for covert reconnaissance and transportation of special operations troops. It is not known whether the machines are new-built 500M-Ds or OH-6As modified to 500M-D standard. Shortly after the aircraft's debut in Grenada various aviation trade journals and defense affairs publications began referring to it as the 'OH-8', though DoD spokesmen have since referred to the light attack version as the 'AH-6A' and the transport/reconnaissance machine as the 'MH-6A'. In early 1990 the Army announced its intention to convert 36 of its AH/MH-6 machines to the NOTAR — no tail rotor — configuration pioneered by MDHC's MD 530N proof-of-concept vehicle. The NOTAR system replaces the standard tail rotor with a gearbox-driven variable pitch fan in the end of the tailboom, which expels pressurized rotor-bleed air both sideways and to the rear to provide longitudinal control. The NOTAR-equipped aircraft will be significantly quieter, and far more agile, than conventional helicopters.

TECHNICAL DATA

Engine:
One 317 shp Allison T63-A-5A turboshaft (OH-6A)
One 420 shp Allison 250-C20B turboshaft (500M-D)

Dimensions:

Main rotor diameter:	26 ft 4 in (OH-6A)
	26 ft 5 in (500M-D)
Tail rotor diameter:	4 ft 2 in (OH-6A)
	4 ft 6 in (500M-D)
Fuselage length:	23 ft 1.5 in (OH-6A)
	21 ft 5 in (500M-D)
Height (to top of main rotor hub):	8 ft 6 in (OH-6A)
	8 ft 11 in (500M-D)

Weight (empty/maximum, in lbs):
1156/2700 (OH-6A)
1295/3450 (500M-D)

Performance:
Speed (cruising/maximum, in mph):
134/150 (OH-6A)
160/175 (500M-D)

Service Ceiling: 15,500 ft (OH-6A)
17,500 ft (500M-D)

Range: 380 miles (OH-6A)
290 miles (500M-D)

Armament:
OH-6A: Provision for XM-27 7.62 mm minigun system or XM-75 40 mm grenade launcher on pylon mounted outside port passenger door, plus (in Vietnam) at least one M-60 7.62 mm machine gun mounted in one or both rear doors.

500M-D: Provision for one XME-27E1 minigun/rocket launcher system, or one XM-230 30 mm 'Chain Gun' cannon, or one or two 7-round 2.75 inch rocket launcher pods, or two to four BGM-71A TOW anti-tank missiles.

Accommodation:
OH-6A: One pilot and one observer, plus up to four passengers, or one pilot and one medic and up to two stretchers.

500M-D: One pilot and one observer, plus up to five passengers, or one pilot and medic and two stretchers.

KAMAN H-2 TOMAHAWK and SEASPRITE

Type: Single-engined attack helicopter prototype (Tomahawk) Twin-engined research helicopter (Seasprite)

Manufacturer: Kaman Aircraft Corporation, Bloomfield, Connecticut.

HISTORY

Originally developed in response to a 1958 U.S. Navy requirement for a ship-based light utility helicopter, the UH-2 first came to the Army's attention in September 1963. Earlier that year the Army had allocated some $4 million for the development of the world's first purpose-built attack helicopter, and at the same time solicited tenders for a low-cost interim gunship that could be used until the more advanced aircraft became available. Kaman had anticipated the Army's need for a stop-gap attack craft and had developed a low-cost design based on the existing Navy UH-2A Seasprite. The single interim gunship prototype, which bore the Navy Bureau number 149785, was handed over to the Army Aviation Test Board for evaluation in October 1963.

The UH-2A interim attack helicopter, which the Army designated H-2 Tomahawk, differed from the standard Navy Seasprite in

The single H-2 Tomahawk prototype in flight during Army evaluations, November 1963. The machine's two nose-mounted gun turrets offered an extremely wide arc of fire, and could be aimed independently or in unison by the co-pilot via a swivelling overhead-mounted sight. Note the load-carrying stub wings, as well as the 'last four' of the aircraft's Navy Bureau Number just behind and below the national insignia. *(Kaman)*

The Compound Seasprite, seen here prior to the addition of its Beech Queen Air wings, carried its auxiliary YJ85 engine on its starboard side just aft of the cockpit door and was able to maintain altitude in the autogyro mode solely on turbojet power. Note the conical mesh screen fitted over the turbojet's intake, as well as the Navy Bureau Number and designation 'HU2K-1' on the vertical tail just below the tail rotor. *(Kaman)*

several ways. The most obvious difference was in armament, for the Tomahawk was fitted with two chin-mounted turrets, each housing two 7.62 mm machine guns. The turrets could be operated independently of one another, or could be 'slaved' together to engage the same target. The aircraft also carried a single door-mounted M-60 machine gun, and was fitted with short stub wings upon which could be carried up to four 7-round pods of 2.75 inch unguided rockets. Other modifications made to the H-2 included the addition of armor plating around the cockpit, engine, transmission, and fuel tanks, and the installation of Army-standard navigation and communications equipment. The Aviation Test Board ultimately judged the Tomahawk to be an extremely capable machine, and in early November 1963 the Army sought and received Congressional authorization to purchase 220 aircraft. However, five days after the 22 November assassination of John Kennedy and the subsequent assumption of the Presidency by Texan Lyndon Johnson the acquisition of the Connecticut-built H-2 was ordered abandoned in favor of further purchases of the Texas-built Bell UH-1 Iroquois.

The decision to abandon the Tomahawk in favor of more Hueys did not mark the end of the Army's involvement with the Seasprite, for in mid-1964 a single UH-2A was selected for use in a joint Army-Navy helicopter research programme intended to explore the mechanics and techniques of high-speed rotor-borne flight. Under an Army Transportation Research Command contract the Seasprite (BuNo 147978) was fitted with a General Electric YJ85 turbojet engine in addition to its existing T58 turboshaft and, so equipped, reached level-flight speeds in excess of 215 mph. In early 1965 the craft was fitted with wings, and in subsequent test flights increased its top speed to more than 225 mph. The extensive tests conducted with the 'compound Seasprite' were of enormous value in determining the capabilities and limitations of high-speed compound rotorcraft. Upon completion of the test programme in early 1966 the aircraft was returned to its original configuration and sent back to the fleet.

A third UH-2 also saw limited Army service. Essentially identical to the H-2 Tomahawk of 1963, this third variant was offered as an interim gunship that could be used in Vietnam until the problem-plagued Advanced Aerial Fire Support System (AAFSS) attack helicopter programme could produce a viable aircraft. The updated Tomahawk competed against a modified Sikorsky S-61 and the Bell Model 209 in an Army 'fly-off' conducted at Edwards Air Force Base, California, between 13 November and 1 December 1965. Both the S-61 and the modified UH-2 performed reasonably well during the competition, but the Army selected the Bell 209 (AH-1 Cobra, q.v.) as its new interim attack helicopter. Both the Kaman UH-2 and Sikorsky S-61 (H-3 q.v.) were returned to their manufacturers following the end of the competition.

TECHNICAL DATA *(All versions, except where noted)*

Engine:
One 1250 shp General Electric T58-GE-8 turboshaft, plus
One 2500 lb st General Electric YJ85 auxiliary turbojet in the 'compound Seasprite'

Dimensions:
Main rotor diameter: 44 ft
Tail rotor diameter: 8 ft
Fuselage length: 36 ft 7 in
Height (to top of main rotor hub): 13 ft 6 in
Wingspan (compound Seasprite): 39 ft 8 in

Weight (empty/gross, in lbs):
6400/9000 (Tomahawk)
7200/11,200 (Compound)

Performance:
Speed (cruising/maximum, in mph):
152/162 (Tomahawk)
190/225 (Compound)

Service Ceiling: 17,400 ft (Tomahawk)
19,900 ft (Compound)

Range: 670 miles (Tomahawk)
450 miles (Compound)

Armament: See text

Accommodation:
Pilot, co-pilot, and crew chief/gunner (Tomahawk).
Pilot, co-pilot, and flight engineer (Compound).

LOCKHEED H-51

Type: Single-engined
(XH-51A) or twin-
engined (XH-51A
Compound) high-speed
research helicopter

Manufacturer: Lockheed-
California Company, Burbank,
California.

HISTORY

The Lockheed Model 186 was designed in response to a 1960
joint Army/Navy requirement for a high-speed, highly manoeuvrable research helicopter. Two examples were ordered in early
1962, with the first of the two making its maiden flight in
November of that year. The aircraft, designated XH-51A, were
operated by both Army and Navy pilots and carried Navy
Bureau numbers (151262 and 151263) in addition to markings
indicating their dual-service status.

In keeping with its intended role of high-speed research
vehicle the XH-51A was far more streamlined than most
contemporary helicopters. The craft's aluminum skin was flush-
riveted to the extensively flush-sealed fuselage frame, the
engine air intake scoops were faired into the upper fuselage
decking, the skid landing gear was retractable, and the main
rotor plane was tilted a few degrees forward of the fuselage
datum line. All these features combined gave the XH-51A an
extremely low aerodynamic drag coefficient, which in turn
resulted in a maximum level speed of 175 mph. The craft's rigid
main rotor, a system pioneered by Lockheed on its earlier
CL-475 research helicopter, made the XH-51A extremely agile
and allowed it to perform flight manoeuvres previously possible
only in fixed-wing aircraft.

The XH-51A's quite impressive performance significantly
improved, however, following the second prototype's 1964
conversion into a compound rotorcraft. The conversion of

The first XH-51A prototype, BuNo 151262, in flight over southern California.
The machine's retractable landing skids (here in the raised position) and
extensive streamlining gave it an extremely low aerodynamic drag
coefficient and helped make it one of the fastest helicopters ever built.
(Lockheed-California)

161

The second XH-51A, BuNo 151263, following its conversion into a compound rotorcraft testbed. The single Pratt & Whitney J60 turbojet, stub wings, and other refinements allowed the XH-51 Compound to set an unofficial rotorcraft level-flight speed record in June 1967. The chin-mounted probe evident in this photograph carried special test instrumentation. *(Lockheed-California)*

151263 included the addition of a pod-mounted Pratt & Whitney J60 turbojet engine, short stub wings fixed to the lower fuselage sides, an enlarged horizontal stabilizer, and other detail changes. The reworked XH-51A Compound made its first flight in September 1964, and in June 1967 set an unofficial helicopter world speed record of 302.6 mph.

The XH-51A and XH-51A Compound were extremely valuable technology testbeds, and many of the systems pioneered or refined in these aircraft were later incorporated in such advanced helicopters as the AH-56A Cheyenne (q.v.). The XH-51As themselves were finally retired from service only in the late 1960s.

TECHNICAL DATA *(Both versions, except where noted)*

Engine(s):
One 500 shp Pratt & Whitney of Canada T74 (PT6B) turboshaft (XH-51A), plus one 2600 lb st Pratt & Whitney J60-P-2 auxiliary turbojet (XH-51A Compound)

Dimensions:

Main rotor diameter:	35 ft
Tail rotor diameter:	6 ft
Fuselage length:	32 ft 4 in (XH-51A)
	34 ft 2 in (XH-51A Compound)
Height (to top of main rotor hub):	8 ft 2.5 in
Wingspan (XH-51A Compound):	16 ft

Weight (empty/gross, in lbs):
2790/4100 (XH-51A)
3100/4450 (XH-51A Compound)

Performance:
Speed (cruising/maximum, in mph):
160/175 (XH-51A)
230/302.6 (XH-51A Compound)

Service Ceiling: 20,000 ft

Range: 260 miles (XH-51A)
275 miles (XH-51A Compound)

Armament: None

Accommodation:
Pilot and co-pilot/flight engineer.

LOCKHEED C-121

Type: Airborne missile   Manufacturer: Lockheed
    tracking platform   Aircraft Corporation, Burbank,
                                    California.

HISTORY

The Army's association with the venerable Lockheed Constellation began in 1963, when a need was indentified for an optical and infrared tracking aircraft to be used during test firings of the Army's then-current generation of guided missiles. This specialized task required a machine capable of serving as a stable camera and sensor platform during long duration flights at relatively high altitudes, traits which in the early 1960s were admirably expressed in the Constellation. The 'Connies' then in service with the Navy and Air Force were used primarily as airborne early warning (AEW) and long range transport aircraft, and thus offered the range, endurance, and performance the missile-tracking role required. The Army therefore arranged to 'borrow' a single Navy EC-121K Warning Star early warning radar variant, which was specifically modified prior to entering Army service.

The modifications made to the Navy EC-121K by the Douglas Aircraft Company's Tulsa (Oklahoma) Division were intended to convert the aircraft into the most advanced airborne optical/infrared tracking platform possible, and included extensive structural changes both inside and out. The aircraft was first stripped of all its AEW-associated equipment, beginning with the dorsal and ventral radars and their protective radomes. The

The Army's sole Constellation, JC-121K 143196, is seen here on the ramp at Douglas Aircraft's Tulsa Division soon after being converted for Army use. Note the dorsal 'greenhouse' with its three optical glass panels, as well as the smaller camera ports in the fuselage side between the wing trailing edge and the open cargo door. (Harry Gann)

dorsal radome was then replaced by a streamlined, non-pressurized 'greenhouse' observation enclosure separated from the main fuselage area by a pressure bulkhead fitted with a removable hatch. The left side of the greenhouse had two 30 inch by 60 inch and one 30 inch by 32 inch optical-glass panels, beneath each of which were motion picture and still camera mounts. In order to provide an unrestricted view for infrared tracking instruments the aircraft's port-side cargo door was set into a track-type mounting to permit opening in flight, and retractable air deflectors were installed just forward of the door to minimize turbulence when the door was open. Additional optical-quality glass viewing windows were installed in the fuselage's port side between the cargo door and the wing's trailing edge, and each of the eighteen-inch diameter ports was equipped with camera mounts. Eight electronic equipment racks were installed along the starboard side of the fuselage interior directly opposite the viewing windows, with an equipment operator's seat anchored to the decking in front of each rack. The airplane's internal electric power and crew oxygen systems were upgraded, and the Connie was fitted with new and highly capable HF, VHF, and UHF radios that provided simultaneous communication with all ground stations and aircraft involved in the missile tests.

The EC-121K Warning Star was developed from the commercial Model 1049 Super Constellation and the first of 142 examples entered Navy service, as the WV-2, in 1954. The aircraft loaned to the Army was one of forty-two machines of the eighth production batch, and retained its Navy Bureau Number (143196) though it was allocated the temporary special testing designation JC-121K. The machine was powered by four Wright R-3350-42 radial engines and retained its wingtip-mounted auxiliary fuel tanks.

The Army's single JC-121K proved well-suited to its role as an airborne optical and infrared missile tracking platform, and at the time this book went to press remained the largest aircraft ever operated by the United States Army. The machine was returned to the Navy in the late 1960s and was ultimately disposed of by that service.

TECHNICAL DATA

Engines:
Four 3400 hp Wright R-3350-42 Turbo Compound radials

Dimensions:
Winspan: 126 ft 2 in
Wing area: 1654 sq ft
Length: 116 ft
Height: 27 ft

Weight (empty/maximum, in lbs):
60,500/143,600 (approximately)

Performance:
Speed (cruising/maximum, in mph): 245/321

Service Ceiling: 22,250 ft

Range: 4600 miles

Armament: None

Accommodation:
Three-four crew and up to twenty-three sensor operators and/or observers.

LOCKHEED V-4 HUMMINGBIRD

Type: Twin-engined VTOL research aircraft

Manufacturer: Lockheed-Georgia Company, Marietta, Georgia.

HISTORY

In June 1961 the Army Transportation Research Command awarded Lockheed-Georgia a contract for the production of a single VZ-10A fixed-wing VTOL research aircraft, a refined version of the company's earlier Model 330 proof-of-concept vehicle. The VZ-10A, which in July 1962 was redesignated XV-4A, was one of three generally similar craft selected for simultaneous Army evaluation, the others being Ryan's XV-5A and Hawker Siddeley's XV-6A (q.v.). The first XV-4A (a second example having been ordered in September 1961) was delivered to the Army in mid-summer of 1962.

The XV-4A Hummingbird was essentially conventional in appearance, with a somewhat stubby fuselage, high 'T'-tail, relatively small non-swept wings, and side-by-side seating for its two-man crew under a standard plexiglas canopy. The craft's two podded Pratt & Whitney JT12A-3 turbojet engines were placed one on either side of the fuselage just above the wing roots, and provided the power for the XV-4A's augmented-jet

The first Hummingbird prototype, 62-4503, hovering during the initial flight tests. Note the open bomb-bay type doors in the upper and lower fuselage; air was drawn into the central ejector ducts through the top doors, mixed with hot engine exhaust, and blown out of the bottom doors to produce vertical lift. This machine made its first successful transition from vertical to horizontal flight in late 1963, but was destroyed in a June 1964 crash that also killed its pilot. *(Lockheed-Georgia)*

ejector lift system. This Lockheed-developed system utilized engine thrust for both vertical and horizontal flight by means of diverter valves fixed in the tailpipe of each engine. For vertical flight the diverter valves were rotated 180 degrees to direct the exhaust of each engine into ejector ducts built into the aircraft's central fuselage. The ducts channelled the exhaust downward through a series of nozzles into a central mixing area, where the exhaust gases were mixed with air drawn in through bomb-bay type doors set into the top of the central fuselage and then expelled through another set of doors in the aircraft's belly. The hot exhaust gases accelerated the air being drawn in through the upper fuselage and blown out through the bottom, thereby providing vertical lift. During the transition to horizontal flight the XV-4A's nose would be lowered some ten degrees to initiate forward movement, after which the diverter valves would be progressively rotated to the rear to provide forward thrust in the normal fashion. Stability in low-speed and hovering flight was provided by engine exhaust bled from the central mixing box and expelled through small nozzles in the aircraft's nose, tail, and wingtips.

The XV-4A made its initial tethered hovering flight in November 1962, and its first successful transition from hovering to forward flight almost exactly one year later. The flight test programme progressed reasonably well until 10 June 1964, when the crash of the first prototype — and the death of its pilot — brought the XV-4A programme to a halt. Though limited flight testing of the second prototype was eventually resumed the Army ultimately decided that the augmented-jet ejector lift system should not be developed further and in 1966 the surviving XV-4A was turned over to the Air Force. The USAF subsequently converted the craft into a direct jet lift testbed, but the machine was totally destroyed in a 1966 crash.

TECHNICAL DATA

Engines:
Two 3300 lb st Pratt & Whitney JT12A-3 turbojets

Dimensions:
Wingspan: 25 ft 10 in
Wing area: 104 sq ft
Fuselage length: 33 ft 11 in
Height: 11 ft 9 in

Weight (empty/gross, in lbs):
5000/7200

Performance:
Speed (cruising/maximum, in mph): 390/520

Service Ceiling: 50,000 ft

Range: 920 miles

Armament: None

Accommodation:
Pilot and co-pilot, though the prototypes were normally operated only by the pilot.

LOCKHEED O-3

Type: Single-engined quiet observation aircraft

Manufacturer: Lockheed Missiles and Space Company, Palo Alto, California.

HISTORY

In July 1966 the Department of Defense Advanced Research Projects Agency (DARPA) completed a study of the feasibility of developing a silent aircraft as one possible means of satisfying an existing need for a covert aerial observation platform for use in Vietnam. The study's favourable conclusions led the Director of Defense Research and Engineering to seek military sponsorship for the construction of an experimental prototype aircraft and the Army, itself acutely aware of the enormous potential of a low-noise reconnaissance and observation vehicle, endorsed the programme and agreed to fund additional research. In April 1967 the Lockheed Missiles and Space Company (LMSC) was awarded a contract for the construction of two prototype aircraft. These two machines, known to both LMSC and the Army by the company designation QT(Quiet Thrust)-2, were the predecessors of the later O-3.

The QT-2 was essentially a highly-modified Schweizer SGS 2-32 all-metal sailplane that had been fitted with a heavily-muffled

One of the two QT-2 prototypes developed by LMSC in conjunction with the Army and DoD is seen here during an early manufacturer's test flight. The aircraft were initially powered by conventional 100 hp piston powerplants, though these were later replaced by more powerful Wankel rotary engines. Both machines were evaluated in Vietnam (in far less colourful markings) from January to April 1968. (Lockheed MSC)

100 hp Continental piston engine (and, briefly, with a 200 hp Curtiss-Wright Wankel rotary). The powerplant was located amidships, directly aft of the machine's small tandem, two-seat cockpit, and drove a large-diameter, slow-turning propeller via belt-drives and an externally mounted drive shaft. The two aircraft were evaluated by the Army's Combat Developments Experimentation Center (CDEC) at Fort Ord, California, in October 1967, and the following month the impressive test results led the U.S. Military Assistance Command, Vietnam (USMACV), to request the two QT-2 machines be sent to Southeast Asia for a sixty-day evaluation under field conditions. This request was approved, and in December 1967 and January 1968 LMSC trained three Navy and two Army pilots to fly the QT-2 prototypes. The aircraft, their crews, and LMSC maintenance personnel were flown to Vietnam in late January 1968, and flight operations were conducted from Soc Trang Army Air Field through the following April. The QT-2 Vietnam evaluation, code-named PRIZE CREW, was a joint Army and Navy operation and was co-managed by the Army Concept Team in Vietnam (ACTIV) and the Naval Research and Development Unit, Vietnam (NRDU-V).

The PRIZE CREW evaluation showed the QT-2 to be a potentially valuable observation platform, though both ACTIV and NRDU-V recommended that the type be modified in several important ways prior to being put into quantity production. The suggested changes included the replacement of the troublesome mid-mounted engine and its external drive shaft with a more orthodox, and more powerful, nose-mounted powerplant driving a larger diameter airscrew. Further, the PRIZE CREW evaluation team recommended that the QT-2's successor have a larger, bubble-style cockpit canopy, more extensive instrumentation, better communications equipment, and wing hard points capable of carrying target-marking rockets and small anti-personnel bombs. And, finally, the team suggested that the advanced quiet observation aircraft be far more streamlined than the QT-2, with flush-riveting throughout and fully retractable main landing gear.

The Army's Aviation Systems Command was named executive agent for the advanced quiet observation aircraft programme soon after the completion of the QT-2 field evaluation, and in July 1968 awarded LMSC a contract for the construction of one prototype and ten pre-production QT-3 aircraft. Though based on the same Schweizer SGS 2-32 sailplane as the QT-2, the QT-3 incorporated many of the changes suggested by the PRIZE CREW evaluation team and therefore differed greatly in appearance from its predecessor. The most obvious changes were the adoption of a conventional nose-mounted engine driving a large six-bladed propeller, a large bubble canopy covering a modified tandem, two-seat cockpit, wings attached lower on the fuselage sides, and fully retractable main landing gear. The QT-3 was

The second YO-3A, 69-18001, in flight over northern California in 1969. The difference in appearance from the earlier QT-2 is obvious, though both aircraft were based on the same SGS 2-32 sailplane. Though it is not readily apparent in this somewhat foreshortened view, the YO-3A's wing spanned an impressive fifty-seven feet. *(Lockheed MSC)*

also better equipped for covert night observation activities, fitted as it was with a sophisticated Night Viewing Aerial Periscope (NVAP) and an equally advanced Infrared Illuminator/ Infrared Designator (IRI/IRD). All eleven QT-3 aircraft were completed by the spring of 1970 and, upon subsequent delivery to the Army, were assigned the designation YO-3A and the serial numbers 69-18000 through -18010.

The YO-3A underwent extensive service testing at Fort Ord and the nearby Hunter Liggett military reservation from 25 May through 25 June 1970, during which one of the ten pre-production aircraft (69-18009) was destroyed in a crash. The surviving nine pre-production machines were subsequently deployed to Vietnam for operational testing under field conditions, with the first observation mission being flown on the night of 27 July 1970. Between that time and the end of the official evaluation period on 30 April 1971 the nine YO-3As flew a total of 1116 missions from bases at Soc Trang, Long Thanh, and Binh Thuy. No aircraft was lost to enemy action during the evaluation period, though one YO-3A — and one crewman — were lost to hostile fire during a follow-up mission conducted in June 1971.

The performance of the YO-3A under combat conditions was judged to be generally mediocre. Though essentially quite capable in its intended role of a quiet, low-altitude night observation platform the YO-3A proved mechanically unreliable, difficult to maintain under field conditions, and prone to groundlooping on takeoff and landing. The YO-3A evaluation team's final report on the Vietnam test project recommended that neither the aircraft nor its mission-related surveillance equipment be developed any further. The Department of the Army concurred with this recommendation and withdrew all surviving YO-3As from Vietnam in early 1972. These aircraft were declared surplus in 1974, and several were subsequently operated by the Federal Bureau of Investigation and, reportedly, the U.S. Border Patrol.

TECHNICAL DATA *(Both QT-2 and YO-3A, except where noted)*

Engine:
One 100 hp Continental O-200A piston (QT-2)
One 200 hp Curtiss-Wright RC 2-60 Wankel rotary (QT-2)
One 210 hp Continental IO-360D piston (YO-3A)

Dimensions:

Winspan:	57 ft
Wing area:	213 sq ft
Fuselage length:	31 ft (QT-2)
	29 ft 4 in (YO-3A)
Height:	12 ft 4 in

Weight (maximum gross, in lbs):
2166 (QT-2)
3700 (YO-3A)

Performance:
Speed (cruising/maximum, in mph):
68/95 (QT-2)
78/138 (YO-3A)

Service Ceiling:	21,000 ft
Range:	385-455 miles
Armament:	None

Accommodation:
Pilot and observer.

LOCKHEED P-2 NEPTUNE

Type: Twin-engined
electronic warfare
aircraft

Manufacturer: Lockheed
Aircraft Corporation, Burbank,
California.

HISTORY

Though best known as a Navy patrol bomber and anti-submarine warfare (ASW) aircraft the Lockheed P-2 Neptune also had a fascinating, if rather brief, career with the Army Security Agency (ASA) during the Vietnam war. During that conflict the ASA was tasked with gathering the signals intelligence (SIGINT) used to locate and identify enemy radio transmitters, as well as with electronic warfare (EW) operations intended to disrupt enemy communications. Aircraft were particularly useful in these tasks, and the Army employed various small fixed-wing types in the SIGINT and EW roles almost from the beginning of America's involvement in the Vietnam conflict. However, by 1965 it had become apparent that a need existed for a SIGINT/EW aircraft that was larger, longer-ranged, and of greater

One of the Army's twelve known AP-2E Neptunes, BuNo 131492, on the ramp in Seattle prior to deployment to Vietnam. These aircraft retained their Navy color schemes, belly-mounted APS-20 search radar, and magnetic amomaly detector (MAD) tail booms, though each machine's plexiglass nose section was eventually replaced by a solid nose cone housing additional ELINT equipment. Aircraft 131485 is currently on display at the Army Aviation Museum at Fort Rucker, Alabama. *(Duane Kasulka via Peter M. Bowers)*

endurance than the OV-1 and RU-8 types which then formed the backbone of the ASA effort. Some consideration was given to converting several CV-2 Caribou transports into EW platforms, but the Air Force was already strenuously lobbying for the removal of all Caribous from the Army inventory and it therefore seemed pointless to extensively modify aircraft that would in all probability soon have to be handed over to the USAF. The Army therefore turned to the Navy, a proven ally in the struggle to form an independent post-World War II Army aviation arm, for assistance in discretely acquiring the necessary aircraft.

Fortunately, in the venerable P-2 the Navy had just the type of airplane the Army needed. The Neptune had been in regular Navy service since 1946, and by 1965 had been produced in seven major variants totalling more than 1050 aircraft. The P-2 had a proven record in SIGINT and EW operations, having undertaken such tasks for both the Navy and (as the RB-69A) the Air Force. More importantly, the type was still in service with several Navy patrol squadrons based in South Vietnam, a fact that would greatly simplify maintenance and logistics needs for an aircraft larger and more complex than most others then used by the Army. Locating suitable machines was not a problem, for several stateside Naval Reserve squadrons still flew Neptunes and late-model aircraft could therefore be loaned to the Army without adversely affecting the readiness of frontline Navy units. In the end at least twelve Naval Reserve P-2s were loaned to the ASA for opertions in Vietnam, with the first aircraft officially turned over in late 1966 or early 1967.

All twelve Neptunes known to have been operated by the Army in Vietnam had been built as standard P2V-5 patrol bombers but, like most late-model examples of that variant, were later modified to P2V-5F configuration through the addition of two wing-mounted J34-WE-34 auxiliary turbojet engines. Under the 1962 Tri-Service designtion system the P2V-5F became the P-2E, and upon entering Army service the type was designated AP-2E*. All twelve machines retained the standard Navy gray-over-white paint scheme and displayed their Navy bureau numbers instead of Army serial numbers. Indeed, to the casual observer only the word 'ARMY' painted in small block letters on the fuselage sides just aft of the national insignia distinguished the aircraft from standard Navy P-2s.

The Army's Neptunes were based at Cam Ranh Bay, South Vietnam, from July 1967 to April 1972 and were operated by the 1st ASA Company (an organization often incorrectly referred to

* This was actually a non-standard designation. The Army Neptunes should have been designated RP-2E by virtue of the nature of their assigned tasks, but by calling them AP-2Es the Army hoped to both disguise their true function and avoid upsetting the Air Force.

by its cover designation of '1st Radio Research Company'). This unit also operated RU-8 and (later) RU-21 ELINT/EW aircraft, and its AP-2Es were apparently equipped with the same sort of sensors as those fitted to the smaller machines. These sensors probably included the Left Foot communications intelligence (COMINT) system, the Cefly Lancer airborne emitter locator, and possibly the early versions of the Cefirm Leader signal detection and automatic jamming system. All twelve known AP-2Es are thought to have been returned to the Navy by the end of 1972 though a single example, BuNo 131485, was eventually transferred to the Army Aviation Museum at Fort Rucker, Alabama.

TECHNICAL DATA

Engines:
Two 3750 hp Wright R-3350-30W Cyclone pistons, plus two Westinghouse J34-WE-34 auxiliary turbojets, each of 3250 lb st.

Dimensions:
Winspan: 103 ft 10 in
Fuselage length
including MAD
ASW tail): 91 ft 2 in
Height: 28 ft 1 in

Weight (empty/gross, in lbs):
40,600/66,400

Performance:
Speed (cruising/maximum, in mph): 207/323

Service Ceiling: 23,000 ft

Range: 4750 miles

Armament:
None normally fitted to Army machines.

Accommodation:
Three crew and up to seven systems operators.

LOCKHEED H-56 CHEYENNE

Type: Single-engined
  attack helicopter

Manufacturer: Lockheed-
California Company, Burbank,
California.

HISTORY

Developed as Lockheed's entry in the Army's Advanced Aerial
Fire Support System (AAFSS) competition, the Cheyenne was a
highly sophisticated compound rotorcraft whose design incorporated several features pioneered in Lockheed's earlier XH-51A
(q.v.). The Cheyenne was named winner of the AAFSS contest in
March 1966, at which time Lockheed was awarded an Army
contract for the production of ten YAH-56A prototypes. The first
of these made its maiden flight in September 1967, and all ten
aircraft (serials 66-8826 through -8835) had been delivered to the
Army for flight testing by July 1968. In January of that year the
Army had placed an initial order for 375 production machines,
and the ten prototypes were subsequently redesignated AH-56A
in early 1969.

  The Cheyenne was, to say the least, a rather exotic-looking
aircraft. The forward end of its long and narrow fuselage was
dominated by an outsized segmented canopy covering a
tandem, two-seat cockpit, while the tailboom supported a large
ventral fin, a conventional anti-torque tail rotor, and a decidedly

The first YAH-56A, 66-8826, on Lockheed's ramp just prior to delivery. This
machine sports the nose-mounted XM-134 minigun system, though this
was usually replaced by an XM-129 40 mm grenade launcher on those later
Cheyennes equipped with the belly-mounted 30 mm antitank cannon.
(Lockheed-California)

The sixth Cheyenne, 56-8831, rolls in toward a ground target during the armament test phase of the AH-56A evaluation. This aircraft is equipped with the belly-mounted 30 mm cannon, and is carrying 2.75 inch rocket pods on its outer wing hardpoints and three-round TOW missile launchers on the inner pylons. Note the modified engine exhaust port, a feature added to all but the first two Cheyennes in order to reduce their infrared signatures by directing hot exhaust gases upward and to the rear. *(Lockheed-California)*

unconventional pusher propeller. A pair of small, low-set stub wings fixed to the fuselage sides contributed to the Cheyenne's hybrid look, as did its retractable, wheeled main landing gear. The AH-56A's ungainly appearance was deceptive, however, for in flight the craft was amazingly agile and extremely fast. The Cheyenne's impressive performance was the product of an innovative propulsion system built around a 3435 shp General Electric shaft turbine engine. This powerplant drove a rigid, four-bladed, gyro-stabilized main rotor, the tail-mounted anti-torque rotor, and the pusher propeller at the extreme end of the tailboom. During vertical and hovering flight all power was applied to the main and anti-torque rotors, while during forward flight all but about 700 shp was shafted to the pusher propeller. In forward flight lift was generated by the stub wings and windmilling main rotor, and in absolutely 'clean' configuration the AH-56A was capable of sea-level speeds in excess of 250 mph.

The Army's AAFSS specifications had called for an aircraft capable of undertaking armed escort, long range interdiction, fire support, and anti-tank operations by day or night and in all weathers, and the Cheyenne had been armed and equipped accordingly. The AH-56A's armament consisted of a nose turret housing either an XM129 40 mm automatic grenade launcher or XM134 7.62 mm multi-barrelled minigun, a 30 mm cannon mounted in a revolving belly turret, and an impressive number of TOW anti-tank missiles and/or pods of 2.75 inch unguided rockets carried on underwing hardpoints. The Cheyenne's day and night, all-weather flight capability was based on an extensive avionics suite which included automatic terrain-following radar, Doppler radar, an inertial navigation unit, and an automatic flight control system that allowed high-speed flight at altitudes as low as fifteen feet.

Despite its technological sophistication, or perhaps because of it, the AH-56A was fated never to enter regular Army service. The flight test programme revealed several significant problems with the aircraft's innovative propulsion system, problems which ultimately resulted in the fatal crash of one of the ten prototypes. In addition, by March 1979 significant cost overruns had increased the per-unit Cheyenne price by more than $500,000, an increase that was unacceptable in light of the Army's continued high expenditures in support of operations in Vietnam. And, finally, the USAF had become increasingly vocal in its opposition to the Army's acquisition of an aircraft as capable as the Cheyenne, and continued to push for the cancellation of the AH-56 project. The Army ultimately decided to develop a cheaper and less sophisicated helicopter in place of the Cheyenne, and in August 1972 formally terminated the AH-56 programme.

TECHNICAL DATA

Engine:
One 3435 shp General Electric T64-GE-16 shaft turbine

Dimensions:

Main rotor diameter:	50 ft 4.8 in
Tail rotor diameter:	10 ft
Pusher propeller diameter:	10 ft
Wingspan:	26 ft 8.5 in
Fuselage length:	54 ft 8 in
Height (to top of main rotor hub):	13 ft 8.5 in

Weight (empty/maximum VTOL, in lbs):
17,725/22,000

Performance:
Speed (cruising/maximum, in mph): 225/253

Service Ceiling: 26,300 ft

Range: 875 miles

Armament: See text

Accommodation:
Pilot and co-pilot/gunner.

McCULLOCH H-30

Type: Single-engined
    observation
    helicopter

Manufacturer: McCulloch
Motors Corporation, Los
Angeles, California.

HISTORY

The Model MC-4 tandem-rotor light helicopter was the first
aircraft to be developed by McCulloch Motors' Aircraft Division,
and made its first flight in March 1951. The Army acquired three
examples of the slightly modified Model MC-4C in 1952 for
engineering test and evaluation, designating the machines YH-
30 and allocating them the serials 52-5837 through -5839.

The YH-30 was a craft of relatively simple construction,
consisting of a steel tube framework to which was attached a
light metal skin. The helicopter's single 200 hp Franklin engine
was mounted horizontally amidships and drove the two inter-
meshing tandem rotors through a single horizontal drive shaft

The first of three YH-30s acquired by the Army for engineering and flight
evaluation, 52-5837 is seen here on later display at the Army Aviation
Museum, Fort Rucker, Alabama. The three evaluation machines were each
fitted with small endplate rudders not found on McCulloch's original MC-4
prototype. *(U.S. Army)*

177

and two right-angled reduction units. Two small endplate rudders were fixed to the rear fuselage to provide additional lateral stability, and the aircraft was equipped with wheeled tricycle landing gear. The craft's two crew members enjoyed better than average visibility to the front and sides, though the view upward was blocked by the overhanging front rotor housing.

The Army's evaluation of the YH-30 showed the helicopter to be somewhat underpowered and its drive system to be overly complex. The type was therefore not procured in quantity, and the three evaluation machines were declared surplus in mid-1953 and disposed of.

TECHNICAL DATA

Engine:
One 200 hp Franklin 6A4-200-C6 piston

Dimensions:
Rotor diameter (each): 22 ft
Fuselage length: 32 ft 5 in
Height (to top of
  aft rotor hub):   9 ft 2 in

Weight (empty/gross, in lbs):
1200/2000

Performance:
Speed (cruising/maximum, in mph):
  85/105

Service Ceiling: 8,000 ft

Range: 200 miles

Armament: None

Accommodation:
Pilot and co-pilot/observer.

McDONNELL V-1

Type: Single-engined V/STOL research aircraft

Manufacturer: McDonnell Aircraft Corporation, St Louis, Missouri.

HISTORY

In June 1951 the Army Transportation Corps, the Air Force Air Research and Development Command, and the McDonnell Aircraft Corporation jointly initiated the development of a single-engined research aircraft incorporating the rotor system of a helicopter with the wings, twin-boom tail surfaces, and pusher propeller of a conventional airplane. McDonnell had already completed the preliminary design studies for just such a hybrid 'convertiplane', the Model M-28, and was therefore able to present a complete mock-up for inspection in November 1951. The mock-up won Army and Air Force approval without the need for major modifications, and the first prototype aircraft (serial 53-4016) was completed in early 1954. The craft had initially been designated the XL-25, though during the course of construction this was changed to XH-35 in the helicopter category and, finally, to XV-1 in the newly created convertiplane category.

The XV-1 was designed to take off and land like a helicopter and undertake forward flight like a conventional fixed-wing aircraft. During vertical flight the single 525 hp radial engine drove two air compressors which channelled air through ducts built into the main rotor blades and expelled it through pressure jets at the blade tips; in forward flight the engine's power was applied to the two-bladed pusher propeller mounted at the aft end of the central fuselage pod. The transition from vertical to horizontal flight was accomplished by transferring power from

The first XV-1 prototype, 53-4016, in flight. The machine's engine is driving the two-bladed pusher propeller, while the rotor is autorotating to supplement the lift generated by the wing. Note the small anti-torque rotors that have been added to the end of each tailboom, and compare the shape of this aircraft's cut down rotor pylon with the unmodified pylon of the second prototype in the photo below. *(McDonnell-Douglas)*

179

The second XV-1 as it appeared in October 1955. This aircraft retains the original 'stepped' rotor pylon, but is otherwise outwardly identical to the first prototype. In October 1956 this machine became the first rotorcraft to achieve 200 mph. *(McDonnell-Douglas)*

the main rotor to the propeller as soon as the XV-1's forward speed exceeded the stalling speed of the main wing. The main rotor was then allowed to autorotate, thereby supplementing the lift generated by the craft's wings.

The XV-1's initial tethered hovering flight occurred on 15 February 1954, and its first free hovering flight took place almost exactly five months later. The second prototype machine, 53-4017, joined the flight test programme in the spring of 1955, and in April of that year the first prototype made the first transition from vertical to forward flight. The flight test programme revealed several design deficiencies which were progressively corrected through the introduction of such modifications as a cut-down rotor pylon, small anti-torque rotors fixed to the end of each tailboom, redesigned landing skids, and other minor detail changes. These modifications undoubtedly improved the XV-1's performance, for in October 1956 the second prototype became the first rotorcraft to achieve 200 mph in level flight. However, the type's mechanical complexity was ultimately judged to be a disadvantage not counterbalanced by its high speed, and the XV-1 programme was consequently cancelled in 1957. Fortunately, and unusually in the case of an experimental aircraft not ultimately adopted for widespread operational use, both XV-1s were preserved rather than being sold for scrap; 53-4016 was handed over to the Army Aviation Museum at Fort Rucker and 53-4017 was acquired by the Smithsonian Institution's National Air and Space Museum.

TECHNICAL DATA

Engine:
One 550 hp Continental R-975-19 radial

Dimensions:
Rotor diameter:	31 ft
Wingspan:	26 ft
Length:	30 ft
Height (to top of rotor hub):	10 ft 9 in

Weight (empty/gross, in lbs):
4277/5505

Performance:
Speed (cruising/maximum, in mph): 138/203

Service Ceiling: 19,800 ft

Range: 593 miles

Armament: None

Accommodation:
Provision for pilot and co-pilot/observer in tandem, though prototypes were normally operated by pilot only.

McDONNELL-DOUGLAS H-64 APACHE

Type: Twin-engined
    attack helicopter

Manufacturer: McDonnell-
Douglas Helicopter Company,
Mesa, Arizona.

HISTORY

The AH-64 Apache originated as Hughes Helicopters' entry in the Army's 1973-1976 Advanced Attack Helicopter (AAH) competition, which was initiated following the forced cancellation of the AH-56 Cheyenne (q.v.) programme. The new AAH design was intended by the Army to be a less sophisticated and less costly aircraft than the Cheyenne, while retaining the latter's ability to undertake day, night and adverse weather anti-armor operations beyond the capabilities of the AH-1 Cobra (q.v.). Preliminary AAH design proposals were submitted by Bell, Sikorsky, Boeing-Vertol and Lockheed, in addition to Hughes, and in June 1973 both Bell and Hughes were awarded contracts for the production of two prototype aircraft. Bell's Model 409 was subsequently designated the YAH-63 (q.v.), while Hughes' Model 77 became the YAH-64.

In accordance with the Army's AAH specifications both the YAH-63 and YAH-64 were powered by twin General Electric T700 turboshaft engines, were capable of carrying up to sixteen Hellfire or TOW missiles, and carried externally-mounted 30 mm cannon for use against troops, soft-skinned vehicles, and other aircraft. Not surprisingly, given their common required attributes, the aircraft were very similar in general appearance. Each had a long slender fuselage with two-seat tandem cockpit forward, mid-mounted stub wings, engine pods on either side of the upper fuselage just below the rotor mast, and a high 'T'-tail. The YAH-64 differed from its competitor, however, in having a four-

The second of two YAH-64 prototypes evaluated by the Army in competition with Bell Helicopter's YAH-63, 73-22249 is seen here during a later test-firing of an early version of the Hellfire anti-tank missile. Note that this Apache has the early-version tail unit with high-mounted horizontal stabilizer, tail rotor mounted half-way up the vertical tail, and extended tail cone. *(U.S. Army)*

YAH-64 79-23257, seen here in flight over southern California in 1980, was the first 'Phase Two' Apache prototype. This machine differed from its predecessors in several ways, the most obvious of which was in having a redesigned tail unit with a repositioned tailplane. Note the Hughes 30 mm Chain Gun beneath the forward cockpit, as well as the four-round Hellfire launchers on the inner hardpoint of each wing. *(MDHC)*

bladed, fully articulated main rotor, a four-bladed tail rotor with angled blades intended to reduce the aircraft's noise signature, and its co-pilot/gunner seated forward of, rather than behind, the pilot. The Hughes craft also carried its single-barrelled 30 mm gun mounted under the lower fuselage rather than below the nose, and was equipped with semi-retractable twin main landing gear and a fixed tail wheel in place of the YAH-63's tricycle arrangement.

The YAH-64 prototypes (serials 73-22248 and -22249) both flew for the first time in the fall of 1975, and both were handed over to the Army for evaluation against the YAH-63 in May 1976. The following December Hughes was named winner of the AAH competition and was subsequently awarded an Army contract for a 'Phase Two' engineering development programme. Modifications introduced during this period included the replacement of the 'T'-tail by an enlarged vertical stabilizer and a low-mounted, movable tailplane, the adoption of a flat-plate canopy, the installation of infrared signature-suppressing engine exhausts, and full-length fuselage side fairings. These changes were incorporated into three additional prototypes, which were also fitted with various avionics and fire-control systems. The sensor suite finally adopted for use on production aircraft includes the Target Acquisition and Designation System (TADS) incorporating television, laser, infrared and optical components, the Pilot's Night Vision System (PNVS), and the Integrated Helmet and Display Sight System (IHADSS).

In January 1984 Hughes Helicopters was acquired by McDonnell-Douglas Aircraft, and soon thereafter the restructured McDonnell-Douglas Helicopter Company (MDHC) delivered to the Army the first of a projected 675 production AH-64A

The Army began taking delivery of production AH-64A aircraft in early 1984, and by mid-1987 more than 200 had entered service. This shot of the third production Apache, 82-23954, shows the type's nose-mounted sensors — PNVS and TADS — to good advantage. *(U.S. Army)*

Apaches. By mid-1986 Apache production at the MDHC facility in Mesa, Arizona, was running at approximately twelve machines a month, and the 300th aircraft was delivered on 7 December 1987. In September 1985 MDHC and the Army began defining the configuration of an advanced AH-64B with an 1100-nautical mile self-deployment range, improved flight controls, a simplified cockpit, more powerful engines, and improved sensors.

The Apache underwent its long-anticipated baptism of fire during the 1989 US invasion of Panama. Twelve AH-64s provided fire support during the operation, using Hellfire missiles and 30mm cannon fire. Three of the aircraft were hit by enemy fire, but were quickly repaired and returned to service. The Army subsequently judged the Apache's overall combat performance in Panama to be 'outstanding,' an evaluation supported by most knowledgeable defense and industry observers.

TECHNICAL DATA

Engines:
Two 1536 shp General Electric T700-GE-700 turboshafts

Dimensions:

Main rotor diameter:	48 ft
Tail rotor diameter:	00 ft
Fuselage length:	49 ft 5 in
Height (to top of rotor hub):	12 ft 6.75 in

Weight (empty/gross, in lbs):
10,268/17,650

Performance:
Speed (cruising/maximum, in mph):
182/232

Service Ceiling: 20,500 ft

Range: 380 miles (on internal fuel

Armament:
One 30 mm Hughes/MDHC Chain Gun, plus up to sixteen Hellfire missiles or seventy-six 2.75 inch unguided rockets carried in pods on wing hardpoints.

Accommodation:
Pilot and co-pilot/gunner.

MISSISSIPPI STATE UNIVERSITY/ PARSONS V-11

Type: Single-engined STOL research vehicle

Manufacturer: Parsons Corporation, Traverse City, Michigan.

HISTORY

In 1964 the Department of Aerophysics and Aerospace Engineering of Mississippi State University (MSU) was awarded an Army contract for the development of a short takeoff and landing (STOL) research aircraft incorporating a suction-type high-lift boundary layer control (BLC) system. The Department had long been a leader in the development of such systems, in which manipulation of the wing's boundary layer air mass greatly improves an aircraft's STOL and low speed flight capabilities. The Army's choice of MSU to develop the new craft was based partly on official satisfaction with the University's work on an earlier proof-of-concept vehicle, the XAZ-1. This machine, which had been funded by the Army and which bore the military serial number 62-12147, was commonly known as the 'Marvelette'.

The MSU 'Marvel', as the 1964 design was unofficially named, incorporated several unique features pioneered on the XAZ-1. Constructed primarily of glassfibre-reinforced plastics, the machine was powered by an internal 317 shp turbine engine driving a tail-mounted, fully-shrouded, two-bladed pusher propeller. The Marvel's wing surfaces and forward fuselage were pierced by nearly one million tiny holes, through which boundary layer air was drawn in flight. The shoulder-mounted wings were equipped with conventional ailerons, but had no

The XV-11's unique BLC system and shrouded propeller were first tested on the Army-funded XAZ-1 'Marvelette' shown here. (MSU)

The sole XV-11 in flight. Note the excellent visibility offered by the pod-like cockpit enclosure. *(MSU)*

flaps. Instead, a form of wing-warping was used to alter the camber of the inner portion of the wing trailing edges. The Marvel's fixed landing gear was of the amphibious 'pantobase' type, with two tandem wheels inside each of the water-tight, pontoon-shaped main units. And, finally, the aircraft's pod-like two-place cabin offered excellent all-around visibility.

The sole XV-11 (serial 65-13070) was fabricated by the Parsons Corporation of Traverse City, Michigan, in the summer of 1966, and the machine was subsequently assembled in Mississippi by University staff after a fire destroyed the Parsons plant. The Marvel's flight test programme, conducted during 1967 and 1968 under the auspices of the Army Aviation Material Laboratories, showed the XV-11 to be an extremely capable STOL performer and provided much valuable information on BLC-based STOL systems. The Marvel was withdrawn from Army service in early 1969, and was subsequently returned to MSU for further University-funded research.

TECHNICAL DATA

Engine:
One 317 shp Allison T63-A-5A turbine

Dimensions:

Wingspan:	26 ft 2.5 in
Wing area:	106 sq ft
Fuselage length:	23 ft 3.75 in
Height:	8 ft 8.25 in

Weight (empty/gross, in lbs):
1958/2620

Performance:
Speed (cruising/maximum, in mph):
184/225

Service Ceiling:	15,000 ft
Range:	265 miles
Armament:	None

Accommodation:
Pilot and co-pilot/observer.

NOORDUYN C-64 NORSEMAN

Type: Single-engined
   utility transport

Manufacturer: Noorduyn
Aviation, Ltd, Montreal,
Quebec.

HISTORY

The Canadian-built Noorduyn Norseman first entered U.S. military service in early 1942 when the USAAF acquired seven examples of the Norseman IV/YC-64 variant for use by famed Norwegian pilot-explorer Bernt Balchen. Balchen, who had volunteered his services to the USAAF the preceeding summer, had been tasked with pioneering an aircraft ferry route between the U.S. and England and had requested that the Norseman be acquired for initial exploration of the route across northeastern Canada, Greenland and Iceland.

The rugged and dependable Norseman's excellent performance with Balchen's exploration team made the aircraft an ideal choice for use as a general utility transport, and during the course of the war the USAAF purchased 749 of the upgraded

The UC-64B Norsemen used by the Army Corps of Engineers were virtually identical to the float-equipped USAAF UC-64A seen here (43-5121), which was itself handed over to the Army in 1947 and operated by the Corps of Engineers until 1949. Three of the -B model machines remained in Army service until replaced by L-20 Beavers in the early 1950s. *(San Diego Aerospace Museum)*

UC-64A (Norseman V). An additional six slightly modified UC-64Bs purchased for use by the Army Corps of Engineers differed from the standard -A model primarily in having twin Edo floats for operation on water. Three of the UC-64Bs and several UC-64As remained in Army service following the 1947 creation of the independent USAF and, though the UC-64As were phased out of service by 1949, the three UC-64Bs continued to provide yeoman service to the Corps of Engineers until replaced by de Havilland of Canada L-20 Beavers (q.v.) in the early 1950s.

TECHNICAL DATA *(Both versions, except where noted)*

Engine:
One 550 hp Pratt & Whitney R-1340-AN-1 radial

Dimensions:
Wingspan:	51 ft 8 in
Wing area:	325 sq ft
Fuselage length:	32 ft 4 in (UC-64A)
	34 ft 3 in (UC-64B, with floats attached)
Height:	10 ft 1 in (UC-64A)
	14 ft 10 in (UC-64B, with floats)

Weight (empty/gross, in lbs):
4250/7200 (UC-64A)
4700/7540 (UC-64B)

Performance:
Speed (cruising/maximum, in mph):
141/155 (UC-64A)
134/155 (UC-64B)

Service Ceiling:	17,000 ft (UC-64A)
	14,000 ft (UC-64B)
Range:	464 miles (UC-64A)
	442 miles (UC-64B)
Armament:	None

Accommodation:
Pilot and co-pilot, plus up to eight passengers.

NORTHROP N-156F

Type: Twin-engined light
strike fighter

Manufacturer: Northrop
Corporation, Hawthorne,
California.

HISTORY

The Northrop N-156F light strike fighter prototype was one of three jet-powered, fixed-wing attack aircraft selected by the Army in 1961 for competitive evaluation in the forward air control (FAC), tactical reconnaissance, and ground attack roles. Like the other two types evaluated, the Fiat G-91 and Douglas A4D Skyhawk (q.v.), the N-156F was chosen for testing primarily because of its relatively simple design, impressive load-carrying capacity, and ability to operate from unimproved forward airfields.

Northrop had begun development of the N-156 family of low-cost, lightweight supersonic aircraft in 1956, with the first design being that of the N-156F single-seat fighter version. Much to Northrop's chagrin the Air Force showed no real interest in the N-156F, though in June 1956 the service's Air Training Command did adopt a two-seat trainer variant as the T-38 Talon. In the spring of 1958 the Department of Defense renewed Northrop's hopes for the fighter version by directing the USAF to procure three N-156F prototypes for engineering and operational evaluation. The first of these aircraft (serial 59-4987) made its initial flight in July 1959, less than four months after the maiden flight of the first T-38. The Air Force's attitude towards the N-156F did not change appreciably despite the aircraft's excellent showing in the evaluations, however, and work on the number three prototype was halted prior to completion because the USAF did not feel that the remaining tests required a third aircraft. At the end of the test period the Air Force announced that it would not procure the N-156F, and Northrop was forced to temporarily suspend work on the fighter version. The company thus viewed the Army's 1961 decision to evaluate the N-156F as a possible reprieve and gladly supplied the first prototype machine and a complete ground support staff for the tests.

The N-156F was of fairly conventional layout with thin, slightly-swept, low-set wings, a fuselage characterized by a narrow area-rule section amidships, a one-piece 'all-moving' tailplane, a rather large vertical fin, and tricycle landing gear. The aircraft was built primarily of aluminium, and Northrop made considerable use of adhesive-bonded honeycomb as a stiffener in critical areas. The N-156F was powered by two afterburning General Electric J85 turbojets mounted side-by-side in the aft fuselage, and could be fitted with up to four 1,000 pound JATO (Jet-Assisted Take Off) bottles for operation from extremely short fields. More than a quarter of the aircraft's total fuselage area consisted of easily-removable access panels to

The Northrop N-156F taxies in following a test flight during the Army's evaluation of the type. Like the two other aircraft against which it was evaluated, the Fiat G.91 and Douglas A4D, the N-156F was a relatively simple aircraft capable of fulfilling both the FAC and tactical reconnaissance roles. *(Northrop)*

simplify field maintenance, and both engines were attached to built-in overhead tracks for easy removal.

The Army's evaluation of the N-156F found it to be a well-built and capable aircraft, easy to maintain under field conditions and capable of carrying a significant offensive load while operating from the most rudimentary forward airstrips. These abilities were ultimately rendered meaningless, however, by the Army's decision to accede to Air Force pressure and abandon the quest for fixed-wing jet aircraft. The sole N-156F tested by the Army was susbsequently returned to Northrop, and was eventually converted into the prototype YF-5A Freedom Fighter.

TECHNICAL DATA

Engines:
Two 3850 lb st General Electric J85-GE-5A turbojets

Dimensions:
Wingspan:	25 ft 3 in
Wing area:	170 sq ft
Fuselage length:	45 ft 1 in
Height:	13 ft 1 in

Weight (empty/maximum, in lbs):
7860/15,460

Performance:
Speed (cruising/maximum, in mph):
562/910

Service Ceiling: 55,600 ft

Range: 2230 miles

Armament:
The N-156F was not equipped with internal guns, but could carry some 5500 lbs of ordnance. Weapons that could be carried included Sidewinder, Falcon, Sparrow and Bullpup air-to-air missiles; 2.75 inch rockets; podded .50 calibre and 20 mm guns; and a variety of bombs.

Accommodation:
Pilot only.

NORTH AMERICAN/RYAN
U-18 NAVION

Type: Single-engined   Manufacturer: North
    liaison and staff   American Aviation, Los
    transport aircraft   Angeles, California.
                             Ryan Aeronautical Company,
                             San Diego, California.

HISTORY

North American Aviation developed the Model NA-154 Navion low-wing cabin monoplane during the last years of World War II specifically for the post-war civil aviation market. However, the Navion's simple but rugged construction, impressive rough field performance, and automobile-type seating for four persons also made it an ideal military liaison and staff transport aircraft, and in late 1946 83 L-17A production machines were purchased for use by the Army (36) and National Guard (47). These aircraft were powered by 185 hp Lycoming engines and differed from the standard civil Navion only in having military-specification communications equipment, additional cockpit instrumentation, and a jettisonable cabin hood. Six of the Army's L-17As were later converted into QL-17A drones through the addition of remote-piloting equipment.

In the summer of 1947 Ryan Aeronautical acquired all Navion design and manufacturing rights from North American, and

The Navion's classic styling, shown here to good advantage by L-17B 48-971, made it one of the more aesthetically pleasing of the Army's early post-World War II fixed wing aircraft. The L-17A, B, and C variants operated by the Army were essentially identical in appearance, differing only in powerplants and minor detail changes. *(Peter M. Bowers Collection)*

soon thereafter opened a Navion production line in San Diego. In early 1948 Ryan was awarded an Air Force-administered contract for 163 L-17Bs fitted with more powerful 205 hp engines; 129 of these machines went to the Army and the remainder to the National Guard. In 1949 Ryan upgraded thirty-five North American-built L-17As with new landing gear, larger fuel tanks, and other detail changes, and these aircraft were subsequently operated by the Army as L-17Cs. In 1951 the Army procured four Ryan Super Navions for operational evaluation with the designation XL-22, though this was later changed to XL-17D. The -D model, essentially similar to the L-17C but powered by a 250 hp engine, was not adopted for service use.

Army Navions saw extensive service in the Far East during the Korean War, being used for troop and VIP transport, aeromedical evacuation and, on more than one occasion, improvised ground attack. By 1957, however, the Navion had been replaced in frontline service by more modern types and all surviving L-17s were subsequently turned over to Army flying clubs or used as unit hacks. In 1962 the few L-17A, B, and C Navions remaining in the Army inventory were redesignated under the Tri-Service System as respectively, the U-18A, B, and C.

TECHNICAL DATA *(All versions, except where noted)*

Engine:
One 185 hp Continental O-470-7 piston (L/QL-17A)
One 205 hp Continental O-470-9 piston (L-17B/C)
One 250 hp Lycoming O-435-17 piston (XL-17D)

Dimensions:

Wingspan:	33 ft 5 in
Wing area:	184 sq ft
Fuselage length:	27 ft 6 in
	28 ft (XL-17D)
Height:	8 ft 8 in

Weight (empty/gross, in lbs):
1782/2750 (L-17A)
1765/2250 (QL-17A)
1812/2905 (L-17B/C)
1860/3100 (XL-17D)

Performance:
Speed (cruising/maximum, in mph):
145/153 (L/QL-17A)
155/163 (L-17B/C)
165/174 (XL-17D)

Service Ceiling: 13,000 ft (L/QL-17A)
15,600 ft (L-17B/C)
18,000 ft (XL-17D)

Range: 560-740 miles

Armament:
None normally fitted, though some L-17s operated in Korea were fitted with improvised underwing pylons for light bombs and rockets.

Accommodation:
Pilot and up to four passengers.

NORTH AMERICAN T-28 TROJAN

Type: Single-engined
trainer and flight
test aircraft

Manufacturer: North
American Aviation,
Inglewood, California.

HISTORY

The Army's connection with the North American T-28 Trojan was a limited one in terms of numbers, only a handful of the aircraft having been acquired, but it was a relationship that spanned more than thirty-five years. Originally developed in response to a 1947 USAF requirement for a relatively sophisticated two-place, propeller-driven trainer that could be used for combined primary and basic flight instruction, the Trojan entered Air Force service in 1949 and in 1952 was adopted by the Navy as well. However, both the Air Force T-28A variant and the more powerful Navy T-28B and T-28C versions were considered far too advanced for Army pilot training needs and, as far as can be determined, the Army made no effort to acquire Trojans for use as pure trainers.

The Army's lack of interest in the Trojan as a training machine did not, however, indicate a total lack of interest in the type. Indeed, military records indicate that at least seven Trojans were transferred to Army control in the years between 1952 and 1976. The first machine operated by the Army was an early production Air Force T-28A (probably 51-3612) evaluated at Fort Rucker sometime during the later stages of the Korean War. The Army felt the T-28 showed some promise as an observation and artillery-direction platform, but nothing apparently came of the tests for the machine was eventually returned to the Air Force. The next time the Trojan appeared in Army service was in the spring of 1966 when four Navy T-28Bs were transferred to the control of the Army Aviation Engineering Flight Activity (AAEFA) at Edwards AFB, California. This organization was then preparing to flight test the Lockhheed AH-56 Cheyenne AAFSS (q.v.), and required an aircraft fast enough and agile enough to serve as an air-to-air photography platform, chase plane, and possible air combat training opponent for the new attack helicopter. A Beech U-21 Ute had already been tested and found unsuitable, and the T-28 seemed to offer the necessary speed and manoeuvrability. Navy records indicate that Trojans bearing the Navy serials 137702, 137716, 138210, and 138327 were transferred to the Army at about this time, and it is known that at least three of the machines were, in fact, evaluated as possible Cheyenne chase planes. It is possible that the fourth T-28B was also so evaluated, though there are unconfirmed reports that it was tested solely for possible use as an electronic intelligence (ELINT) platform. In the end the Trojan was deemed incapable of matching the Cheyenne's anticipated acceleration and manoeuvrability, and in 1967-1968 the Army instead acquired three extensively modified F-51D Mustangs (q.v.) for use as AH-56 chase aircraft.

Trojan 138327 of the AAEFA in flight near Edwards AFB in early 1987. The AAEFA Trojans carried several colour schemes during their nearly twenty years of service though the markings shown here — gloss white upper surfaces, gloss green undersurfaces, yellow stencils, and full-size national insignia — were the most long-lived. The T-28s assigned to ASOTB retained the gloss red and white Navy trainer schemes in which they were delivered. *(U.S. Army)*

The four T-28s were subsequently transferred to other duties, with three being retained by the AAEFA for airspeed calibration testing and miscellaneous test support duties. The fourth machine (138210) was flown to Fort Bragg, North Carolina, where it was soon joined by two other ex-USN T-28Bs (137747 and 140018). All three aircraft were assigned to the Army's Airborne Special Operations Test Board (ASOTB), an agency tasked with testing and evaluating new parachute delivery systems and methods intended for U.S. military use. The stable and manoeuvrable Trojans were ideally suited for use as camera-equipped test observation machines, and were used to record hundreds of in-flight tests prior to their early 1987 replacement in AASOTB service by ex-USN T-34C Mentors (q.v.).

The Edwards-based AAEFA T-28s continued to serve until they too were replaced by T-34C Turbo Mentors (q.v.), early in 1987. All three Trojans were subsequently retired from the Army inventory and passed to various air museums, with 138327 going to the McClellan Air Force Base Museum in California. This aircraft was the last T-28 in service with the active duty U.S. military forces until turned over to the McClellan Museum on 27 March 1987.

TECHNICAL DATA *(All versions, except where noted)*

Engine:
One 800 hp Wright R-1300-1A radial (T-28A)
One 1425 hp Wright R-1820-86 radial (T-28B/C)

Dimensions:

Wingspan:	40 ft 1 in
Wing area:	268 sq ft
Fuselage length:	33 ft
Height:	12 ft 8 in

Weight (empty/gross, in lbs):
6425/8500

Performance:
Speed (cruising/maximum, in mph):
265/300 (T-28A)
310/343 (T-28B/C)

Service Ceiling: 35,500 ft

Range: 1100 miles

Armament:
T-28A aircraft had provision for two wing-mounted .50 calibre machine guns and could be fitted with under-wing hardpoints capable of carrying light practice bombs. T-28B and -C variants did not have provision for armament.

Accommodation:
Pilot and trainee or observer.

NORTH AMERICAN/CAVALIER
F-51 MUSTANG

Type: Single-engined flight
test support aircraft

Manufacturer: North
American Aviation,
Inglewood, California.
Cavalier Aircraft Corporation,
Sarasota, Florida.

HISTORY

Almost immediately following the March 1966 selection of the
Lockheed YAH-56A Cheyenne (q.v.) as winner of the Advanced
Aerial Fire Support System (AAFSS) competition the Army began
searching for a propeller-driven aircraft fast enough and agile
enough to serve as a chase plane for the Cheyenne during the
latter's flight test programme. After initial evaluations of a
modified Beech U-21 Ute and a Navy T-28 Trojan showed both
types to be incapable of matching the anticipated acceleration
and manoeuvrability of the YAH-56 prototypes, the Army
evaluated a modified F-51D Mustang (serial 0-72990) obtained
from the Air Force. The aircraft, originally built by North
American Aircraft and one of the few Mustangs remaining in

The first F-51D acquired by the Army for evaluation in the AH-56 chase plane
role was 0-72990, seen here parked on the Edwards ramp in May 1973. This
machine was built in 1944 for the USAAF, but did not see combat in World
War II and was transferred to the Royal Canadian Air Force in 1953. The
Canadians sold it to a private U.S. owner in 1959, and it was reacquired by
the USAF in the early 1960s. Though upgraded by Cavalier Aircraft prior to
being obtained by the Army in 1967, this Mustang was not as extensively
modified as the two later machines. *(Peter Mancus via Jim Sullivan)*

0-72990 leads 68-15795 in a formation flight over the Sierra Nevada soon after the second aircraft's delivery to the Army in 1968. Note that 68-15795 sports a taller vertical stabilizer and, barely discernible in this shot, wingtip fuel tanks. These were the only immediately obvious differences between the two types of Cavalier-modified Mustang used by the Army. *(U.S. Army)*

U.S. military service, had been completely modernized by the Florida-based Cavalier Aircraft Corporation. The Army's flight testing of the modernized Mustang showed it to be exceptionally well-suited to the chase plane role, and in early 1967 the Army therefore placed an order with Cavalier for two even more extensively modified F-51Ds. These aircraft (serials 68-15795 and -15796) were delivered to the Army in 1968.

Contrary to popular belief these latter two machines were not dual-control TP-51s; both had been built as standard -D model aircraft and were brought up to Cavalier Mk. 2 configuration prior to their delivery to the Army. Modification to this standard included the removal of all weapons and weapon-related equipment, the complete updating of all avionics and communications systems, total overhaul and strengthening of the airframe, the addition of two 110 gallon wingtip fuel tanks, the installation of an observer's seat and a gyro-stabilized camera mount immediately behind the pilot's position, and the addition of a fourteen-inch extension to the vertical stabilizer. Both aircraft were powered by upgraded Packard-built V-1650-7 Merlin engines fitted with two-stage, dual-speed superchargers, and were significantly faster and more agile than 'stock' F-51Ds.

The flight characteristics of the Army's three Cavalier Mustangs were quite similar to those of the YAH-56A, especially in terms of acceleration, and the modified F-51s were quite successful in the chase plane role. The aircraft were used primarily as camera platforms from which the Cheyenne flight tests were filmed, though on several occasions they took a more active role in the flight test programme by engaging YAH-56s in simulated air-to-air combat. Following the 1972 termination of the Cheyenne programme the three Mustangs were shifted to other tasks, including the testing of advanced communications and electronic intelligence equipment. One of the aircraft (68-15795) was even fitted with a 106 mm recoilless rifle and used to evaluate the weapon's value in attacking fortified ground targets. All three Mustangs were finally withdrawn from service in the mid-1970s; 68-15795 and 0-72990 were subsequently turned over to U.S. Air National Guard units for preservation and display, while 68-15796 was acquired by the Army Aviation Museum at Fort Rucker, Alabama.

TECHNICAL DATA *(Both versions, except where noted)*

Engine:
One 1595 hp Packard V-1650-7 Merlin piston

Dimensions:

Wingspan:	37 ft (0-72990)
	40 ft 1.5 in (68-15795/15796, over tip tanks)
Wing area:	272.3 sq ft
Fuselage length:	32 ft 2.5 in
Height:	12 ft 2.5 in

Weight (empty/gross, in lbs):
7500/10,500

Performance:
Speed (cruising/maximum, in mph): 260/457

Service Ceiling: 42,000 ft

Range: 2000 miles

Armament: None

Accommodation:
Pilot and observer/camera operator.

PIASECKI H-25 ARMY MULE

Type: Single-engined utility
  helicopter

Manufacturer: Piasecki
Aircraft Corporation, Morton,
Pennsylvania.

HISTORY

Originally designed to meet a U.S. Navy requirement for a
shipboard utility helicopter, the Piasecki Model PV-18 first flew
in 1948 and entered regular Navy service the following year as
the HUP-1 Retriever. In 1950 the Army, in the process of rapidly
enlarging its helicopter fleet, evaluated several examples of the
improved HUP-2 variant and judged the type suitable for use in
the general utility role. A total of seventy H-25A aircraft (serials
51-16572 to -16641) were subsequently procured through an Air
Force-managed contract, with the first of these entering regular
Army service in early 1953.

H-25A 51-16612 in the hover, December 1954. Note the circular fuselage
door and reversed tricycle landing gear. The majority of the Army's Mules
were turned over to the Navy beginning in 1955, and the type was
withdrawn from Army service entirely by 1958. *(U.S. Army)*

The Army Mule, as the H-25 was officially named, was a single engined, tandem rotor aircraft of fairly conventional design. The type was basically similar in general layout to the HUP-2, sharing that aircraft's all-metal fuselage, fixed three-point landing gear, and 550 hp Continental R-975-42 engine. The H-25A differed from the Navy variant primarily in having hydraulically-boosted controls, a strengthened floor with cargo tie-down fittings, and modified doors intended to ease the loading and unloading of stretchers.

Though a rugged and fairly capable aircraft the H-25A ultimately proved unsuited to the rigors of front-line Army service, and fifty of the seventy examples procured were turned over to the Navy beginning in 1955. Those Army Mules that remained in Army service were used mainly as training or medical evacuation aircraft, and the type was totally withdrawn from Army service by 1958.

TECHNICAL DATA

Engine:
One 550 hp Continental R-975-42 radial

Dimensions:
Rotor diameter (each): 35 ft
Fuselage length: 31 ft 10 in
Height (to top of
   aft rotor head):   12 ft 6 in

Weight (empty/maximum, in lbs):
3928/6125

Performance:
Speed (cruising/maximum, in mph):
   92/115

Service Ceiling: 12,700 ft

Range: 355 miles

Armament: None

Accommodation:
Pilot, co-pilot, and up to five passengers
or three stretchers.

PIASECKI VZ-8

Type: Single- or twin-
    engined VTOL
    research vehicle

Manufacturer: Piasecki
    Aircraft Corporation,
    Philadelphia, Pennsylvania.

HISTORY

In 1957 Piasecki Aircraft was awarded an Army Transportation
Research Command contract for the development of a 'flying
jeep'-type VTOL research vehicle capable of operating at
extremely low altitudes at speeds up to 70 mph. Piasecki, at that
time a leader in vertical lift research and development, produced
an innovative design dubbed the Model 59K Sky Car. The craft
was built around two tandem, three-bladed, ducted rotors
driven by two 180 hp Lycoming piston engines. Both powerplants
were connected to a single central gearbox so that both rotors
would continue to turn even if one engine failed. The Sky Car
had fairly conventional helicopter-type controls which provided
directional stability through a series of hinged vanes mounted
under each rotor duct. The craft had fixed tricycle wheeled
landing gear, and accommodated its single pilot and one
passenger in seats sited between the two rotor ducts.

    The first of two Model 59 examples ordered by the Army
made its initial free flight in October 1958 and, renamed Airgeep
by Piasecki, was turned over to the Army shortly thereafter. The
machine was subsequently given the designation VZ-8P (the P
indicating Piasecki) and the serial number 58-5510. Shortly after
being accepted by the Army the VZ-8P was fitted with a single

The first VZ-8P (58-5510), seen here with designer Frank Piasecki at the
controls during an early test flight, featured a raised and slightly angled rear
propeller duct intended to reduce airflow interference effects from the front
duct. Note the tufting attached to the cuneiform control vanes beneath the
front duct to measure air flow patterns. *(U.S. Army)*

Soon after the VZ-8P was accepted by the Army the machine's piston engines were replaced by a single Turbomeca Artouste IIB turbine, the exhaust shroud for which can be seen extending from the aircraft's port side in this photo. Note that the change in powerplant was accompanied by a reduction in the size of the rear propeller duct. *(Bowers Collection)*

425 shp Turbomeca Artouste IIB turbine engine in place of its twin Lycoming pistons, and its first turbine-powered flight took place in June 1959. The craft was subsequently loaned to the Navy for evaluation (as the Model 59N), and upon its return to the Army its Artouste IIB was replaced by a lighter and more powerful AiResearch 331-6 turbine.

The second VZ-8P (serial 58-5511) incorporated several significant design changes and was, accordingly, dubbed the Model 59H Airgeep II by Piasecki and the VZ-8P (B) by the Army. This vehicle's most obvious differences from its predecessor were an angled rear duct, the installation of two 400 shp Artouste IIC engines, zero-altitude zero-speed ejection seats for the pilot and added co-pilot/gunner, seating for up to three passengers, and the addition of powered tricycle landing gear meant to improve ground handling and provide a measure of overland mobility. The Airgeep II made its first non-tethered flight in the summer of 1962.

Neither version of the VZ-8P was dependent upon surface-effect lift for flight and, though intended to operate within a few feet of the ground in order to make the best use of natural cover, both were quite capable of flying at altitudes of several thousand feet. Both versions were found to be quite stable and relatively capable craft, able to hover or fly beneath trees and between buildings or other obstacles. In addition, the Airgeep was found to be a surprisingly effective weapons platform, able to engage targets with only the weapon and its sight visible above the line of defilade. This remains a unique talent, for even modern battlefield helicopters must rise above the line of defilade to fire their weapons (which are mounted below the rotor plane) thus revealing themselves and providing a much greater target area*.

---

* Interestingly, the Airgeep was also a forerunner of modern stealth aircraft: its ducts shielded the turning rotors, thus making them invisible to both radar and the human eye and giving the VZ-8P a much better chance of remaining undetected on the battlefield than was — or is — enjoyed by the helicopter.

The second VZ-8P, 58-5511, during its first non-tethered test flight. This machine featured a sharply-angled rear duct, twin turbine engines, powered landing gear, and crew ejection seats. *(Piasecki Aircraft)*

Despite its many positive qualities the Airgeep, like most 'flying jeeps' developed during this period, was ultimately judged by the Army to be mechanically ill-suited to the rigors of field operations. The 'flying jeep' concept was eventually abandoned in favor of the further development of conventional battlefield helicopters, and both VZ-8P examples were dropped from the Army's inventory in the mid-1960s.

TECHNICAL DATA *(All versions, except where noted)*

Engine(s):
Two 180 hp Lycoming O-360-A2A pistons (VZ-8P)
One 425 shp Turbomeca Artouste IIB turbine (VZ-8P)
One 550 shp AiResearch 331-6 turbine (VZ-8P)
Two 400 shp Turbomeca Artouste IIC turbines (VZ-8P[B])

Dimensions:
Rotor diameter: 7 ft 5 in (VZ-8P)
8 ft 2 in (VZ-8P[B])
Length overall: 26 ft 1 in (VZ-8P)
24 ft 5 in (VZ-8P[B])
Height: 6 ft 8 in (VZ-8P)
5 ft 10 in (VZ-8P[B])
Width: 9 ft 5 in (VZ-8P)
9 ft 3 in (VZ-8P[B])

Weight (empty/gross, in lbs):
1848/2350 (VZ-8P)
2611/3670 (VZ-8P[B])

Performance:
Speed (cruising/maximum, in mph):
50/65 (VZ-8P)
70/85 (VZ8P[B])

Service Ceiling: 3000 ft

Range: 25 miles (VZ-8P)
35 miles (VZ-8P[B])

Armament:
Though neither machine ever actually fired live ordnance, both were experimentally fitted with a single forward-facing dummy recoiless rifle fixed between the crew seats just above the rotor ducts.

Accommodation:
Pilot and one passenger/observer (VZ-8P)
Pilot, optional co-pilot/gunner, and up to three passengers (VZ-8P[B]).

PIASECKI 16H-1A

Type: Single-engined
compound research
helicopter

Manufacturer: Piasecki
Aircraft Corporation,
Philadelphia, Pennsylvania.

HISTORY

Beginning in early 1964 the Army and Navy jointly funded modifications to Piasecki Aircraft's Model 16H-1 Pathfinder compound research helicopter as part of an ongoing study of advanced high-speed rotorcraft technology. The 16H-1 had originally been developed as a company private venture and, as such, had first flown in February 1962. The modified version, designated the 16H-1A Pathfinder II by Piasecki, made its first tethered test ascents in October 1965.

Like its predecessor, the Pathfinder II was a high-speed compound rotorcraft which utilized a conventional fully articulated, three-bladed main rotor for vertical lift and a tail-mounted, ducted 'ringtail' pusher propeller for directional and anti-torque control. After takeoff, power was applied to the pusher propeller for forward propulsion, and in cruising flight the craft's small wings helped off-load the rotor and increase forward speeds.

The 16H-1A first flew in November 1965, and logged more than 150 flight hours during the course of the joint Army-Navy test programme. *(Piasecki)*

The Pathfinder II differed from the earlier 16H-1 primarily in having a more powerful General Electric T58 shaft turbine engine, a longer and more streamlined fuselage with increased cabin accommodation, a larger main rotor, increased-span stub wings, strengthened main landing gear, redesigned engine air intakes, and upgraded electronics.

The Pathfinder II made its first free flight in November 1965, and quickly proved itself to be an extraordinarily fast and manoeuvrable machine. Forward speeds in excess of 225 mph were not uncommon, and the 16H-1A was capable of flying backwards and sideways at speeds of up to 35 mph. The evaluation programme provided a wealth of valuable information on compound rotorcraft technology and operations, much of which was later used in the development and testing of the AH-56 Cheyenne (q.v.). Joint Army-Navy sponsorship of the 16H-1A ended in late 1966, at which time the craft was returned to Piasecki for further company-funded research.

TECHNICAL DATA

Engine(s):
One 1250 shp General Electric T58-GE-8 shaft turbine

Dimensions:

Main rotor diameter:	44 ft
Tail propeller diameter:	5 ft 6 in
Wingspan:	22 ft
Fuselage length:	37 ft 3 in
Height (to top of rotor hub):	11 ft 4 in

Weight (empty/maximum, in lbs):
4800/10,800

Performance:
Speed (cruising/maximum, in mph): 175/230

Service Ceiling: 18,700 ft

Range: 450-950 miles

Armament: None

Accommodation:
Crew of two, plus up to six passengers.

PILATUS V-20 CHIRICAHUA

Type: Single-engined STOL
utility transport

Manufacturer: Pilatus
Flugzeugwerke AG, Stans,
Switzerland

HISTORY

In the late 1970s the Army began casting about for a STOL-capable single-engined transport aircraft to be used by the Army Aviation Detachment assigned to the Berlin Brigade. The Detachment already operated several UH-1 Iroquois helicopters in the VIP transport role but needed fixed-wing aircraft of greater endurance and capacity to conduct 'show-the-flag' patrols of 'The Ring', the area of Allied air space that includes all of West Berlin and portions of East Berlin and East Germany. The Berlin-based unit's needs were unique, in that the aircraft selected would be required to operate at low speeds and low altitudes within one of the most restricted and busiest military air traffic regions in the world. Following preliminary evaluation of several aircraft types the Army selected the Swiss-built Pilatus PC-6 Turbo-Porter as being the best qualified, and in 1979 ordered two examples. The machines were designated UV-20A Chiricahuas* and were assigned the serial numbers 79-23253 and -23254.

The civil Turbo-Porter was developed from the earlier piston-powered PC-6 Porter, and first flew in the late 1960s. The Army's UV-20s are based on the civil model PC-6/B2H2 variant, which was type-certified in 1970, and differ from that model primarily in having military-specification avionics and communications equipment. The Chiricahua is an all-metal, high-wing cabin monoplane and is powered by a single 680 shp PT6A-27

The United States Army's entire UV-20 inventory in formation flight over the Swiss countryside prior to delivery. Both aircraft are painted in the gloss olive green and white colour scheme with high-visibility national insignia. *(Pilatus)*

Despite its rather ungainly appearance, the UV-20 is an extremely capable STOL aircraft ideally suited to the particularly demanding mission of the Berlin Brigade's Aviation Detachment. This photo shows the aircraft's characteristic high wing, squared tail and oversized tyres to good advantage. *(Pilatus)*

turboprop engine driving a fully-feathering, three-bladed Hartzell reversible-pitch propeller. The machine's single-spar wing is fitted with electrically-operated double-slotted flaps on the inboard sections and single-slotted ailerons on the outboard sections. The capacious cabin provides some 107 cubic feet of cargo space, and the interior can be configured to carry up to eleven passengers, eight parachutists or three stretchers and four attendants. This load-carrying capability is particularly important, for the Berlin Brigade's UV-20s are often called upon to perform such additional duties as aeromedical evacuation, VIP transport, and the dropping of parachutists during air shows.

---

* Like most recent Army aircraft, the UV-20A is named after an American Indian tribe. The Chiricahuas were an Arizona off-shoot of the Apaches.

TECHNICAL DATA

Engine:
One 680 shp Pratt & Whitney of Canada PT6A-27 turboprop

Dimensions:

Wingspan:	49 ft 8 in
Wing area:	310 sq ft
Fuselage length:	35 ft 9 in
Height:	10 ft 6 in

Weight (empty/gross, in lbs):
2685/4850

Performance:
Speed (cruising/maximum, in mph): 150/174

Service Ceiling: 25,000 ft

Range: 850 miles

Armament: None.

Accommodation:
See text.

PIPER L-4

Type: Single-engined
observation and
liaison aircraft

Manufacturer: Piper Aircraft
Corporation, Lock Haven,
Pennsylvania

HISTORY

The fact that the majority of Piper L-4s operated by the Army had disappeared from the inventory prior to 1947 would, at first glance, seem to place the petit yet durable 'Cub' outside the scope of this book. However, three factors argue for its inclusion in any work dealing with post-World War II Army aviation or aircraft. First, the L-4 was operated in greater numbers than any other liaison or observation type during the formative years of what would eventually become the modern Army's air arm, and it played a significant role in shaping the operational doctrine that guided Army aviation activities until the early years of the Vietnam War. Second, examples of several L-4 variants did, in fact, remain in the Army's inventory into the early 1950s. And, third, the L-4 provided the basic airframe from which two other significant Army aircraft were developed.

The ubiquitous Piper L-4 first entered Army service in 1941, when it was one of three commercial light plane types selected for evaluation in the artillery observation and general liaison roles. Like the other two aircraft chosen for testing, the Taylorcraft Model D (Army designation L-2) and Aeronca Model 65TC Defender (L-3), the Piper J3C-65 Cub was a light, two-place, high-wing monoplane of simple metal and fabric construction. Powered by a 65 hp Continental engine, the YO-59, as the service test Cubs were designated, was capable of a top speed of about 83 mph. Speed was not an especially important factor in the evaluation, however, and the Cub's good short-field performance and ease of maintenance made it an ideal Army co-operation machine. Shortly after delivery of the four evaluation aircraft Piper was awarded a contract for the first of an eventual 5375 production machines. The Army ultimately used ten variants (excluding the TG-8 non-powered glider trainer), the characteristics of which were as follows:

O-59:
First production model, 144 of which were acquired in 1942. This aircraft was essentially identical to the YO-59, and was equipped with a six-volt radio, wind-driven generator, and reel-mounted trailing antenna. Both the YO-59 and O-59 were redesignated L-4 in mid-1942.

O59A:
Very similar to the O-59, but incorporated a modified cabin enclosure intended to improve visibility. Approximately 671 were built as O-59As, with an additional 277 examples delivered

Though normally associated with World War II, the L-4 served the Army well into the 1950s. This particular aircraft, L-4J 45-55263, was photographed near Fort Rucker in 1952. *(U.S. Army Transportation Corps Museum)*

as L-4A following the variant's redesignation in mid-1942. In 1948 a few surviving machines were redesignated ZL-4A to indicate their obsolete status.

L-4B:
Essentially identical to the L-4A, except for deletion of radio antenna and wind-driven generator. A total of 980 were built. The few examples still in the Army inventory in 1948 were redesignated ZL-4B.

L-4C:
Designation given to eight commercial model J3L-65 Cubs impressed into service after America's entry into the Second World War. These aircraft were powered by 65 hp Lycoming O-145-B1 engines, and had interiors somewhat more plush than those of the purpose-built military variants.

L-4D:
Five commercial model J3F-65 Cubs were assigned this designation upon impressment in 1943. Generally similar to the L-4C, but powered by the 65 hp Franklin 4AC-176 engine.

L-4E:
The Army impressed seventeen commercial model J4E aircraft in 1942 for the training of glider pilots. The L-4E was powered by the 75 hp Continental A75-9 engine, and had side-by-side rather than tandem seating.

L-4F:
Designation assigned to forty-three impressed commercial model J5A Cubs. Had the same powerplant as, and was essentially similar to, the L-4E, but could seat an additional person in the rear of the cabin. Also used to train glider pilots.

L-4G:
Impressed commercial model J5B. Identical to the L-4F except in having a 100 hp Lycoming GO-145-C2 engine. A total of forty-one were impressed, and all were used for glider pilot training during World War II. At least one example remained in Army service as late as mid-1948.

L-4H:
Similar to the L-4B, the L-4H had improved communications and operational equipment and was fitted with a fixed-pitch propeller. This version was produced in the greatest numbers, with a total of 1801 machines entering the inventory between 1943 and 1945. Army records indicate that several dozen examples of this variant were still in service at the outbreak of the Korean War, and many were pressed into service in the Far East pending the arrival there of more advanced types.

L-4J:
Basically identical to the L-4H, but equipped with a variable-pitch propeller. A total of 1680 examples were built, with deliveries beginning in 1945. At least 150 of these aircraft remained in Army service when the United States entered the Korean War.

TECHNICAL DATA (All versions, except where noted)

Engine:
One 65 hp Continental O-170-3 piston (YO/O-59, L-4/A, B, H, J)
One 65 hp Lycoming O-145-B1 (L-4C)
One 65 hp Franklin 4AC-176 (L-4D)
One 75 hp Continental A-75-9 (L-4E, F)
One 100 hp Lycoming GO-145-C2 (L-4G)

Dimensions:
Wingspan: 35 ft 3 in
Wing area: 179 sq ft
Fuselage length: 22 ft 4 in
Height: 6 ft 8 in

Weight (empty/gross, in lbs):
730/1220 (YO/O-59, L-4/A, B, C, D, H, J)
745/1335 (L-4E, F)
800/1450 (L-4G)

Performance:
Speed (cruising/maximum, in mph):
75/87 (YO/O-59, L-4/A, B, C, D, H, J)
81/93 (L-4E, F)
100/110 (L-4G)

Service Ceiling:
9300 ft (YO/O-59, L-4/A, B, C, D, H, J)
10,250 ft (L-4E, F)
13,500 ft (L-4G)

Range:
190 miles (YO/O-59, L-4/A, B, C, D, H, J)
230 miles (L-4E, F)
450 miles (L-4G)

Armament:
None normally fitted, though aircraft operating in combat areas were sometimes equipped with defensive small arms mounted on the window sills or under the wings.

Accommodation:
Pilot and observer.
Instructor and one or two students (L-4F/G).

PIPER L-18

Type: Single-engined
    observation and
    liaison aircraft

Manufacturer: Piper Aircraft
Corporation, Lock Haven,
Pennsylvania

HISTORY

In early 1949 Piper Aircraft developed an upgraded version of the L-4J intended to fill the U.S. Government's requirement for a light observation aircraft which could be supplied to friendly nations under various military aid programmes. The L-18A, as the proposed craft was designated, proved unsuitable, however, and no orders were placed. Instead, some 105 examples of the standard commercial model PA-11 Cub 95 were purchased as L-18Bs and allocated to the Turkish Army under the Mutual Security Programme (MSP). A few that were not accepted by the Turks for one reason or another were turned over to the Army for flying club use. The Army was at the same time searching for an observation and liaison craft to replace its existing L-4s, L-5s and L-16s, and judged the L-18B to be basically suitable for field use. In late 1949 Piper was therefore awarded a contract for 838

The L-18C was essentially identical to the L-18B aircraft provided to various foreign countries under the MAP agreements. The machine seen here, 55-4749, was the last L-18 variant delivered to the American military, having been originally built for the Air Force in 1955. The aircraft was later turned over to the Army, and is seen here experimentally equipped with the Whittaker tandem-wheel landing gear system. This device, which consisted of dual main wheels fixed one behind the other, was intended to both improve rough field handling and keep trainee pilots from inflicting unnecessary landing injuries on their aircraft. (Bowers Collection)

examples of the similar L-18C; 108 of these machines were later transferred to foreign governments under Military Assistance Programme (MAP) agreements.

The L-18B and -C were essentially identical to the earlier L-4J, having nearly the same dimensions and just slightly higher empty and gross weights. Both versions were powered by a 90 hp Continental engine driving a two-bladed, fixed-pitch wooden propeller. Though its performance was somewhat better than that of the L4, the L-18 never proved entirely satisfactory from the Army's point of view. It did, however, provide a basis for the development of the more capable L-21/U-7, and carried out many important frontline tasks during the early stages of the Korean War.

TECHNICAL DATA *(Both versions, except where noted)*

Engine:
One 90 hp Continental O-205-1 (C90-8F) piston

Dimensions:

Wingspan:	35 ft 3 in
Wing area:	179 sq ft
Fuselage length:	22 ft 4.5 in
Height:	6 ft 7 in

Weight (empty/maximum, in lbs):
800/1500

Performance:
Speed (cruising/maximum, in mph): 100/110

Service Ceiling: 13,500 ft

Range: 450 miles

Armament: None.

Accommodation:
Pilot and observer/passenger.

PIPER U-7

Type: Single-engined
    observation and
    liaison aircraft

Manufacturer: Piper Aircraft
    Corporation, Lock Haven,
    Pennsylvania

HISTORY

Shortly after accepting its first Piper L-18Cs the Army acquired two examples of the slightly larger and somewhat more powerful Piper PA-18 Cub 135. These aircraft, designated YL-21 and assigned the serial numbers 51-6495 and -6496, were evaluated in the observation and liaison roles and found to be rather more capable than the L-18. The Army subsequently procured 150 production L-21A models (serials 51-15654 through -15803), all of which were powered by 125 hp Lycoming engines, and all 150 were delivered by 31 December 1951. Several of these aircraft were later converted to full dual-control trainers and operated in that role with the designation TL-21A.

In 1952 the Army began procurement of the L-21B, which differed from the -A models only in having a more powerful 135 hp engine, wing flaps, and provision for a high-flotation, tandem-wheel undercarriage. A total of 584 L-21Bs was delivered,

Based on the Piper PA-18 Cub 135, the L-21 was found to be somewhat more capable than the earlier L-18. The Army acquired 150 L-21As and 584 L-21Bs, the survivors of which became, respectively, U-7A and U-7B in 1962. This particular aircraft is a U-7A, which did not have the flaps or slightly more powerful engine of the U-7B.
(Gordon S. Williams via Peter M. Bowers)

211

though many of these were later transferred to friendly nations under various military aid programmes. The Army used the L-21B extensively overseas, particularly in the Far East, though the type was ultimately supplanted in frontline service by the vastly superior Cessna L-19/0-1 Bird Dog. The few L-21Bs that remained in the Army inventory in 1962 (mainly with the Reserve components) were redesignated U-7A.

TECHNICAL DATA *(Both versions, except where noted)*

Engine:
One 125 hp Lycoming O-290-11 piston (YL-21, L-21A)
One 135 hp Lycoming O-290-D2 (L-21B)

Dimensions:
Wingspan: 35 ft 3 in
Wing area: 179 sq ft
Fuselage length: 22 ft 7 in
Height: 6 ft 6 in

Weight (empty/gross, in lbs):
950/1580

Performance:
Speed (cruising/maximum, in mph):
115/123 (YL-21, L-21A)
125/137 (L-21B)

Service Ceiling: 18,500 ft (L-21A)
21,600 ft (YL-21, L-21B)

Range: 650 miles

Armament: None.

Accommodation:
Pilot and observer/passenger.

PRINCETON UNIVERSITY GEM

Type: Single-engined ground
    effect research vehicle

Manufacturer: James
Forrestal Research Center of
Princeton University,
Princeton, New Jersey

HISTORY

The Princeton Model X-3 ground effect machine (GEM) was the larger of two research vehicles developed by the University's Forrestal Research Center during the late 1950s in order to explore both the theoretical and practical aspects of air cushioned 'flight'. In 1959 the Army agreed to help fund the ongoing development and testing of the X-3 (and, during the same general period, of the similar Curtiss-Wright Aircar, q.v.) as part of its own continuing exploration of the possible military applications of unconventional aircraft.

The saucer-shaped X-3 was constructed of steel tubing and aluminium ribs covered by fabric, and was twenty feet in diameter. The machine's single pilot sat in a fully enclosed cockpit faired into the upper deck just behind the saucer's leading edge. The X-3's air cushion was created by a main vertical-lift engine buried in the central fuselage and driving a horizontally-mounted four-bladed wooden propeller. The propeller drove air downward through a nineteen square-foot annular nozzle in the saucer's bottom to create the vehicle's

The X-3B GEM 'flying' at an altitude of approximately sixteen inches. Note the 45 hp propulsion engine in the tail cut-out, as well as the tufts of yarn attached at various points over the craft to aid in determining air flow patterns. The X-3A was essentially identical in appearance to the machine shown here, though the X-3C differed in having twin rudder-equipped tail fins. *(U.S. Army Transportation Corps Museum)*

peripheral air curtain. A smaller engine and propeller placed within a cutout in the single horizontal tail fin provided forward propulsion. In its original X-3A form the Princeton GEM had a 44 hp lift engine and a 5 hp propulsion unit, though in the modified X-3B that appeared in late 1960 these were replaced by, respectively, 185 hp and 45 hp engines. In the X-3C version introduced in late 1961 the single tail fin was replaced by twin rudder-equipped fins supporting a single full-width horizontal 'trimmer' stabilizer geared to the attitude of the machine. This trimmer produced greater longitudinal stability and helped eliminate the X-3's previous tendency to pitch its leading edge upward during forward 'flight'. In each of its three incarnations the X-3 carried fuel for both the lift fan and forward propulsion engine in two 15 U.S. gallon Piper Comanche wingtip tanks fixed to the outboard edges of the upper decking.

During the period of Army involvement in the funding of the Princeton X-3 the U.S. military had no type-classification for air cushion vehicles and the machine, which was never assigned a military aircraft serial number, was therefore known to the Army simply as the Princeton GEM. The craft provided both Princeton and the Army with a wealth of information about the mechanics of air cushioned 'flight' and, equally as important, helped create official interest in the military potential of air cushion vehicles that far outlasted the 1962 end of Army participation in the X-3 development programme.

TECHNICAL DATA *(All versions, except where noted)*

Engines:
One 44 hp Nelson H-63B lift fan and one 5 hp Power Products forward propulsion unit (X-3A)
One 180 hp Lycoming VO-360-A1A lift fan and one 45 hp Power Products forward propulsion unit (X-3B/C)

Dimensions:
Lift fan diameter: 4 ft 10 in
Fuselage diameter at base: 18 ft 2 in
Fuselage diameter overall: 20 ft

Weight (empty/maximum, in lbs):
1240/1600 (X-3A)
X-3B/C unknown

Performance:
Speed (cruising/maximum, in mph):
13/25 (X-3A)
30/50 (X)-3B/C)

Normal operating height above ground:
12 to 24 in (X-3A)
12 to 48 in (X-3B/C)

Armament: None.

Accommodation:
Pilot only.

RYAN VZ-3

Type: Single-engined V/STOL
        research aircraft

Manufacturer: Ryan
Aeronautical Company, San
Diego, California

HISTORY

The increasing interest shown by the Army in non-helicopter V/STOL flight during the mid- and late 1950s resulted in a flurry of contracts being awarded to various aircraft companies for the production of fixed-wing research prototypes. In 1956 Ryan Aeronautical was awarded such a contract covering the development, construction and flight testing of a single aircraft of the deflected-slipstream type. The resultant Model 92 Vertiplane was designated VZ-3 and allotted the serial number 56-6941.

The VZ-3 was a single-seat, high-wing, 'T'-tail monoplane powered by a single 1000 shp Lycoming turboshaft buried in the

Ryan workers put the finishing touches on the sole VZ-3 prior to its delivery. Note the large diameter propellers and the wingtip endplates for the aircraft's huge full-span flaps. *(San Diego Aerospace Museum)*

The same aircraft during the course of flight testing, its full-span flaps about sixty per cent deployed. Note that a nose wheel and a small ventral fin have been added, as has a revised nozzle on the jet exhaust outlet. This machine is now in the collection of the Army Aviation Museum at Fort Rucker, Alabama. *(U.S. Army Transportation Corps Museum)*

central fuselage. The engine drove two three-bladed, large-diameter wooden propellers, one of which was mounted beneath each wing. The wings themselves were equipped with huge full-span retracting flaps which, when lowered completely, formed a tight seal with the wing endplates and deflected the propeller slipstream directly downward to produce vertical lift. Additional directional stability was provided by a variable-deflection jet exhaust nozzle in the aircraft's tail, and by retractable spoilers set into the upper surfaces of each wing. The VZ-3 was built with a tail wheel undercarriage, though this was changed to a tricycle arrangement prior to the beginning of flight testing, and its enclosed cockpit was equipped with an ejection seat and conventional airplane controls.

The VZ-3's maiden flight took place in January 1959, following three months of extensive testing in NASA's low-speed wind tunnel complex at Moffet Field, California. Four weeks into the joint Army/Office of Naval Research test programme the craft was badly damaged in a landing accident caused by a propeller malfunction; the subsequent repairs included the removal of the canopy enclosure and the installation of a more powerful Martin-Baker ejection seat. Flight testing resumed in the summer of 1959, and the VZ-3 subsequently proved to be an able, if unspectacular, V/STOL performer. The craft was never able to perform a vertical take-off, but it was able to lift off at a speed of 25 mph after a roll of only thirty feet. The VZ-3 could also hover at near-zero air speeds at altitudes from one hundred to 3750 feet, transition from hovering to forward flight with relative ease, and safely undertake near-vertical high-speed descents far beyond the capabilities of contemporary helicopters.

In February 1960 the sole VZ-3 was turned over to NASA for further evaluation. The machine was almost completely destroyed on its first NASA test flight and required an extensive rebuild prior to the resumption of NASA flight tests in late 1961. The aircraft was presented to the Army Aviation Museum at Fort Rucker, Alabama, following the completion of its NASA evaluation in 1963.

TECHNICAL DATA

Engine:
One 1000 shp Lycoming T53-L-1 turboshaft

Dimensions:
Wingspan:	23 ft 5 in
Fuselage length:	27 ft 8 in
Height:	10 ft 8 in

Weight (empty/gross, in lbs):
1750/2600

Performance:
Speed (cruising/maximum, in mph): 80/155

Service Ceiling: 5500 ft

Range: 300 miles

Armament: None

Accommodation:
Pilot only.

RYAN V-8

Type: Single-engined
flex-wing research
vehicle

Manufacturer: Ryan
Aeronautical Company, San
Diego, California

HISTORY

The Ryan XV-8A flexible-wing research vehicle was developed under an Army Transportation Research Command contract awarded in mid-1962. The craft, designated the Model 164 by Ryan, was a revised version of the firm's earlier Flex Wing aerial utility vehicle prototype. That machine, which had first flown in May 1961, had itself been built to flight test the innovative 'powered kite' lifting body concept originated by NASA's Langley Research Center. Design work on the XV-8A began in August 1962, and the first of two projected prototypes made its first flight in June 1963. In the event, the Army acquired only the one example (serial 63-13003), the other having been cancelled during the construction phase.

The XV-8A, which was universally if unofficially known as the 'Fleep', consisted of a delta-shaped flexible wing attached by a

The sole Fleep, 63-13003, just prior to an early test flight. The rather ungainly-looking XV-8 was actually a surprisingly stable aircraft, and its delta-shaped Rogallo wing, rudimentary cockpit, the aft-mounted pusher propeller all became standard features on the first generation of ultralight civil aircraft. *(U.S. Army)*

pivoting tubular pylon to a load-bearing metal keel. This keel in turn supported a rudimentary single-seat cockpit, a small central cargo tie-down/passenger seating area, a single 210 hp piston engine, a V-shaped tail unit, and tricycle landing gear. The craft's Rogallo-type 'parasol' wing was constructed of fabric-covered aluminium tubing, had inflatable leading edges of variable rigidity, and could be folded into a relatively small package for storage or shipment aboard larger aircraft. The XV-8A had no flaps, and trimming was achieved by varying the incidence of the wing.

The sole XV-8A was extensively flight tested at the Army's Yuma, Arizona, test station between July 1963 and July 1964. Though the craft was primarily a research and proof-of-concept vehicle, the Army hoped that it might be developed into an easily operated and simple to maintain 'flying jeep'. The craft did, in fact, prove to be extremely easy to operate, but the Army nonetheless chose not to pursue further development of the flexible-wing lifting body concept following the termination of the XV-8 test programme.

TECHNICAL DATA

Engine:
One 210 hp Continental IO-360-A piston

Dimensions:

Wingspan:	33 ft 5 in
Wing area:	450 sq ft
Fuselage length:	19 ft 6 in
Height:	14 ft 6.5 in

Weight (empty/maximum, in lbs):
1115/2300

Performance:
Speed (cruising/maximum, in mph): 57/65

Service Ceiling: 1500 ft

Range: 120 miles

Armament: None.

Accommodation:
Pilot and up to six passengers.

RYAN V-5

Type: Single-engined VTOL
research aircraft

Manufacturer: Ryan
Aeronautical Company, San
Diego, California

HISTORY

In November 1961 the Army Transportation Research Command awarded the General Electric Corporation a $10.5 million contract for the development of two VZ-11 VTOL research aircraft incorporating the 'fan-in-wing' system that GE and Ryan Aeronautical had been jointly working on since 1959. As prime contractor, GE was responsible for the vehicles' engines and lift fan systems and, after conducting an essentially cosmetic industry-wide airframe design competition, GE selected Ryan as the sub-contractor responsible for designing and building the airframes. Construction of the two Ryan Model 143 aircraft began in June 1962, at which time the machines (serials 62-4505 and -4506) were redesignated XV-5. The first prototype made its maiden flight on 25 May 1964, followed shortly thereafter by the second example.

Both XV-5 prototypes are seen here parked on the ramp at Edwards Air Force Base early in the flight test programme. The aircraft have their nose fan doors open, and both carry day-glow orange test markings on nose, wingtips and tail. The aircraft nearest the camera, 62-4505, was destroyed in April 1965 during an attempted transition from vertical to forward flight. *(Ryan via SDAM)*

The second XV-5A, 62-4506, on the taxiway at San Diego's Lindberg Field prior to delivery to the Army. This machine was extensively damaged in an October 1964 crash, rebuilt in a modified form, and ultimately transferred to NASA for testing as the sole XV-5B. *(Ryan via SDAM)*

The XV-5's layout was basically conventional, with a slender if rather slab-sided fuselage, side-by-side seating for two crew men, a high 'T' tail, slightly swept mid-position wings, and fully retractable tricycle landing gear. The engine air intake was placed above and to the rear of the canopy in order to avoid most of the turbulence generated by the two GE X353-5B main lift fans, one of which was buried in the inboard half of each wing. The counter-rotating fans were each driven by exhaust gases cross-ducted onto them from both of the XV-5's two J85 turbojet engines; the failure of one powerplant was therefore not catastrophic, for both fans would continue to turn and could produce up to sixty per cent of the total thrust available during normal twin-engined operation. Trim and pitch control during vertical flight were provided by a small GE X376 fan which was mounted in the aircraft's nose and driven by engine exhaust.

To initiate vertical flight the XV-5 pilot opened the hinged butterfly-doors covering the wing fans and applied full engine power to all three fan units. Once the craft had reached a safe hovering height the small louvres fixed to the bottom of each main fan were rotated to the rear and the XV-5 began to move forward. At approximately 175 mph the aircraft achieved wing-borne flight and the pilot closed the fan doors and diverted the engine thrust to the two tailpipes beneath the fuselage.

Transition from horizontal to vertical flight was achieved by simply reversing the process.

The XV-5 was one of three similar VTOL craft selected for simultaneous Army evaluation, the others being Lockheed's XV-4 Hummingbird and Hawker Siddeley's XV-6 Kestrel (q.v.). During the course of its 1964 to 1966 flight test programme the XV-5 proved itself to be significantly more capable than the XV-4, a machine whose augmented jet-ejector lift system was both more complex and less effective than the Ryan aircraft's fan-based system. The XV-5's range of performance was impressive, for the craft was able to hover almost motionless at a hundred feet or reach nearly 550 mph in level flight. However, it was not a particularly easy aircraft to fly as evidenced by the fact that 62-4505 was destroyed in April 1965 while attempting the transition from vertical to horizontal flight. The extensive damage sustained by the second prototype in an October 1964 accident helped convince the Army to abandon further development of the XV-5 and concentrate its (ultimately unsuccessful) efforts to acquire high-performance VTOL aircraft on the Hawker Siddeley XV-6. The damaged second XV-5 was eventually rebuilt in modified form and transferred to NASA control as the XV-5B.

TECHNICAL DATA

Engine:
Two 2658 lb st General Electric J58-GE-5 turbojets

Dimensions:
Wingspan:	29 ft 10 in
Wing area:	260 sq ft
Fuselage length:	44 ft 6.25 in
Height:	14 ft 9 in

Weight (empty/maximum, in lbs):
7541/12,300 (VTOL)

Performance:
Speed (cruising/maximum, in mph): 345/547

Service Ceiling: 40,000 ft

Range: 1000 miles

Armament: None.

Accommodation:
Pilot and co-pilot/observer.

SEIBEL H-24

Type: Single-engined utility
helicopter prototype

Manufacturer: Seibel
Helicopter Company, Wichita,
Kansas

HISTORY

The Seibel Helicopter Company was formed in 1947 by Charles M. Seibel, an engineer formerly employed by Bell Helicopter, and the S-4A Sky Hawk was the second of the firm's designs to fly. Both the Army and the Air Force expressed interest in the Sky Hawk, and in 1951 the Army ordered two examples for operational and engineering evaluation in the observation, utility and aeromedical evacuation roles. The machines were delivered near the end of 1951, designated YH-24, and assigned the serial numbers 51-5112 and -5113.

The YH-24 was of extremely simple welded steel-tube construction, and was unique in having a stepped, two-deck fuselage structure. The long lower deck supported the pilot's seat and control panel, as well as a small passenger/cargo area that was unobstructed and accessible from the rear. The shorter upper deck, directly above the passenger/cargo area, carried the

The first YH-24, 51-5112, in flight shortly after delivery in December 1951. Plastic and canvas enclosures have been fitted over the cockpit and passenger/cargo space, though both areas were normally left unenclosed. The machine has also been fitted with what appear to be small, fixed horizontal stabilizers attached to the fuselage frame just aft of the nose wheel. *(U.S. Army)*

craft's single 125 hp Lycoming engine, fuel and oil tanks, and the complete main rotor assembly. A tapered alloy tail boom was attached to the rear of the upper deck, and carried a two-bladed anti-torque rotor at its tip. The pilot's position and passenger/cargo area were not normally enclosed, though they were provided with roll-down fabric and clear plastic panels for use in bad weather. During the course of the Army's evaluation, the fuselage of the second YH-24 (51-5113) was shortened and widened to allow the installation of a co-pilot's seat beside that of the pilot, and the machine was later fitted with skid landing gear in place of its original wheeled tricycle undercarriage.

Though a relatively robust and easily maintained aircraft, the YH-24 was ultimately judged to be unsuitable for Army service, primarily because its load-carrying ability was considered to be too limited to successfully accomplish the aeromedical evacuation and general utility tasks for which it had been evaluated. The two YH-24 prototypes were subsequently dropped from the Army inventory during the latter part of 1952.

TECHNICAL DATA *(Both examples, except where noted)*

Engine:
One 125 hp Lycoming 0-290-D piston

Dimensions:
Main rotor diameter: 29 ft 1.5 in

Tail rotor diameter: 5 ft 7 in

Fuselage length: 27 ft 10 in
24 ft 6 in (second prototype, after modification)

Height (to top of
rotor hub): 10 ft

Weight (empty/gross, in lbs):
960/1540

Performance:
Speed (cruising/maximum, in mph):
58/65

Service Ceiling: 4300 ft

Range: 98 miles (YL-26)

Armament: None

Accommodation:
Pilot and one passenger or one stretcher (as originally built).
Pilot, co-pilot and one passenger or stretcher (as modified).

SHORTS SD3-30

Type: Twin-engined medium utility transport

Manufacturer: Short Brothers Aviation Ltd., Belfast, Northern Ireland

HISTORY

In the summer of 1985 the Army purchased four ex-civil Shorts 330 twin-turbine medium-range airliners for use as logistical support aircraft at the sprawling U.S. Pacific Missile Range complex centred on Kwajalein Atoll in the Marshall Islands. The British-built machines were procured as replacements for the several ageing de Havilland C-7A Caribous that had performed the range support tasks since the mid-1970s. The purchase of the four 330s made the Army the second U.S. military service to acquire the type for cargo transport and general utility use, the Air Force having taken delivery of eighteen C-23A Sherpa freighter versions beginning in October 1984. The Army's 330s had originally been owned by California-based Golden West Airlines, but had passed to the control of the Federal Aviation Administration and were subsequently put up for sale by that agency. The Army allocated the four the serial numbers 85-25343 through -25346, but the aircraft were not type-classified and are therefore officially referred to as SD3-30s. Each machine was overhauled and modified to military standard by Field Aviation in Calgary, Canada, prior to delivery to the Army.

The Army's SD3-30s were built as commercial model 330 series 200 airliners, and they retain nearly all of that variant's standard features. These include a distinctive squared fuselage, strut-braced shoulder-mounted wings, twin tailfins, retractable tricycle landing gear, a large cargo-loading door in the forward port side, and two 1020 shp PT6A-45R turboprop engines. The machines do not have the C-23A's full-width rear cargo-loading ramp and are thus unable to transport outsize cargo, but each does have the ability to carry several D-type commercial cargo

One of four such aircraft purchased by the Army in 1985, Shorts SD3-30 85-25345 is seen here about to land at Kwajalein. Two additional aircraft were purchased off the British civil register in 1987. *(Shorts)*

Though similar in general layout to the Army's existing SD3-30s, the ten C-23A machines ordered for the Army National Guard will be identical to the USAF Sherpa shown here. A true cargo aircraft, the C-23A has a full-width rear loading ramp, slightly different engines, and fewer fuselage windows than the airliner-configured SD3-30. *(Shorts)*

containers in a storage area just aft of the two-place cockpit. In addition, each SD3-30 has eighteen to twenty standard airliner seats in an aft passenger compartment separated from the forward cargo storage area by a removable partition. The modifications made to the Army's 330s included the installation of military-specification communications equipment, additional cargo tie-down fittings, and wall-mounted stretcher attachment points.

In late 1987 the Army purchased two additional 330 aircraft (formerly G-BIFK and G-BIOE on the UK civil register) second-hand in Britain, also for range support duties in the Pacific. And in October 1988 the Army National Guard awarded Shorts a $60 million contract covering the purchase of ten standard C-23A Sherpa transports, which will be used to carry aviation spares between ARNG bases in the continental U.S. The C-23s will be virtually identical to the USAF's Sherpas, which perform the same task in Europe, and will replace the ARNG's remaining C-7 Caribou (q.v.).

TECHNICAL DATA

Engines:
  Two 1020 shp Pratt & Whitney of Canada PT6A-45R turboprops

Dimensions:

Wingspan:	74 ft 8 in
Wing area:	453 sq ft
Fuselage length:	58 ft
Height:	16 ft 3 in

Weight (empty/maximum, in lbs):
  14,727/22,900

Performance:
  Speed (cruising/maximum, in mph): 184/254

Service Ceiling: 11,500 ft

Range: 600-800 miles

Armament: None.

Accommodation:
  Two to three crew, plus eighteen to twenty passengers.

SIKORSKY H-18

Type: Single-engined light
    utility helicopter
    prototype

Manufacturer: Sikorsky
Aircraft Division of United
Aircraft, Stratford, Connecticut

HISTORY

Sikorsky's long and eventful partnership with Army aviation can accurately be said to have started during the Second World War when the company's XR-4, the first helicopter built for military service, was delivered to the USAAC. Two other Sikorsky designs, the R-5 and R-6, also entered Army Air Force service before VJ Day, and all three types made important contributions both to the American war effort and to the development of military rotary-wing doctrine. However, it is the H-18 that holds the distinction of being the first Sikorsky helicopter to be procured for service evaluation by the Army Ground Forces, as distinct from the USAAF.

Design work on the Sikorsky Model S-52 began in late 1945, and the craft made its first flight in the summer of the following year. The first American helicopter to be equipped with all-metal main and anti-torque rotor blades, the S-52 had a semi-monocoque, pod-and-boom type fuselage, a single 425 hp Franklin engine, quadricycle wheeled landing gear, and a fully-enclosed cabin that could seat up to three people. The machine's performance was quite impressive by the standards of the day; indeed, the commercial S-52 set three international speed and altitude records in 1948.

The YH-18 was of standard pod-and-boom construction, with quadricycle landing gear and accommodation for four persons. The machine shown here, 49-2889, was the second of four examples procured by the Army for service test and evaluation. *(Sikorsky)*

The S-52's performance was certainly a factor in the Army's 1949 decision to purchase four examples of the slightly modified Model S-52-2 for service test and evaluation. The Army's four YH-18As (serials 49-2888 through -2891) were essentially similar to the standard commercial S-52, differing primarily in their ability to carry a fourth passenger. Extensive testing showed the YH-18A to be quite capable in the light utility and observation roles, but the Army ultimately decided not to procure the type in quantity. One aircraft was later converted into the sole H-39 turbine-powered research helicopter (q.v.) and the S-52-2 eventually served the Navy, Marine Corps and Coast Guard as the HO5S.

TECHNICAL DATA

Engine:
One 245 hp Franklin 0-425-1 piston

Dimensions:
Main rotor diameter: 33 ft

Tail rotor diameter: 5 ft 4 in

Fuselage length: 28 ft 10 in

Height (to top of
   rotor hub):   8 ft 8 in

Weight (empty/gross, in lbs):
1650/2700

Performance:
Speed (cruising/maximum, in mph): 92/110

Service Ceiling: 15,800 ft

Range: 358 miles

Armament: None.

Accommodation:
Pilot and up to three passengers.

SIKORSKY H-19 CHICKASAW

Type: Single-engined medium utility helicopter

Manufacturer: Sikorsky Aircraft Division of United Aircraft, Stratford, Connecticut

HISTORY

Developed by Sikorsky during the late 1940s, the Model S-55 made its first flight in November 1949. The Air Force ordered five YH-19 prototypes for service test and evaluation shortly thereafter, and in 1951 purchased fifty H-19A production machines. Near the end of 1951 the Air Force accepted the first of an eventual 270 more powerful and slightly modified H-19B aircraft, and at the same time loaned a single H-19A to the Army for operational evaluation in the utility transport and aeromedical evacuation roles. The H-19 performed both with far greater ability than any other helicopter then in Army service, and in the fall of 1951 the Army ordered the first batch of an eventual seventy-two H-19C aircraft (serials 51-14242 through -14313). In late 1952 orders were placed for the first of some 301 examples of the more capable H-19D variant, sixty-one of which were transferred to friendly nations under various military assistance programmes.

The H-19 was of all-metal pod-and-boom construction, had quadricycle wheeled landing gear, and carried its single piston engine in its nose. The engine was linked to the gear drive of the three-bladed main rotor by a long extension shaft, and was easily accessible via two large clamshell doors. The innovative arrangement of powerplant and drivetrain allowed the place-

This H-19C displays the Chickasaw's characteristic pod-and-boom layout, quadricycle landing gear, and elevated cockpit to good advantage. Note, however, that though this machine has the C model's straight tailboom, it does not have the variant's standard inverted 'V' tail fins on the lower part of the boom. *(Peter M. Bowers Collection)*

The H-19D differed from the H-19C primarily in having a more powerful engine, redesigned tailboom, and repositioned horizontal tail surfaces. The Chickasaw was the Army's first true transport helicopter, and it saw extensive service from the Korean War through the Vietnam conflict. *(Sikorsky)*

ment of a large and unobstructed box-like passenger/cargo cabin directly below the main rotor blades, thus ensuring that loads of varying sizes and composition would not adversely affect the craft's centre of gravity. The H-19's two-man cockpit was placed above and slightly forward of the passenger/cargo cabin, with the seats placed one either size of the drive shaft, and offered excellent visibility to the front and sides. The craft's high-set tailboom carried a vertical tailplane and a two-bladed anti-torque rotor, and was faired into the rear of the fuselage by a triangular fin. The Army's H-19C was essentially identical to the Air Force H-19A and, like that aircraft, was powered by a 600 hp R-1340-57 engine and had two small fins fitted to the lower rear of the tailboom in an inverted 'V'. The H-19D was the Army's version of the Air Force -B model and shared that aircraft's more powerful 700 hp engine, downward-sloping tailboom, repositioned horizontal tail fins, and smaller-diameter tail rotor.

The H-19 Chickasaw holds the distinction of being the Army's first true transport helicopter and, as such, played an important role in the initial formulation of Army doctrine regarding air mobility and the battlefield employment of troop-carrying helicopters. The Chickasaw made its combat debut during the last stages of the Korean War (having arrived in Korea in

January 1953 in the hands of the 6th Transportation Company), and went on to serve in Southeast Asia during the first years of the Vietnam War. In 1962 the H-19C and H-19D were redesignated as, respectively, the UH-19C and UH-19D, and examples of both variants remained in Army service well into the mid-1960s.

TECHNICAL DATA *(Both versions, except where noted)*

Engines:
One 600 hp Pratt & Whitney R-1340-57 Wasp radial (UH-19C)
One 700 hp Wright R-1300-3 Cyclone radial (UH-19D)

Dimensions:
Main rotor diameter: 53 ft

Tail rotor diameter: 4 ft 5 in

Fuselage length:　42 ft 2 in (UH-19C)
　　　　　　　　　42 ft 3in (UH-19D)

Height (to top of
rotor hub):　　13 ft 4 in

Weight (empty/gross, in lbs):
4795/7500 (UH-19C)
5250/7900 (UH-19D)

Performance:
Speed (cruising/maximum, in mph):
85/101 (UH-19C)
91/112 (UH-19D)

Service Ceiling: 10,500 ft (UH-19C)
　　　　　　　　　 12,500 ft (UH-19D)

Range:　　　　 450 miles (UH-19C)
　　　　　　　　　 385 miles (UH-19D)

Armament:
None normally fitted, though H-19s used for armament tests at Fort Rucker during the late 1950s were experimentally equipped with a variety of automatic weapons and rockets. In addition, H-19s serving in Southeast Asia in the early 1960s were sometimes equipped with door-mounted .30 or .50 calibre machine guns for self-defence and suppression of enemy fire near landing zones.

Accommodation:
Two crew and up to ten troops or eight stretchers.

SIKORSKY H-39

Type: Single-engined   Manufacturer: Sikorsky
     research helicopter   Aircraft Division of United
                              Aircraft, Stratford, Connecticut

HISTORY

In late 1953 the Army awarded Sikorsky a contract for the experimental conversion of two existing H-18 (q.v.) helicopters from piston to turbine power. The two aircraft selected for conversion were 49-2890 and -2891, the third and fourth H-18s built, with the former to be used for flight testing and the latter for static engineering evaluation. Sikorsky allotted the two craft the company designation S-59, and began the conversion work in early 1954.

The H-39 retained the H-18's basic pod-and-boom layout, but differed from the earlier machine in several significant ways. The most obvious difference was, of course, in powerplant. The H-39 was powered by a single 400 shp XT51-T-3 Artouste II turbine engine, which drove a new, fully-articulated, four-bladed

The H-39 was the Army's first turbine-powered helicopter and, as the legend just visible here on the aircraft's starboard door indicates, in 1954 it captured the world records for helicopter speed and altitude. Note also that the H-39's main landing gear retracted forward and inward. *(Sikorsky)*

main rotor. Other changes included a modified tail rotor, strengthening of the fuselage, incorporation of retractable wheeled landing gear, and the addition of updated electronics.

The H-39 was the Army's first turbine-powered helicopter, and was for a time the world's fastest rotorcraft. On 26 August 1954 Army Warrant Officer Billy Wester flew the craft to a new world helicopter speed record of 156.005 mph; less than two months later WO Wester and his H-39 set a new world helicopter altitude record by reaching 24,521 feet. The H-39 provided the Army with much valuable information on the capabilities of turbine-powered helicopters, and the success of its three-year evaluation was instrumental in bringing Army aviation into the turbine age.

TECHNICAL DATA

Engine:
One 400 shp Turbomeca XT51-T-3 Artouste II turbine

Dimensions:
Main rotor diameter: 35 ft

Tail rotor diameter: 6 ft 4 in

Fuselage length: 41 ft

Height (to top of rotor hub): 9 ft 7 in

Weight (empty/gross, in lbs):
2105/3361

Performance:
Speed (cruising/maximum, in mph): 138/156

Service Ceiling: 17,900 ft

Range: 280 miles

Armament: None.

Accommodation:
Pilot and up to three passengers.

SIKORSKY H-34 CHOCTAW

Type: Single-engined
    medium utility
    helicopter

Manufacturer: Sikorsky
Aircraft Division of United
Aircraft, Stratford, Connecticut

HISTORY

The H-34 was originally developed to meet a Navy requirement for a single-engined medium helicopter that could replace the Sikorsky HO4S (Model S-55/H-19) in the anti-submarine warfare (ASW) role. Designated the Model S-58 by Sikorsky and XHSS-1 by the Navy, the new aircraft incorporated several features that had first appeared on the S-55, including a nose-mounted engine and a cockpit located above and slightly forward of a spacious, box-like passenger/cargo compartment. However, the S-58 was larger and heavier than its predecessor, with a more powerful 1525 hp engine and a completely redesigned, downward-sloping tail section. The S-58 also differed from the S-55 in having larger-diameter, four-bladed main and tail rotors and three-point, tail-wheel landing gear.

    The prototype XHSS-1 made its first flight in March 1954, and the type entered regular Navy service in August 1955 as the HSS Seabat. A troop transport variant was simultaneously acquired by the Marine Corps as the HUS Seahorse, and one example of this type was loaned to the Army for service test

H-34A 54-2899 shows off the type's distinctive profile while departing McChord Air Force Base, Washington, during the late 1950s. The Army's two Choctaw variants were almost identical in outward appearance.
(Peter M. Bowers)

and evaluation. The Army had placed preliminary orders for production H-34A troop transport variants of the Navy XHSS-1 in April 1953 and the performance of the borrowed Marine Seahorse, which was essentially identical to the H-34 version, confirmed the Army's belief that the type would be a vast improvement over the H-19s then in service.

The Army accepted the first of 437 new-construction H-34As in April 1955; an additional twenty-one HUS-1 aircraft transferred from the Marine Corps during Fiscal Year 1955 were also designated H-34A (though at least five further USMC Seahorses operated by the Army between 1955 and 1957 retained their original Navy Bureau numbers). The H-34A's performance was, as hoped, markedly superior to that of the H-19, as evidenced by the fact that in 1956 an early production example flown by Army Captains Claude E. Hargett and Ellis Hill set new world helicopter speed records on courses of 100, 500 and 1000 km. The H-34A was also the first helicopter judged safe enough for routine use by the U.S. President, and in 1957 the Army organized an Executive Flight Detachment equipped with specially modified Choctaws. These aircraft were fitted with extensive sound-proofing, plush VIP interiors, and upgraded communications equipment, and were designated VH-34A*.

In 1960 Sikorsky began modifying Army H-34As (and Air Force H-34As and -Bs) to -C model standard through the addition of automatic flight stabilization systems and other detail changes. By January 1962 the Army had 190 H-34Cs and 179 H-34As in its inventory; under the Tri-Service designation system introduced later that year the aircraft were redesignated as, respectively, CH-34C and CH-34B. Several -C model aircraft were subsequently modified to VH-34C standard for VIP transport duties.

Though the CH-34 was arguably the most capable Army transport helicopter of the early 1960s (prior to the widespread introduction of the UH-1 Iroquois), it did not see extensive Army service in Vietnam**. The Army's 1962 decision to deploy the Vertol CH-21 Shawnee to Southeast Asia instead of the faster and more capable Choctaw was based on two considerations. First, in accordance with then-current Army doctrine regarding the area-standardization of aircraft types, the CH-21 was already widely deployed in the Pacific area and the continental United States, whereas all but about thirty of the Army's CH-34s were based in western Europe. It was therefore logical and logistically preferable that the CH-21, which was considered acceptable if somewhat past its prime, should be chosen for deployment to Southeast Asia. The Army's second reason for sending the Shawnee rather than the Choctaw was a somewhat negative opinion of the Choctaw's combat survivability, a belief based on French experience in North Africa. French forces had used both the CH-21 and the CH-34 in Algeria, the former flown by the Army and Air Force and the latter by the Navy, and official evaluations had indicated that the Shawnee was more likely to survive multiple hits by ground fire than was the CH-34. The French belief that the location and 'fragile' construction of the Choctaw's fuel tanks made the craft extremely vulnerable to ground fire seemed to validate the U.S. Army's decision to deploy the Shawnee to Vietnam pending the introduction into widespread service of the UH-1 Iroquois. The approximately twenty Army H-34s that did eventually reach Vietnam proved no more vulnerable than any other aircraft in the theatre, however, and ably carried out missions ranging from combat assault to aeromedical evacuation and general cargo transport. Most of these twenty aircraft were turned over to the South Vietnamese during the course of the war, though a few were ultimately reclaimed by the Army prior to the final collapse of the Saigon Government.

The CH-34 Choctaw remained in frontline Army service well into the late 1960s, and was standard equipment in many Army Reserve and National Guard aviation units for considerably longer. Indeed, the last Choctaw was not officially retired until the early 1970s, by which time the type's duties had been divided between the UH-1H Iroquois and the CH-47 Chinook.

---

* In 1962 the Executive Flight Detachment was transferred to the control of the Marine Corps, at which time the Detachment's Army and USMC VH-34As, -Cs and -Ds were replaced by eight VIP-configured Sikorsky VH-3A Sea Kings (q.v.), four of which were operated in Army markings.

** Though Navy and Marine Corps HSS Seabat and HUS Seahorse variants did.

TECHNICAL DATA *(All versions, except where noted)*

Engine:
One 1525 hp Wright R-1820-84 radial piston

Dimensions:
Main rotor diameter: 56 ft

Tail rotor diameter: 9 ft 4 in

Fuselage length: 46 ft 9 in

Height (to top of
rotor hub): 14 ft 3.5 in

Weight (empty/gross, in lbs):
7675/13,000

Performance:
Speed (cruising/gross, in mph):
97/122

Service Ceiling: 9500 ft

Range: 210 miles

Armament:
None normally fitted; however, several H-34s were experimentally fitted with various armament suites during tests conducted at Forts Bragg and Rucker in the late 1950s and early 1960s.

Accommodation:
Two to three crew, plus up to eighteen passengers or eight stretchers and two attendants.

SIKORSKY H-37 MOJAVE

Type: Twin-engined heavy transport helicopter

Manufacturer: Sikorsky Aircraft Division of United Aircraft, Stratford, Connecticut

HISTORY

Sikorsky originally developed the Model S-56 twin-engined heavy lift helicopter in response to a 1950 Marine Corps requirement for an assault transport able to carry twenty-three fully equipped troops. In 1951 the Navy ordered four XHR2S-1 prototypes for USMC evaluation, and the first of these made its maiden flight in December 1953. In 1954 the Army borrowed one of these preproduction machines, designated it the YH-37, and subjected it to rigorous operational and maintenance evaluations before returning it to the Marines. On the basis of the large helicopter's excellent showing during the Army evaluation, Sikorsky was in late 1954 awarded a contract for nine production H-37A Mojaves. The first of these reached Fort Rucker during the summer of 1956, at about the same time the HR2S-1 naval variant was entering regular Marine squadron service. The Army subsequently placed orders for a further 85 H-37As, and all ninety-four aircraft were delivered by June of 1960.

At the time of its introduction into the Army inventory the H-37A was the largest helicopter in U.S. military service. It was also Sikorsky's first multi-engined helicopter, and in developing it

The fourth production H-37A, 54-996, hovers during a manufacturer's pre-delivery flight test. The Army acquired ninety-four -A model Mojaves, all but four of which were ultimately modified to H/CH-37B standard. *(Sikorsky)*

The most obvious visual difference between the CH-37 and the Navy HR2S-1W prototype evaluated by the Army was the latter's huge chin radome covering the AN/APS-20E search radar. The Navy ultimately abandoned further development of the HR2S-1W because severe airframe vibration severely degraded the radar's performance. Though this aircraft retains its Navy Bureau Number on the fuselage, the stenciling just aft of 'Guppy's' cockpit windows identifies it as a U.S. Army HR2S-W [sic].
(Peter M. Bowers Collection)

the company chose to break with then-current industry practice by using a single five-bladed main rotor instead of two fore- and aft-mounted tandem rotors. The Mojave's designers chose not to locate the aircraft's engines in the upper section of the fuselage, as was common with most other contemporary heavy lift helicopters, but instead placed the 1900 hp Pratt & Whitney radials in nacelles fixed to the ends of short shoulder-mounted stub wings; the engine nacelles also accommodated the machine's fully retractable, twin-wheeled main landing gear legs. The H-37's innovative engine arrangement gave the craft an unobstructed cargo bay of nearly 1500 cubic feet, large enough to carry three Jeeps, twenty-four stretchers, or up to twenty-six fully-equipped troops. The Mojave's nose section was equipped with large clam-shell doors which allowed vehicles to be driven straight into the cargo area, with the cockpit placed above and slightly to the rear of the doors to ensure good visibility forward and to the sides. The H-37's tailboom was very similar in appearance to that of the H-34, in that it sloped downward toward the tailwheel and ended in a sharply upswept vertical tail unit carrying a four-bladed anti-torque rotor.

In 1961 Sikorsky began converting the Army's H-37As to -B model standard by installing automatic flight stabilization systems, crash-resistant fuel cells and modified nose doors. All but four -A model aircraft were eventually converted; in 1962 these were redesignated CH-37A, while the modified machines became CH-37B. Records indicate that the Army also evaluated one of the Navy's two radar-equipped HR2S-1W airborne early warning (AEW) aircraft. This machine (BuNo 141646) retained the AEW variant's large chin-mounted radome and AN/APS-20E search radar, and was operated in Army markings and two-tone 'Arctic' paint scheme.

The CH-37 was developed just prior to the widespread adoption of the turbine engine as a standard helicopter powerplant and, as a result, the type was forced to rely on larger, heavier and less powerful pistons. This did not prove to be an insuperable handicap, however, for the Mojave ultimately proved to be a more than capable heavy lifter when properly employed. Perhaps the best illustration of such employment occurred in Southeast Asia during the summer and fall of 1963. In June of that year four CH-37Bs were temporarily deployed to Vietnam to assist in the recovery of downed U.S. aircraft. By the following December the Mojaves had recovered an estimated $7.5 million worth of equipment, most of which was sling-lifted out of enemy-dominated areas virtually inaccessible by any other means. That the CH-37 did not see more extensive service in Vietnam is primarily the result of its replacement in the Army inventory by the turbine-powered Sikorsky CH-54 Tarhe (q.v.), a machine that weighed slightly less than the CH-37 but which could carry nearly four times as many troops or five times as much cargo. The last CH-37 was withdrawn from Army service in the late 1960s.

TECHNICAL DATA *(All versions, except where noted)*

Engines:
Two 1900 hp Pratt & Whitney R-2800-50 radials (early production -A models)
Two 2100 hp Pratt & Whitney R-2800-54 radials

Dimensions:
Main rotor diameter: 72 ft
Tail rotor diameter: 15 ft
Fuselage length: 64 ft 3 in
Height (to tail rotor hub): 22 ft

Weight (empty/gross, in lbs):
20,831/31,000 (CH-37A)
21,450/30,000 (CH-37B, HR2S-1W)

Performance:
Speed (cruising/maximum, in mph):
115/130 (CH-37A)
110/125 (CH-37B, HR2S-1W)

Service Ceiling: 8700 ft

Range: 145 miles (with max payload)

Armament:
None normally fitted, though those aircraft deployed to Vietnam were equipped with two to three .30 or .50 calibre machine guns mounted in the windows on either side of the fuselage.

Accommodation:
Two to three crew, plus up to twenty-six troops or twenty-four stretchers.

SIKORSKY H-3 SEA KING

Type: Twin-engined heavy transport helicopter

Manufacturer: Sikorsky Aircraft Division of United Aircraft, Stratford, Connecticut

HISTORY

The tri-service Executive Flight Detachment was formed under Army command in 1957 expressly to provide helicopter transportation for the President of the United States and other senior American political and military leaders. The unit was initially equipped with VIP-configured Sikorsky H-34 (q.v.) aircraft, though just prior to the 1962 transfer of command from the Army to the Marine Corps the Detachment began re-equipping with eight Sikorsky HSS-2Z Sea Kings. These machines had been purchased by the Navy and thus bore Navy Bureau numbers 150610 through 150617, though at various times between two and five of the aircraft carried full Army markings. All eight examples were redesignated VH-3A under the 1962 Tri-Service designation system.

The VH-3A was derived from the standard Model S-61B/SH-3A anti-submarine warfare (ASW) helicopter, which had been developed as the XHSS-2 in response to a 1957 Navy requirement. The Sea King entered regular Navy service in 1961 as the HSS-2, becoming the SH-3A the following year. Those same

VH-3A 150617, shown here departing Andrews AFB, Maryland, in 1969, was one of several Executive Flight Detachment (EFD) Sea Kings operated in Army markings. The machine sports the EFD's high gloss olive green and white paint scheme, and carries the emblem of the Military District of Washington just behind and slightly below the engine air intakes.
(E. M. Sommerich via Peter M. Bowers)

attributes that made the type a perfect ASW platform — long range, twin engine reliability, automatic flight stabilization, and a relatively large payload capacity — also made it an ideal VIP and staff transport. The VH-3A was outwardly identical to the standard SH-3A, having a water-tight boat-type hull, outrigger floats into which the main landing gear retracted, and a folding tailboom. The VIP machine also retained the SH-3A's twin 1250 shp General Electric turbines and five-bladed main and tail rotors, but dispensed with the ASW variant's dipping sonar, sonobuoy dispensers, Magnetic Anomaly Detector (MAD) gear, and surface-search radar. The modification to VIP-transport standard included the installation of extremely comfortable plush interiors, extensive sound-proofing, upgraded communication and navigation systems, and additional passenger safety devices including, according to some sources, armour plating around the passenger compartment and dynamic components.

During the period immediately following its service introduction the H-3 Sea King was the world's fastest production helicopter, and the basic design spawned a number of specialized variants used by the armed forces of at least seventeen nations. In 1965 Sikorsky even entered a modified, heavily armed S-61 in the Army's Interim Advanced Aerial Fire Support System (AAFSS) attack helicopter competition; it's failure to gain Army acceptance in that contest was perhaps more a result of the Army's confusion about what it wanted in an AAFSS helicopter than of any lack of ability on the S-61's part. The VH-3As of the Executive Flight Detachment were thus the only Sea Kings to see regular Army service, and they remained in that service until replaced by Marine Corps-owned and -crewed VH-3Ds in the 1970s.

TECHNICAL DATA

Engines:
Two 1250 shp General Electric T58-GE-8C (or -8F) turboshafts

Dimensions:
Main rotor diameter: 62 ft

Tail rotor diameter: 6 ft 8 in

Fuselage length: 54 ft 9 in

Height (to top of main rotor hub): 16 ft 10 in

Weight (empty/gross, in lbs):
10,890/20,500

Performance:
Speed (cruising/maximum, in mph): 133/160

Service Ceiling: 10,800 ft

Range: 625 miles

Armament: None

Accommodation:
Two to four crew, plus up to nine passengers.

SIKORSKY H-54 TARHE

Type: Twin-engined
heavy-lift helicopter

Manufacturer: Sikorsky
Aircraft Division of United
Aircraft, Stratford, Connecticut

HISTORY

In 1958 Sikorsky began design work on the Model S-60 twin-engined heavy-lift helicopter, a machine that incorporated the pod-mounted piston engines and dynamic components of the earlier Model S-56/CH-37. The S-60's fuselage was extremely simple, consisting of a central 'backbone' which supported the podded engines, main and tail rotor systems, and a nose-mounted crew cabin. Bulk cargo and passengers were intended to be carried in large rectangular pods that could be attached to the underside of the aircraft's central spine, whereas vehicles and other out-sized loads were to be sling-hoisted. One S-60 was built for Navy evaluation, but the craft was found to be underpowered for its intended roles and Sikorsky took the design back to the drawing boards for extensive reworking. The reconfigured machine, which was allotted the company

Despite its advancing age the ungainly-looking Tarhe remains one of the world's most capable military heavy lift helicopters. In this view CH-54A 68-18455 totes one of the interchangeable universal pods specially designed for the Tarhe; the pods could carry up to eighty-seven troops or be configured for use as portable hospitals, command posts or barracks. Note the CH-54's exposed dynamic components, as well as the rectangular filters fitted over the turbine intakes immediately above and behind the machine's cockpit. *(Sikorsky)*

The second production CH-54B, 69-18464, proves its mettle by sling-lifting an entire battery of 105 mm howitzers at one time. The -B model Tarhe is both heavier and more powerful than the -A model, though the only obvious outward difference between the two is the former's dual-wheeled main landing gear. Note the rear-facing enclosure immediately aft of the cockpit; from this position the freightmaster controls the cargo lifting equipment and, if required, can fly the aircraft during lifting operations. *(U.S. Army)*

designation S-64A, made its first flight in May 1962 under the watchful eyes of Army observers.

The S-64A retained the S-60's unique (and somewhat insect-like) layout but was more streamlined and was powered by two 4500 shp Pratt & Whitney T73-P-1 turboshafts mounted atop the central spine directly beneath the six-bladed, fully-articulated main rotor. The switch to turbine power produced significant increases in both performance and lifting ability, and in June 1963 the Army ordered six examples for operational test and evaluation. These aircraft, designated YCH-54A Tarhes* and allotted the serial numbers 64-14202 through -14207, were delivered to the Fort Benning-based 478th Aviation Company beginning in June 1964. This unit subsequently took four of the machines to Vietnam for a thorough field evaluation, upon the successful conclusion of which the Army placed orders for fifty-four CH-54A production aircraft. In 1969 these machines were joined by the first of an eventual thirty-seven CH-54Bs (serials 69-18462 through -18498). The -B model Tarhe differed from the earlier -A primarily in having more powerful engines, high-lift rotor blades, a modified main rotor gearbox and rotor head, a payload capacity increased by some 5000 pounds, and dual-wheeled main landing gear. The CH-54B went on to set several international helicopter payload and time-to-altitude records that are only now being broken by the latest generation of Western and Soviet heavy-lift rotorcraft.

The first production CH-54s began reaching Vietnam in 1965, and the type quickly proved its value as a 'flying crane' by routinely sling-lifting such outsized and weighty cargoes as artillery pieces, armoured vehicles and recovered aircraft. The Tarhes' universal cargo pods also proved very useful, for they could be used to carry up to eighty-seven troops in addition to serving as mobile hospitals, command posts or barracks. On several occasions, CH-54s even served as makeshift bombers; they were among the few American aircraft in Southeast Asia that were capable of carrying, and dropping, the 10,000 pound 'daisy-cutter' bombs used to create instant helicopter landing zones by flattening all vegetation (and most structures) within an area several hundred yards in diameter.

During the late 1960s and early 1970s the Tarhe was gradually superseded in front-line service by the CH-47B and -C Chinook (q.v.), and all surviving CH-54s were subsequently transferred to the Army Reserve and National Guard. Withdrawal from front-line units did not signal the Tarhe's immediate demise, however, for as of early 1986 seventy-one -A model machines are shared among Georgia, Kansas, Mississippi, Nevada and Pennsylvania, while the twenty-six surviving -Bs serve in Alaska, Alabama and Connecticut. These scrupulously maintained machines remain among the most capable aircraft available to the Army, and current plans call for the CH-54 to remain active in the Reserve and Guard until well into the 1990s.

---

* A Wyandot Indian name meaning 'crane'. Despite being officially assigned this name, the CH-54 is almost universally known as the Sky Crane.

TECHNICAL DATA *(All versions, except where noted)*

Engines:
Two 4500 shp Pratt & Whitney T73-P-1 turboshafts (YCH/CH-54A)
Two 4800 shp Pratt & Whitney T73-P-700 turboshafts (CH-54B)

Dimensions:
Main rotor diameter: 72 ft
Tail rotor diameter: 15 ft 4 in
Fuselage length: 70 ft 3 in
Height (to top of main rotor hub): 18 ft 7 in

Weight (empty/gross, in lbs):
19,234/42,000 (YCH/CH-54A)
19,980/47,000 (CH-54B)

Performance:
Speed (cruising/maximum, in mph): 105/126

Service Ceiling: 9000 ft

Range: 230 miles

Armament:
None normally fitted, though in Vietnam CH-54s were sometimes used to transport and drop 10,000 lb ground-clearing bombs.

Accommodation:
Three to four crew.

SIKORSKY H-59

Type: Single-engined rotor systems research helicopter

Manufacturer: Sikorsky Aircraft Division of United Technologies, Stratford, Connecticut

HISTORY

In late 1971 the Army Air Mobility Research and Development Laboratory awarded Sikorsky a contract for the development of a single-engined research helicopter prototype designed specifically to flight test the company's Advancing Blade Concept (ABC) rotor system. The resultant Model S-69, which was allotted the military designation XH-59A and the serial number 71-1472, made its first flight in July 1973.

The XH-59A's ABC system consisted of two three-bladed, coaxial, contra-rotating rigid rotors, both of which were driven by the craft's single 1825 shp PT6T-3 Turbo Twin Pac engine. During high-speed flight only the advancing blades of each rotor generated lift; this off-loaded the retreating blades and thereby eliminated the aerodynamic restrictions caused by blade-stall and the high mach number effect of the advancing blade tip. This, in turn, produced greater stability and manoeuvrability while eliminating the need for either a supplementary lift-generating wing or an anti-torque tail rotor. The XH-59A's streamlined fuselage more closely resembled that of a conventional airplane than a helicopter, having a cantilever tail unit with twin endplate rudders, side-by-side seating for the two crewmen, and fully retractable tricycle landing gear.

The XH-59A's coaxial, contra-rotating rigid rotor system is clearly visible in this photo of the rebuilt first prototype. This machine, which originally bore the serial 71-1472, was reserialled 73-21942 after being rebuilt to the same compound rotorcraft standard as the second XH-59A through the addition of two J60 turbojets. *(Sikorsky)*

The crash of the first XH-59A early in the flight test programme led to the construction of a second prototype incorporating several significant control system modifications. This second machine (73-21941) flew for the first time in 1975, and in 1977 was converted into a compound rotorcraft through the installation of two 3000 lb st J60-P-3A turbojet engines. The modified machine was jointly evaluated by the Army, Navy, and NASA beginning in 1978, and was later able to reach and maintain speeds in excess of 320 mph in level flight. The first prototype was ultimately rebuilt as a compound rotorcraft under a NASA contract and subsequently test flown (with the new serial 73-29142) by mixed Army, Navy, and NASA crews at NASA's Moffet Field, California, test facility. Both XH-59A aircraft were officially transferred to NASA following the 1981 end of joint Army/Navy participation in the tri-partite flight test programme.

TECHNICAL DATA *(Both versions, except where noted)*

Engine(s):
One 1825 shp Pratt & Whitney of Canada PT6T-3 Turbo Twin Pac and, in the second prototype, two 3000 lb st Pratt & Whitney J60-P-3A auxiliary turbojets

Dimensions:
Main rotor diameter: 36 ft (each)
Fuselage length: 40 ft 9 in
Height: (to top of
upper rotor hub): 13 ft 2 in

Weight (gross, in lbs):
9000 (first prototype, with PT6T-3 only)
11,000 (second prototype, with J60 turbojets)

Performance:
Speed (cruising/maximum, in mph):
125/184 (first prototype)
115/322 (second prototype)

Service Ceiling: 15,000 ft

Armament: None.

Accommodation:
Two crew.

SIKORSKY H-60 BLACKHAWK

Type: Twin-engined utility helicopter

Manufacturer: Sikorsky Aircraft Division of United Technologies, Stratford, Connecticut

HISTORY

Like the Boeing-Vertol YUH-61A (q.v.), the Sikorsky Model S-70 was developed in response to the Army's 1972 requirement for a simple, robust, and reliable Utility Tactical Transport Aircraft System (UTTAS) helicopter intended to eventually replace most of the Army's UH-1 Iroquois. In August 1972 both Sikorsky and Boeing-Vertol were awarded Army contracts for the production and initial testing of three UTTAS prototypes, the Sikorsky machines (serial numbers 73-21650 through -21652) being designated YUH-60A. The first example made its maiden flight in October 1974, and all three prototypes entered competitive testing against the Boeing-Vertol YUH-61A in March 1975. The YUH-60A was declared the winner of the UTTAS competition in December 1976, and almost immediately thereafter the Army awarded Sikorsky a contract for the first fifteen production UH-60A Blackhawks.

The Blackhawk's general shape and external dimensions were dictated by the Army's requirement that one complete UTTAS helicopter be air transportable within the cargo bay of a single C-130 Hercules (with the additional requirement that two helicopters fit within a single C-141 Starlifter, and six within

The fourth production UH-60A Blackhawk, 77-22717, during a pre-delivery factory test flight. Delivery of production aircraft began in 1979, with the aviation components of the 82nd and 101st Airborne Divisions being the first to equip with the type. *(Sikorsky)*

247

The YEH-60A prototype on its first flight, September 1981. Note the extended whip antenna and four boom-mounted dipole antennae. *(Sikorsky)*

each C-5 Galaxy). The UH-60 is thus a long and low-set craft with a streamlined pod-and-boom layout, and is characterized by a downward-sloping tail boom fitted with a moving stabilator, a sharply-swept vertical tail, and a four-bladed anti-torque rotor canted twenty degrees off the vertical to produce added lift and thus allow a reduction in the main rotor diameter. The tips of each of the Blackhawk's four fully-articulated, high-lift main rotor blades are swept twenty degrees to reduce control loads and the effects of high Mach numbers, and all four blades can be manually folded. The UH-60A can be fitted with an External Stores Support System (ESSS) consisting of two stub wings, one fixed to either side of the central fuselage above and just forward of the main cabin doors. These stub wings can carry auxiliary fuel tanks, electronic countermeasures (ECM) equipments, machine gun, cannon or rocket pods, up to sixteen Hellfire anti-tank missiles, or four M-56 landmine dispensers.

The UH-60's design also incorporates a variety of structural features that allow the aircraft to remain in flight after sustaining heavy damage and that provide maximum protection for the crew and passengers in a crash or while under hostile fire. In the Blackhawk these features include an immensely strong yet flexible and crashworthy cabin box, wheeled landing gear able to absorb very heavy vertical impacts, extensive armour plating around the cockpit and dynamic components, self-sealing fuel tanks, widely-separated and redundant electronic and hydraulic systems, and main rotor blades that can withstand hits by explosive or incendiary projectiles up to 23 mm in size.

The first production UH-60A was delivered to the Army in 1979, with the aviation components of the 101st and 82nd Airborne Divisions being the first frontline units to transition to the new helicopter. The Army awarded Sikorsky the first of two multi-year Blackhawk construction contracts in early 1982, and by early 1988 more than 900 examples were in Army service in the utility transport, aeromedical evacuation, and special warfare-support roles. The Army also acquired examples of two electronic warfare (EW) Blackhawk variants, designated EH-60A and EH-60B. Development of the former began in October 1980 when Sikorsky was awarded an Army contract to modify one UH-60A (probably 79-23301) for evaluation under the Quick Fix II

The YEH-60B prototype, seen here lifting off on its maiden flight in February 1981, was developed specifically to carry the SOTAS radar. The aircraft was fitted with main landing gear legs which could be retracted in flight in order to allow the SOTAS system's nineteen-foot antenna to rotate through a full 360 degrees. This photo also shows the Blackhawk's characteristic canted anti-torque tail rotor to good advantage. *(Sikorsky)*

EW programme. The modifications included preparation of the airframe for later installation of the AN/ALQ-151 multi-role tactical EW system, the addition of four dipole antennae mounted in pairs on either side of the tailboom, and the installation of a deployable whip antenna beneath the aft section of the main cabin. The EH-60A was also equipped with the AN/ALQ-144 infrared countermeasures set and flare/chaff dispensers in addition to the standard AN/APR-39(V)1 radar warning receiver. The YEH-60A EW Blackhawk flew for the first time in September 1981, and in October 1984 the Tracor Aerospace Group won an Army contract for the conversion of forty UH-60As to EH-60A standard. Flight testing of a planned 132 production -A model EW Blackhawks began in April 1986, though budget restraints ultimately led the Army to acquire only 66 production machines. The last of these was delivered in September 1989, and soon afterwards the type's designation was changed from EH-60A to EH-60C.

While the EH-60C is intended to locate, classify and disrupt enemy signals traffic, the EH-60B was developed specifically to carry the Stand-Off Target Acquisition System (SOTAS) radar. The EH-60B was characterized by the long box-shaped SOTAS scanner mounted below the main cabin, and was equipped with backward-retracting main landing gear legs to allow the SOTAS antenna to rotate a full 360 degrees in flight. The sole EH-60B prototype made its maiden flight in February 1981, but the SOTAS development programme was cancelled the following September and the aircraft was subsequently converted to EH-60A/C standard.

THe UH-60A underwent its baptism of fire during the 1983 U.S. invasion of Grenada, and there proved itself to be a dependable and capable successor to the Huey. The Blackhawks deployed to Grenada were fired upon by weapons ranging from small arms to 23 mm cannon, and in the Army's official report on the conflict the craft's sturdy construction, mechanical reliability, and ability to absorb significant damage and still fly were singled out for special mention.

Further development of the UH-60 continues as the manufacturer seeks to improve the basic airframe and the Army works to adapt the Blackhawk to a wider variety of operational tasks. In January 1988 the Army accepted the first of nine UH-60A machines especially equipped for use by the commanders-in-chief (CINCs) of various Army commands. These 'CINC Hawks' are fitted with additional radio equipment, satellite communications gear, M-130 flare and chaff dispensers, and other airborne survivability equipment. And in September 1987 Sikorsky submitted a propoal for a Blackhawk derivative intended specifically to support the Army's special operations forces. This

The Blackhawk's External Stores Support System (ESSS) allows the aircraft to carry a variety of weapons, electronic warfare equipment or, as shown here, up to four auxiliary fuel tanks. *(Sikorsky)*

A Blackhawk takes aboard Jamaican troops of the Caribbean Peacekeeping Force during the 1983 American invasion of Grenada. This operation was the UH-60's baptism of fire, and the aircraft proved itself to be a tough and dependable successor to the venerable UH-1 Iroquois. *(Sikorsky)*

aircraft, the MH-60K, will feature a long-range fuel system incorporating both additional internal tankage and the pylon-mounted auxiliary fuel tanks of the Air Force HH-60 combat rescue helicopter, and will have uprated engines, a 'glass' cockpit built around multiple CRT displays, advanced communications and navigation equipment, Forward-Looking Infrared Radar (FLIR), an air-to-air refuelling probe, heavier defensive armament, and additional troop seating. Sikorsky has announced its intention to begin flight testing the MH-60K in early 1989, and current Army planning calls for the acquisition of up to twenty-one aircraft. And in the summer of 1986 Sikorsky began preliminary design work on what was originally called a B-model Blackhawk incorporating an advanced composite main rotor system with larger-diameter blades, more powerful engines, the stronger gearbox developed for the Navy's SH-60B Seahawk variant, a redesigned nose intended to improve pilot visibility, a modified cockpit with improved instrumentation, and upgraded electronics. By late 1988 this aircraft had entered the final design definition stage with the designation UH-60M.

TECHNICAL DATA *(All versions, except where noted)*

Engines:
Two 1560 shp General Electric T700-GE-700 turboshafts

Dimensions:

Main rotor diameter:	53 ft 8 in
Tail rotor diameter:	11 ft
Fuselage length:	50 ft 0.75 in
Height: (to top of main rotor hub):	12 ft 4 in

Weight (empty/gross, in lbs):
10,624/20,250 (UH-60A)
EH-60A/B unknown

Performance:
Speed (cruising/maximum, in mph):
167/184

Service Ceiling: 19,000 ft

Range: 375 miles

Armament:
Two door-mounted M-23D or M-60 7.62 mm machine guns. The ESSS stub wings can carry machine gun, cannon or 2.75 inch rocket pods, up to sixteen Hellfire missiles, or four M-56 mine dispensers. Electronic warfare variants are not normally armed.

Accommodation:
Crew of three (all versions). UH-60A can carry eleven to fourteen troops or four stretchers. EW variants carry two to five systems operators.

SIKORSKY S-72 RSRA

Type: Multi-engined rotor
systems research
helicopter

Manufacturer: Sikorsky
Aircraft Division of United
Technologies, Stratford,
Connecticut

HISTORY

Certainly one of the more exotic-looking rotorcraft yet developed, the Sikorsky S-72 was designed in response to a joint Army/NASA requirement for a high-speed helicopter propulsion and rotor systems testbed. The S-72 was selected in October 1973 over a competing Bell Helicopter design, and in January 1974 Sikorsky was awarded an Army/NASA contract for the construction of two machines. The Rotor Systems Research Aircraft (RSRA), as the S-72 was officially named, was intended from the start to be capable of operating with podded auxiliary turbofan engines and airplane-style wings, and the initial production contract therefore also covered the fabrication of one set of wings and the adaption of two General Electric turbofans for later installation on the completed aircraft. The first RSRA made its maiden flight as a helicopter in October 1976 and the second prototype, built from the start as a compound with wings and turbofans already attached, made its initial ascent in April 1978.

In designing the S-72, Sikorsky's engineers mated a new, highly streamlined glass fibre and alloy fuselage to the twin 1400 shp GE turboshaft engines and five-bladed main rotor system of the proven Model S-61/H-3 Sea King (q.v.). The new craft's sharply-swept T-tail supported a conventional rudder, a five-bladed anti-torque rotor, a low-set tailplane equipped with

The first RSRA following installation of wings and turbofan engines. The S-72's five-bladed main rotor system was taken from an S-61 helicopter, while the engine pods are those of a Lockheed S-3 Viking anti-submarine warfare aircraft. In an emergency the crew can jettison the main rotor blades and fly the machine back to base as a normal jet aircraft or, if necessary, abandon the machine using ejection seats. (Sikorsky)

The first S-72 RSRA prior to installation of wings and auxiliary turbofan engines. The RSRA was intended from the start to be a compound machine, and this view clearly shows the faired-over wing joints and already installed engine attachment hardware. *(Sikorsky)*

elevators, and a ventral fin incorporating a non-retractable tail wheel. In the compound configuration the S-72 was fitted with low-set, variable-incidence wings, each of which incorporated conventional ailerons and flaps. When fitted, the RSRA's turbofan engines were carried one on either side of the forward fuselage just aft of the cockpit. The fitting of the conventional wings, tail surfaces, and auxiliary engines allowed the S-72 to flight test experimental rotor systems that would not, by themselves, support the aircraft's weight. In an emergency the crew was able to use explosive charges to jettison any main rotor system being tested and either eject from the aircraft or, if conditions permitted, fly it back to base as a conventional airplane.

Testing of both RSRA helicopters was conducted jointly by the Army and NASA until 1980, when the latter agency assumed overall control of both machines. In early 1984 Sikorsky was awarded a NASA/Defense Advanced Research Projects Agency (DARPA) contract to convert one of the S-72s into a demonstration testbed for the company's experimental X-wing system.

TECHNICAL DATA

Engines:
Two General Electric T-58-GE-5 turboshafts, plus two removable 9275 lb st General Electric TF-34-GE-400A turbofans

Dimensions:

Main rotor diameter (normal S-61 rotor system):	62 ft
Tail rotor diameter:	10 ft 7.5 in
Wingspan (when attached):	45 ft 1 in
Fuselage length:	70 ft 7 in
Height: (to top of S-61 rotor hub):	14 ft 6 in

Weight (empty/gross, in lbs):
14,490/18,400 (helicopter)
21,022/26,200 (compound)

Performance:
Speed (cruising/maximum, in mph):
160/184 (helicopter)
230/361 (compound)

Service Ceiling: 10,000 ft

Armament: None.

Accommodation:
Pilot and co-pilot in cockpit, flight engineer in rear cabin.

SIKORSKY S-75 ACAP

Type: Twin-engined composite airframe research helicopter

Manufacturer: Sikorsky Aircraft Division of United Technologies, Stratford, Connecticut

HISTORY

Like the Bell D292 (q.v.), the Sikorsky Model S-75 helicopter was developed as part of the Army's Advanced Composite Airframe Programme (ACAP), the goal of which is the development of an all-composite helicopter fuselage which is considerably lighter and less costly to build than the predominantly metal airframes now in general use. Both Sikorsky and Bell were awarded contracts in February 1981 for the design, construction and initial testing of two ground test airframes and one flying prototype, all three to be built entirely of such composite materials as glass-reinforced plastic (GRP), graphite and Kevlar. Sikorsky's S-75 ACAP aircraft flew for the first time in July 1984.

The S-75 is a hybrid machine that uses the twin turboshaft engines, transmission and main and tail rotors of Sikorsky's successful S-76 civil transport helicopter mated to an entirely new composite airframe. Most of the aircraft's basic load-

The S-75 ACAP's basic load-bearing structure is built of a graphite/epoxy material, while most external surfaces are of bullet-resistant Kevlar. The machine meets or exceeds all existing military crashworthiness standards, as well as the weight- and cost-saving criteria set out in the original ACAP specification. *(Sikorsky)*

bearing structure is built of graphite or a graphite/epoxy blend, while the floors, roof and most exterior surfaces are of more ballistically-resistant Kevlar. In keeping with the Army's requirement that the ACAP aircraft meet or exceed all existing military crashworthiness standards, the S-75 is equipped with specially designed impact-resistant crew and passenger seats and high strength pneumatic shock absorbers on its non-retracting tricycle landing gear. The machine is operated by two crew members, and can carry up to six passengers in its one hundred cubic-foot rear cargo cabin.

Evaluation of the S-75 was still under way as this book went to press, but in tests already completed the machine was found to have exceeded the weight- and cost-saving criteria set by the Army in the original ACAP specification.

TECHNICAL DATA

Engines:
Two 650 shp Allison 250-C30S turboshafts

Dimensions:

Main rotor diameter:	44 ft
Tail rotor diameter:	8 ft
Fuselage length:	43 ft 8 in
Height: (to top of main rotor hub):	13 ft 2 in

Weight (empty/gross, in lbs):
6421/8470

Performance:
Speed (cruising/maximum, in mph):
159/184

Service Ceiling: 13,500 ft

Range: 398 miles

Armament: None.

Accommodation:
Two crew, plus up to six passengers.

STINSON L-5 SENTINEL

Type: Single-engined liaison and observation aircraft

Manufacturer: Stinson Aircraft Division of Consolidated Vultee, Wayne, Michigan

HISTORY

The Army first procured the Stinson Sentinel in 1941, when six commercial model 105 Voyagers were purchased for evaluation in the observation and liaison roles. These six machines, which were designated YO-54, were followed in 1942 by 275 O-62 production models. The O-62 retained the civilian Voyager's high-wing layout, fabric-covered metal-tube construction, and 185 hp Lycoming O-435-1 engine, but differed from the commercial three-seat craft in having a two-seat tandem cockpit, a slightly larger fuselage, higher operating weights, and military-standard instruments and communications equipment. Following the mid-1942 delivery of the 275th aircraft the O-62 designation was changed to L-5, and seven distinct variants were ultimately produced:

Sentinel 44-17377 at a forward Korean airfield in July 1950. The camera-equipped -C model retained its stretcher-carrying capability, and was thus the first 'all-purpose' Sentinel variant. Note that this particular aircraft wears the sort of hastily-applied, non-standard camouflage paint scheme common to many Army observation and liaison aircraft in the first months of the war. *(Peter M. Bowers Collection)*

L-5:
Designation given to 1731 aircraft produced immediately after the change in type classification; identical to standard O-62.

L-5A:
Beginning in late 1942 Stinson produced 688 -A model Sentinels, which differed from the basic O-62/L-5 only in having upgraded twenty-four-volt electrical systems. Also, from the first L-5A onward all L-5 variants were delivered without the landing gear strut fairings that had been standard equipment on preceding models.

L-5B:
In 1943 Stinson began modifying the first of an eventual 679 L-5As to -B model standard by installing an upward-hinged hatch aft of the cockpit to allow loading of a single stretcher.

L-5C:
Designation applied to some 200 L-4Bs fitted with carrying brackets for single-mount K-20 aerial cameras. This model retained the ability to carry a single stretcher, and can therefore be considered the first all-purpose L-5 variant.

L-5E:
Essentially an L-5C fitted with drooping ailerons operating in conjunction with the flaps; the first of 558 new-construction examples appeared in mid-1944.

XL-5F:
Designation allocated to a single L-5B (serial 44-17103) experimentally fitted with a 185 hp Lycoming 0-435-2 engine. The modification was not adopted and the craft was subsequently modified to L-5C standard.

L-5G:
Final Sentinel variant, identical to the L-5E except in having a 190 hp 0-435-11 engine. A total of 115 were built during the Second World War, though an additional machine was constructed in 1959 for use as a glider tug at the U.S. Air Force Academy.

The L-5 was the second most common liaison and observation aircraft in U.S. service during the Second World War, being outnumbered only by the Piper L-4 (q.v.). The Sentinel was initially operated solely by Army Air Force pilots, and did not reach Army Ground Forces aviation units until 1943. The type quickly proved itself to be an excellent liaison and observation platform, and served with distinction in every theatre of war. Many L-5s were unceremoniously scrapped or sold off in the years immediately following the hostilities, though, quite fortunately as it later turned out, the type did remain in service with several active and Reserve units. Sentinels were among the first U.S. aircraft to see action in Korea following the outbreak of war in 1950, and it was in the back seat of an Army L-5 that South Korean President Syngman Rhee was evacuated from Seoul during the initial North Korean advance on the capital. Though obsolescent and increasingly vulnerable to enemy fire, the L-5 (supported by those Piper L-4s still in service) formed the backbone of the Army's fixed wing aviation operations in Korea during the conflict's first crucial months, and carried out a wide range of vital tasks until ultimately replaced in front line service by the newer and more capable Cessna L-19 Bird Dog (q.v.). Following its removal from combat the L-5 served as crew trainer, unit hack, and instructional airframe, and the type had almost entirely disappeared from the Army inventory by the late 1950s. Army records do indicate, however, that several later-model Sentinels were being used for covert operations in Southeast Asia as late as 1961, and at least five Army-owned L-5s were redesignated U-19A under the 1962 Tri-Service Designation System.

TECHNICAL DATA (All versions, except where noted)

Engine:
One 185 hp Lycoming 0-435-1
One 185 hp Lycoming 0-435-2 (XL-5F)
One 190 hp Lycoming 0-435-11 (L-5G)

Dimensions:

Wingspan:	34 ft
Wing area:	155 sq ft
Fuselage length:	24 ft 1 in
Height:	7 ft 11 in

Weight (empty/gross, in lbs):
1550/2020

Performance:
Speed (cruising/maximum, in mph):
100/130
105/135 (L-5G)

Service Ceiling: 15,800 ft

Range: 425 miles

Armament: None.

Accommodation:
Pilot and observer, or pilot and one stretcher.

SUD-OUEST HO-1

Type: Single-engined observation helicopter

Manufacturer: Sud-Ouest Aviation, Paris, France

HISTORY

In late 1956 the Army leased three examples of Sud-Ouest's diminutive Model SO 1221 Djinn two-place light turbine helicopter for evaluation in the observation role. The Djinn, which had first flown in December 1953, was already in service with the French Army as an observation craft and its success in that role, coupled with its relatively low per-unit cost and fairly basic maintenance requirements, piqued the Army's interest. The machines obtained by the Army (serials 57-6104 through -6106) were the first helicopters acquired under the new HO (helicopter, observation) classification, and were designated YHO-1.

The SO 1221 was of welded steel-tube construction and was powered by an innovative cold-jet propulsion system developed by Sud-Ouest for its earlier Ariel II and III helicopters. In the Djinn this system used a modified Turbomeca Palouste IV engine as a turbo-generator to feed compressed air through the rotor shaft to ejectors built into the tips of each rotor blade; this provided the benefits of a ramjet without the weight penalties imposed by blade-tip combustion chambers. The Djinn had no tail rotor, directional stability being achieved by directing the

The first YHO-1 acquired by the Army, 57-6104, hovers during an early test flight. The tubing visible between the upper part of the engine and the rotor head fed compressed air from the machine's modified Palouste IV turbine to ejectors in the rotor blade tips. *(U.S. Army Transportation Corps Museum)*

engine's exhaust onto a large central rudder set between small endplate fins at the end of the aircraft's cantilever tail. The craft's small and rather spartan two-seat cockpit was surrounded by a sectioned bubble-type enclosure and transparent side doors, which combined to provide excellent visibility forward and to both sides. Cockpit instrumentation was quite basic in the standard SO 1221, and the three YOH-1s were consequently fitted with additional U.S. military-standard avionics and communications equipment for their Army evaluation. The Djinn's landing gear was of the skid type, with small retractable wheels to facilitate ground handling.

The Army's engineering and operational evaluation of the YOH-1 found the aircraft to be well built, relatively easy to maintain under field conditions, and an exceptional observation platform. The Djinn was not adopted for service use, however, primarily because the Army faced continuing budgetary constraints and some domestic political opposition to the procurement of French, rather than American (or Canadian) aircraft. In early 1958 all three YOH-1s were returned to Sud-Ouest for ultimate delivery to the French Army.

TECHNICAL DATA

Engine:
One 240 shp Turbomeca Palouste IV turbo-generator.

Dimensions:
Main rotor
diameter: 36 ft 1 in

Fuselage length: 17 ft 4 in

Height (to top of
rotor hub):   8 ft 5 in

Weight (empty/gross, in lbs):
794/1765

Performance:
Speed (cruising/maximum, in mph):
62/80

Service Ceiling: 9280 ft

Range: 118 miles

Armament:
None as evaluated by U.S. Army, though French Army variants had been experimentally equipped with Nord SS-10 wire-guided anti-tank missiles.

Accommodation:
Pilot and observer

VERTOL H-21 SHAWNEE

Type: Single-engined
    utility helicopter

Manufacturer: Vertol Aircraft
Corporation, Morton,
Pennsylvania

HISTORY

In 1949 the U.S. Air Force ordered eighteen examples of the Piasecki Model PD-22 single-engined, tandem-motor helicopter for evaluation in the SAR and general transport roles. The YH-21 Work Horse, as the type was designated, made its maiden flight in April 1952. The Air Force was quite pleased with the YH-21, and eventually purchased thirty-two production H-21A SAR models and 163 of the more powerful H-21B assault transports.

The Army became aware of the H-21's potential as a medium utility helicopter soon after the type's maiden flight, and in 1952 awarded Piasecki a contract for the production of the H-21C variant. This aircraft retained the H-21B's extensive armor plating and ability to carry two external fuel tanks, but had such additional features as increased troop capacity and a 4000-pound capacity belly sling hook. The Army procured 334 H-21C Shawnees, with deliveries beginning in August 1954. In addition, the Army obtained at least sixteen H-21B aircraft from the USAF; the majority of these machines were ultimately brought up to H-21C standard, and all were known as Shawnees despite their origins as Work Horses. The Army also funded Vertol's* development of the XH-21D, which was essentially a standard H-21C whose single piston engine had been replaced by two General Electric T58 shaft turbines. Two H-21Cs were so modified and flight tested in 1957 and 1958, but the variant was not adopted for production. In 1962 the H-21B and H-21C were redesignated as, respectively, the CH-21B and CH-21C.

Despite its rather ungainly appearance the H-21 Shawnee was a very capable and well-liked machine, and the type ultimately secured for itself a unique place in post-World War II Army aviation history. It was a Shawnee dubbed 'Amblin' Annie' that made the first non-stop helicopter flight from one coast of the United States to the other, being refuelled in flight from a U-1A Otter. More significantly, the H-21 was the first American military helicopter type to be deployed in appreciable numbers to South Vietnam: the first four Shawnee units arrived in that country between December 1961 and September 1962. Inevitably, perhaps, the H-21 also gained the dubious distinction of being the aircraft in which America's first Vietnam casualties

---

* In 1955 Frank Piasecki was forced out of the firm he had founded and to which he had given his name. He then formed a new Piasecki Aircraft Corporation and went on to develop other innovative aircraft types. The original Piasecki firm was renamed Vertol, which in 1960 became a Division of the Boeing Company known as Boeing-Vertol. The firm is now Boeing Helicopter Company.

Shawnee 51-15888, the eighth production H-21C, sling-lifts a jeep during flight testing at Fort Rucker, October 1954. The Army -C model machines retained the armor plating and external fuel tank connections of the USAF H-21B, but differed in having an increased troop capacity and other detail changes. *(U.S. Army)*

were killed; four Army aviators died in July 1962 when their Shawnee was shot down near the Laotian-Vietnamese border. The machine gun-equipped H-21s used in Vietnam were also, of necessity, the first American military helicopters to be fitted with door-mounted defensive weapons as a matter of course. Several additional aircraft were experimentally fitted with a variety of offensive weaponry and used as interim gunships pending the arrival in Southeast Asia of the first units of armed UH-1 Iroquois in the summer of 1963. The H-21 remained the backbone of the Army's aviation effort in South Vietnam until finally supplanted by the UH-1 in 1964, and most Shawnees were withdrawn from the active inventory within the following year.

TECHNICAL DATA

Engine(s):
One 1425 hp Wright R-1820-103 Cyclone radial (H-21B/C).
Two 1050 shp General Electric T-58 shaft turbines (XH-21D).

Dimensions:
Rotor diameter
(each):   44 ft

Fuselage length: 52 ft 6 in

Height: (to top of
aft rotor hub):   15 ft 9 in

Weight (empty/gross, in lbs):
8950/15,200

Performance:
Speed (cruising/maximum, in mph):
98/127

Service Ceiling: 9450 ft

Range: 265 miles

Armament:
In Vietnam, typically one or two door-mounted .50 calibre M-2 or 7.62 mm M-60 machine guns. Those aircraft used as interim gunships were armed with a combination of 2.75 inch rocket pods, 20 mm cannon, and 7.62 mm multi-barrel machine guns.

Accommodation:
Pilot, co-pilot, crew chief and (in Vietnam) one or two gunners, plus up to twenty troops or twelve stretchers.

VERTOL H-16 TRANSPORTER

Type: Twin-engined heavy-lift helicopter prototype

Manufacturer: Vertol Aircraft Corporation, Morton, Pennsylvania

HISTORY

In 1946 the Army Air Forces awarded Piasecki Aircraft a contract for the development of a tandem rotor helicopter intended for use in the long-range search and rescue (SAR) role. The resultant Piasecki Model PV-15 was originally given the military designation XR-16 (R denoting rotorcraft under the World War II system), though this was changed to XH-16 in June 1948. The Air Force placed an order for two service test and evaluation aircraft in June 1949, and subsequently allocated the serial numbers 50-1269 and -1270 for these machines.

At the time of its inception the H-16 was the largest helicopter in the world, having a fuselage almost as capacious as that of the contemporary Douglas DC-6/C-54. Though originally intended for the SAR role the Transporter, as the H-16 was ultimately named, evolved during the design process into a heavy-lift craft equipped with a tail loading ramp and optimized for troop and cargo transport. In this role the aircraft could carry up to forty troops or three light trucks within its fuselage, the interior of which was kept clear of obstructions by mounting the engines and all dynamic components in the upper fuselage. The H-16 was also capable of transporting large exterior cargo pods,

YH-16 50-1269 during an Army evaluation flight in 1955. This machine was judged to be underpowered and was subsequently fitted with two 2100 shp turbine engines. *(Piasecki Aircraft)*

and was equipped with variable-height landing gear legs in order to accommodate pods of varying sizes.

The first Transporter (serial 50-1269) was powered by two 1650 hp Pratt & Whitney piston engines and made its first flight in October 1953 with the designation YH-16. During construction the second prototype (50-1270) was modified to Model PV-45 standard through the replacement of its piston engines with two 1800 shp Allison turboshafts. The change in powerplants and inclusion of various structural modifications prompted a redesignation to XH-27 in October 1952, though this was changed to YH-16A prior to the aircraft's first flight in 1955. Both H-16 variants were at times fitted with varying types of experimental horizontal tail surfaces, one of which incorporated large end-plate rudders, but none of these designs were adopted for permanent use.

The Air Force ultimately decided against procuring the H-16 for operational use, and in 1955 the YH-16 was turned over to the Army for evaluation. The Army found the piston-driven Transporter to be underpowered and therefore awarded the reorganized Vertol company a contract for the machine's conversion to turbine power. The aircraft was duly equipped with two 2100 shp Allison turboshafts, modified to carry up to fifty troops, and redesignated YH-16B. Despite these improvements the type was ultimately judged to be unsuited to sustained operations under field conditions, and the Army terminated the H-16 test programme in mid-1956.

TECHNICAL DATA (All versions, except where noted)

Engines:
Two 1650 hp Pratt & Whitney R-2180 pistons (XH/YH-16)
Two 1800 shp Allison YT-38-A-10 turboshafts (XH-27/YH-16A)
Two 2100 shp Allison T56-A-5 turboshafts (YH-16B)

Dimensions:
Rotor diameter: 82 ft

Fuselage length: 77 ft 7 in

Height:
(to top of
aft rotor hub):   25 ft

Weight (empty/gross, in lbs):
22,035/37,650 (XH/YH-16)
22,506/33,580 (XH-27/YH-16A)
25,450/45,700 (YH-16B)

Performance:
Speed (cruising/maximum, in mph):
100/128 (XH/YH-16)
105/145 (XH-27/YH-16A)
125/156 (YH-16B)

Service Ceiling: 18,000 ft (XH/YH-16)
22,850 ft (XH-27/YH-16A)
15,600 ft (YH-16B)

Range: 210 miles (XH/YH-16)
244 miles (XH-27/YH-16A)
216 miles (YH-16B)

Armament: None.

Accommodation:
Two to three crew, plus:
forty troops or thirty-two stretchers and five attendants (XH/YH-16, XH-27/YH-16A)

Forty-seven troops or thirty-eight stretchers and five attendants (YH-16B)

VERTOL VZ-2

Type: Tilt-wing V/STOL
    research vehicle

Manufacturer: Vertol Aircraft
    Corporation, Morton,
    Pennsylvania

HISTORY

During the mid-1950s the Army became particularly interested in the possible military applications of V/STOL aircraft, and consequently contracted with several aircraft manufacturers for the development of such vehicles. Among the many innovative designs to appear during this V/STOL era was Vertol's Model 76, the first aircraft in the world to make use of the tilt-wing concept. The single example produced (serial 56-6943) was funded jointly by the Army and the Office of Naval Research (ONR), and made its first hovering flight in the summer of 1957.

The VZ-2 was powered by a single fuselage-mounted YT53-L-1 turbine engine driving, via extension shafts, two rotor/airscrews attached to the tilting wing. For vertical takeoff and landing the leading edge of the wing, and its attached propellers, would be rotated to point directly upwards. Once the machine had reached a safe height the wing would slowly be rotated downward into the normal flight position, and the craft would

The sole VZ-2, seen here in horizontal flight above the California desert in 1958. The small ducted fan visible just above the tail wheel was used to provide additional lateral stability. *(Boeing-Helicopters)*

fly off in the conventional fashion. Unlike other contemporary tilt-wings the VZ-2 was also equipped with two small tail-mounted ducted fans meant to provide additional lateral control. The aircraft's most characteristic features were its high T-tail and helicopter-style bubble cockpit enclosure.

The Vertol VZ-2 made its first transition from vertical to horizontal flight, and back again, in July 1958, and was evaluated by NASA as well as by the Army and Navy prior to its transfer to sole NASA control in the early 1960s.

TECHNICAL DATA

Engine:
One 825 shp Lycoming YT53-L-1 turbine

Dimensions:

Rotor diameter:	9 ft 6in
Wingspan:	24 ft 11 in
Wing area:	110 sq ft
Fuselage length:	26 ft 5 in
Height:	10 ft 4 in

Weight (empty/gross, in lbs):
2500/3200

Performance:
Not recorded

Armament: None.

Accommodation:
Pilot and observer

VERTOL HC-1

Type: Twin-engined
    medium transport
    helicopter

Manufacturer: Vertol Aircraft
Corporation, Morton,
Pennsylvania

HISTORY

In May 1957 Frank Piasecki and his Vertol design team began work on a new company-funded twin-engined, tandem rotor cargo helicopter designated the Model 107. The aircraft was essentially a turbine-powered update of Piasecki's proven CH-21 (q.v.) and was intended to fill an anticipated Army requirement for a medium assault transport helicopter capable of lifting an entire infantry platoon and all its associated equipment.

The first Model 107 prototype made its maiden flight on 22 April 1958 and three months later the Army ordered ten examples, designated YHC-1A, for service test and evaluation. However, prior to the delivery of the first article the Army decided Vertol's larger and more capable Model 114 (later better known as the CH-47 Chinook, q.v.) better fulfilled the revised medium assault transport requirement, and consequently reduced the YHC-1A order to just three aircraft. These machines (serials 58-5514 through -5516) were used primarily to familiarize

A recoilless rifle-equipped Mule utility vehicle rolls from the second of the Army's three YHC-1s, 58-5518, during a field evaluation. All three machines were used primarily to familiarize Army flight crews with the handling characteristics of tandem rotor turbine helicopters prior to the introduction of the CH-47 Chinook. *(U.S. Army Transportation Corps Museum).*

Army flight crews with the capabilities of turbine-powered helicopters, and all three were eventually returned to the manufacturer. Vertol continued development of the Model 107, which later served in large numbers with the U.S. Navy and Marine Corps as the CH-46 Sea Knight.

TECHNICAL DATA

Engines:
Two 1050 shp General Electric T58-GE-6 turbines

Dimensions:
Rotor diameter: 48 ft 4 in (each)

Fuselage length: 44 ft 7 in

Height:
(to top of
aft rotor hub):   16 ft 10 in

Weight (empty/gross, in lbs):
11,715/18,700

Performance:
Speed (cruising/maximum, in mph):
155/168

Service Ceiling: 13,700 ft

Range: 115 miles

Armament: None.

Accommodation:
Three crew and up to twenty-two passengers/troops.

APPENDIX

U.S. ARMY AIRCRAFT DESIGNATION SYSTEMS SINCE 1947

During the period covered by this volume, United States Army aircraft have been officially type-classified under, successively, the 1924, 1948, 1956 Army, and 1962 Tri-Service military aircraft designation systems. In addition, Army aircraft acquired from the Navy, Marine Corps or Coast Guard prior to 1962 would have previously borne still another designation unique to the sea services. A basic understanding of each system is essential to any study of post-World War II Army aviation, both to fully understand the origin of the Army's current aircraft designations and to reduce the confusion the multiplicity of designations can cause when attempting to trace the origin and disposition of individual Army aircraft. Each designation system is briefly outlined below.

1924 System:
Instituted in May 1924 as a revision of the 1919 Air Service designation system. The 1924 method retained the basic concept of alphabetic type prefixes established under the earlier system, though these were increased in number (from twenty-three to thirty-two) and simplified. The basic type prefixes from this system with which we are concerned in this study are:

AT   Advanced Trainer

BT   Basic Trainer

C   Transport

F   Photographic

L   Liaison

O   Observation

R   Rotary Wing

Examples: C-64 Norseman, L-15 Scout.

The 1924 system also introduced the status prefix X for experimental, and the status prefixes Y for service test and Z for obsolete were added in 1928.

1948 System:
Eliminated a number of designations adopted during the course of World War II, and adopted single-letter basic type codes. Those with which the reader is most likely to come in contact in this volume are:

C   Transport

H   Helicopter

L   Liaison

T   Trainer

U   Utility

V   Vertical Take-off/Landing Covertiplane

X   Research

Examples: H-26 Jet Jeep, U-18 Navion, Bell V-3.

1956 Army System:

In 1956 the Army introduced its own aircraft designation system, which used the following two-letter codes to indicate aircraft type and role:

AC   Airplane, cargo

AO   Airplane, observation

AU   Airplane, utility

HC   Helicopter, cargo

HO   Helicopter, observation

HU   Helicopter, utility

VZ   Vertical Take-off/Landing research aircraft

Examples: AO-1 Mohawk, HU-1 Iroquois, VZ-9 Aerocar.

1962 Tri-Service System:

Since 1962 the American military services have used a single unified aircraft designation system which is essentially an expanded version of the 1948 system. The current system uses single letter type codes, and those that are normally applied to Army aircraft include the following:

A   Tactical support

C   Transport

E   Electronic surveillance

H   Helicopter

O   Observation

T   Trainer

U   Utility

V   Vertical/Short Take-off/Landing research

X   Research

Aircraft Code Prefix and Suffix Letters:
Single-letter aircraft designation prefixes and suffixes have traditionally been, and remain, an integral part of the United States armed forces military aircraft designation system. The prefixes are used to indicate an aircraft's status or secondary role, and those most often applied to Army aircraft include:

A   Tactical Support

J   Temporary special testing

M   Special operations support

N   Permanent special testing

R   Reconnaissance

T   Trainer

U   Utility

V   Staff Transport

X   Experimental

Y   Service test

Examples: AH   = tactical support helicopter

MH   = special operations support helicopter

VH   = staff transport helicopter

RU   = reconnaissance-dedicated fixed-wing utility aircraft

YUH = service test utlity helicopter

There are, of course, anomalies in every system, and the prefix code system is no exception. For example, one would expect the designation UV-18 to indicate a utility version of a staff transport or XV-4 to indicate an experimental staff transport. Such is not the case, however, for in both examples cited the 'V' indicates V/STOL aircraft. Thus UV-18 and XV-4 indicate, respectively, a utility version of a V/STOL aircraft and an experimental or research version of a V/STOL aircraft.

The suffixes applied to an aircraft designation tend to be far more straightforward, for each successive letter of the alphabet (excluding I and O) indicates a successive development or variant of the basic aircraft. Thus, U-12A would indicate the first production model of the U-12, U-12B the second, and so on.

As is obvious from the above short introduction, American military aircraft designation systems can be quite confusing at first glance. It doesn't take long to puzzle out most of the facts, however, when one has a good guide to the maze. Perhaps the best such guide is John M. Adrade's *U.S. Military Aircraft Designations and Serials Since 1909* (Midlands Counties Publications, Leicester, UK, 1979), on which I relied for much of the information in this appendix.

BIBLIOGRAPHY

Andrade, John M. *U.S. Military Aircraft Designations and Serials Since 1909,* Midland Counties Publications, Leicester, 1979.

ap Rees, Elfan. *World Military Helicopters,* Jane's Publishing Company Ltd., London, 1986.

Butterworth, W. E. *Flying Army,* Doubleday & Company, Garden City, 1971.

Francillon, Rene J. *McDonnell-Douglas Aircraft Since 1920,* Putnam & Company, London, 1979.

Gunston, Bill. *Military Helicopters,* Arco Publishing Company Inc., New York, 1981.

Jennings, M. G. *U.S. Military Aircraft Directory,* Ari International, London, 1986.

Jessup, Stuart M., and Mower, Andy G. W. *United States Military Aircraft Serials,* Seefive Publications, Hounslow, 1985.

Kaman, Charles H. *Kaman: Our Early Years,* Curtiss Publishing Company, Indianapolis, 1985.

Nalty, Bernard C., Watson, George M. and Neufeld, Jacob. *The Air War Over Vietnam,* Arco Publishing Inc., New York, 1981.

Piasecki Aircraft. *The Piasecki Story of Vertical Lift,* Piasecki Aircraft, Lakehurst, New Jersey, n.d.

Politella, Dario. *Operation Grasshopper: The Story of Army Aviation in Korea,* Longo Company, Wichita, Kansas, 1956.

Polmar, Norman, and Kennedy, Floyd D. *Military Helicopters of the World,* Naval Institute Press, Annapolis, 1981.

Sullivan, Jim. *P2V Neptune in Action,* Squadron/Signal Publications, Carrollton, Texas, 1985

Swanborough, F. G. *Vertical Flight Aircraft of the World,* Aero Publishers, Fallbrook, California, 1965.

Taylor, Michael J. H., and Taylor, John W. R. *Helicopters of the World,* Charles Scribner's Sons, New York, 1976.

————. *Jane's Pocket Book of Research and Experimental Aircraft,* Collier Books, New York, 1981.

Ten Eyck, Andrew. *Jeeps in the Sky: The Story of the Light Plane,* Commonwealth Books, New York, 1946.

Tierny, Richard, and Montgomery, Fred. *The Army Aviation Story,* Colonial Press, Northport, Alabama, 1963.

Weinert, Richard P. *A History of Army Aviation, 1950-1962,* United States Continental Army Command, Fort Monroe, Virginia, 1971.

United States Army. *Army Aircraft Characteristics,* U.S. Army Transportation School, Fort Eustis, Virginia, 1955.

United States Army. *U.S. Army Aircraft: Photographs and Descriptions,* Department of the Army, Washington, DC, 1969.